LAST OF THE
BLUE LIONS

LAST OF THE BLUE LIONS

The British Lions 1938 tour of South Africa

Steve Lewis

SPORTS
BOOKS

Published by SportsBooks Ltd

Copyright: Steve Lewis ©
April 2009

SportsBooks Limited
PO Box 422
Cheltenham
GL50 2YN
United Kingdom
Tel: 01242 256755
Fax: 0560 3108126
email   randall@sportsbooks.ltd.uk
Website   www.sportsbooks.ltd.uk

Cover designed by Alan Hunns.

Front cover by Alan Hunns

A CIP catalogue record for this book is available from the British Library.

ISBN 9781899807 84 0

Printed in the UK by CPI Bookmarque, Croydon, CR0 4TD

About the author

Steve Lewis is a Welshman who started a lifelong affinity with the game of rugby union after standing behind the posts at Rodney Parade, Newport, watching the fifth Springboks scrape home 3-0 in a match that the home team should have won at a canter – the record books never lie but they don't always tell the truth! For an awestruck eleven-year-old the 'black and ambers' were the business; schoolwork and the opposite sex would have to wait. Then it was Wales – Gareth, JPR, Gerald and Mervyn – Barry was never good enough to tie David Watkins' bootlaces! In 1974 two dreams were satisfied when he visited South Africa to follow Willie John McBride's British Lions.

After writing three books on Newport RFC, followed by two on Welsh rugby, the author grabbed the bull by the horns, crossed Offa's Dyke and took on the might of English rugby single-handedly. He lived to tell the tale and in *Last of the Blue Lions* completes a personal Triple Crown: books on club, country and the institution that has become the British and Irish Lions.

His previous books include *Who Let The Dogs Out? – The Revival of Newport Rugby, The Priceless Gift – Wales' International Rugby Captains* and most recently *One Among Equals – England's International Rugby Captains*.

Steve Lewis lives in Newport with his wife Catherine – the cat that wouldn't take no for an answer long since consigned to the great cattery in the sky.

Contents

Foreword

I was thirteen years old when I attended my first international rugby match. Ireland played Wales at Ravenhill, Belfast in March 1939. Victory would have secured the Triple Crown but Irish hopes were dashed, the visitors winning 7-0.

Many of the players involved that day had toured South Africa with the British Lions in 1938 under the captaincy of Ireland's Sam Walker. The Ulsterman was not included against Wales but fellow tourists Harry McKibbin, Vesey Boyle, George Cromey, George Morgan, Bob Alexander and Blair Mayne all took their places in the Irish team. Of the Welsh fifteen, Haydn Tanner and Bill Travers also toured with Walker's Lions.

The outbreak of war in September 1939 brought many international careers to an end and there were several players who would surely have gone on to become legends of the game but for the temporary end of international rugby. However, there were some who featured when the Championship resumed in 1947. Watching that match at Ravenhill in 1939 I would never have thought it possible that eight years later I would play against a Welsh team captained by Tanner and in 1949 one that would also include Travers.

The war years saw many of the 1938 Lions join the armed forces. Sadly Bob Alexander, a gifted wing forward, was killed in action in Italy. Blair Mayne was one of his country's most decorated soldiers of the Second World War and he was on the committee at Queen's University, Belfast, during my student days.

1

Following the war Sam Walker and Vivian Jenkins became respected commentators on the game, Walker with the BBC and Jenkins as a journalist with *The Sunday Times*. Harry McKibbin and Bill Clement were senior administrators in the game and in due course they were elected president of the Irish Rugby Football Union and secretary of the Welsh Rugby Union.

The 1938 British Lions were certainly a remarkable group of men. They achieved a good record against provincial opposition and despite losing the first two Tests and the series, the Lions gained much recognition by defeating the Springboks in the third Test at Cape Town. That match saw an outstanding second half performance by the Lions who after trailing 13-3 at half-time played some of their best rugby of the tour in the second-half to win the Test 21-16. Eight Irishmen played on that memorable day, something unlikely ever to happen again.

Now, with the publication of *Last of the Blue Lions* the full story of the 1938 British Lions tour is finally told, the book filling a gap not only in Lions history but also in the history of the game of rugby football.

Jack Kyle
January 2009

ACKNOWLEDGEMENTS

I first considered writing a book on the 1938 British Lions tour to South Africa in January 1997. The British and Irish Lions, as they are now known, were due to visit South Africa that summer. The first tour to the country since 1980, it would also be the sixth since the Second World War. All of the post-war tours are well documented with comprehensive accounts available to followers of the game but there was little written about those that had gone before. But there was a problem. Almost sixty years had passed since the party of twenty-nine players had set off on the great adventure and any surviving members of the 1938 squad would be in their mid-eighties circa 1997. How much would they recall of those far-off days?

When Bunner Travers answered the telephone I knew immediately that I had come up trumps – of course he remembered the 1938 tour and yes, he would be happy to meet me. Which pub did I suggest? We decided on the Ruperra, a village inn some five or six hundred yards from Bunner's home and no, he didn't need a lift, he would walk. I watched from the car park as the upright figure made his way down the lane. Back ramrod straight and dressed in a blazer together with collar and tie, the imposing figure drew nearer and when I introduced myself my hand disappeared into something resembling a shovel. This was the first of several meetings with the 'Prince of Hookers' and it was during these meetings that the 1938 tour was brought to life, leaving me with no doubt that the story had to be told. Subsequent conversations with Bill Clement and Vivian Jenkins only confirmed this

3

and in the summer of 1997 I set about researching the tour in detail.

David McLennan and Paul Dobson were a great help in pointing me in the right direction in Cape Town and made the necessary introductions. Staff at the city's South African Library were most generous with their time and sent the microfiche containing more than a hundred items as promised. Thomas Graham, then museum manager at the South African Rugby Football Union, provided detailed copies of the tour itinerary and expenses journal. More recently, Durban-based Hymie Sibul and Don Vale generously allowed access to their extensive collections of memorabilia and Gerhard Buraan took the photograph used on the cover of the book. In the UK, staff at Newport Library were always on hand to assist with the various pieces of equipment that invariably go wrong when this novice gets his hands on them. Ronnie Chambers in Northern Ireland dug deep in search for some minute details and was instrumental in introducing me to Jack Kyle. Nowadays the term 'great' is very misused and as a consequence much of its impact has been lost but when talking about the truly great players of the game the name Jack Kyle will never be excluded. I am very grateful to one of 'the first of the red Lions' for taking the time to write the foreword to *Last of the Blue Lions*. John Hill in Hexham expressed a desire to be involved in the early stages of the project and when contacted ten years later readily gave access to his collection of Lions-related material.

With the contacts made and the material sourced, in due course a manuscript finally saw the light of day and all that remained was to find a publisher. Randall Northam of SportsBooks agreed to take the project on board and it is thanks to him that the 1938 British

Acknowledgements

Lions now have a place in the bibliography of rugby football.

Finally, my wife Catherine once again put up with the moods and rants experienced during the gestation period which on this particular undertaking proved to last much longer than usual.

Steve Lewis,
March 2009

INTRODUCTION

When the British and Irish Lions set out on an eleven-match tour of New Zealand in May 2005 it was widely canvassed that the squad was better prepared than any of those that had preceded it. This was the twenty-seventh time a group of players had travelled to the southern hemisphere in the guise of a British team. Sir Clive Woodward, the man behind England's Rugby World Cup triumph of 2003, was appointed head coach of the party some months prior to departure and his search for the personnel most suited to his requirements left no stone unturned.

At his disposal was a budget reported to be in excess of £6 million. This enabled him to select a squad of forty-six players and a back-up team that included four assistant coaches, one from each of the home unions, a medical team, lawyer, chef and media manager. It was a group of personnel the size of which no country had ever deemed necessary to accommodate when setting out on a similar venture. Sir Clive and his men were on a mission – to defeat the All Blacks in the three-match Test series and in doing so write their own chapter in the history books by becoming only the second team from the British Isles to achieve such success following the 1971 Lions who triumphed under the leadership of John Dawes and the coaching genius that was Carwyn James.

The appropriate number of press and television personnel were on hand to ensure that the eight-week tour was comprehensively covered and every minute of each match would be transmitted live to the four corners of the world. Success and failure, euphoria and disappointment. These are just some of the tapestry of emotions that are part and parcel of sport – for every winner there has to be a loser. And lose the Lions most certainly did.

Despite the unprecedented budget and the attention given to detail a series whitewash saw the Lions struggle to come second in a two-horse race. The mid-week matches may have been won with no small amount of style and panache but that is not what matters, in fact it counts for nothing – if the Test series is lost all else is quickly forgotten. Respected observers of the game have gone to great lengths in their efforts to try and analyse where the 2005 tour went so terribly wrong but regardless of any conclusions other than the obvious – that the All Blacks were superior in damn near every position on the park – the most disturbing aspect of the post-mortem questioned the future of such tours. Should they be shorter? Should they be longer? Should they only include Test matches? Or, should they be dropped from the fixture list? This last option is not realistic as the revenue such tours generate is enormous and whatever the disappointing efforts of the class of 2005 suggest the British and Irish Lions can rightly claim to be one of the last great touring experiences in world sport.

Direct comparisons with earlier tours are fraught with danger. The days when some thirty players would play twenty-five or more matches and be away from home for four or five months are long gone. The game is now in the domain of the professional sportsman whose contractual obligations to club or region mean that such prolonged absences from the 'day job' must be seen as a thing of the past. Contrast the gentlemen and scholars who formed the nucleus of the early tours and those who followed, men who often had to give up work to realise a sporting ambition. The advent of professional rugby ensured that such drastic measures would no longer enter the equation but equally, so has the public expectation increased. If a tour is deemed to be a failure, if the Test series is lost, there is no hiding place for those involved. Such was the scenario in 2005.

That Lions tours now bear little resemblance to what went before has to be accepted. Times change and the game has endeavoured to adapt to the demands of the modern era – touring included. But has it ever been any different? From rugby football's inception in the mid-nineteenth century through to the professional sport which it is in the twenty-first there has been a continual process of change. Every aspect of the Laws of the game has been reviewed and amended at frequent intervals in the search for the perfect team sport, one which meets all the requirements to reach a global audience in a way that only Association Football has succeeded in doing.

In 1987 the first Rugby World Cup (RWC) took place in New Zealand. Played every four years the tournament has become one of the major sporting events in the calendar with only the Olympic Games and the football World Cup attracting greater interest. Secure in its future the RWC thrives. Each of the six tournaments held to date has surpassed the previous one. The event gets bigger, better and more financially viable, continuing to surpass all expectations. And at the end of the extravaganza one nation is officially declared world champions, a title held until the next tournament regardless of what fate awaits during the intervening four years.

Before the advent of a world cup it was difficult

to identify the most successful nation in the rugby-playing world. Teams representative of the British Isles had started touring the southern hemisphere as far back as 1888 when a 'missionary' party visited Australia and New Zealand but it was three years later in 1891 that the British Isles first played Test rugby while on a visit to South Africa, albeit with a squad of players only drawn from England and Scotland. When a second tour to South Africa took place in 1896 the composition of the squad was made up of English and Irish players and it was in the final Test of this tour that the hosts claimed a first success over the visitors, one which would be built on with alarming regularity in years to come.

In the twentieth century tours to the southern hemisphere were a regular feature in the rugby calendar but their duration of anything up to six months often prevented the best players from taking part, thereby denying a true measurement of the relevant playing strength found in the two hemispheres. This aside, the success of New Zealand and South Africa on their visits to Britain was sufficient to suggest that global rugby supremacy was to be found south of the equator. With Australia yet to make a significant impact on the rugby stage this conclusion in turn led to the inevitable question – which of the two southern hemisphere juggernauts was the greater? New Zealand or South Africa? The All Blacks or the Springboks? A question that remained unanswered until well into the twentieth century.

The two countries tied a three-match series in New Zealand in 1921, winning one Test each with the third drawn. In 1928 the spoils of a four-Test series in South Africa were also shared, the All Blacks and the

Springboks each winning two matches. It was not until 1937 that the issue would be resolved and even then the outcome went to the wire. That year saw South Africa return to New Zealand and when the teams lined up at Eden Park, Auckland for the third and final Test once again it was all square, both countries successful in one of the earlier matches. Played on 25 September in front of 55,000 spectators, the final Test can rightly be viewed as the first time in the history of rugby union that the winner could lay claim to the unofficial title of world champions – there was a lot at stake.

Come the end of September, the Springboks had been on the road for almost five months. The tour started in Australia where ten of the eleven matches were won and after fifteen matches in New Zealand only defeat in the first Test blotted the copybook. The Springboks lost the Wellington Test 13-7 but levelled the series three weeks later with a 13-6 victory in Christchurch. These scores suggest there was little to choose between the two teams but only a draw in Auckland could prevent one of them laying claim to being the best in the world.

That South Africa had won twenty-four of the twenty-six matches played going into the third Test was an impressive statistic in itself but it was the style of play and the way in which the Springboks totally dominated the opposition that had most impressed onlookers. Gone was the dour, forward-orientated rugby that had characterised Springbok rugby since the end of the First World War. In its place was a much more expansive, entertaining style of play though one still based on the ability of a dominant pack of forwards to win quality, prime possession.

Back home on the high veldt and in the coastal

provinces Springbok supporters were struggling to
come to grips with the way their team was playing,
often doubting the accuracy of the reporting. Recent
years had seen New Zealand in 1928 and Australia
in 1933 both visit South Africa and in 1931–32 the
Springboks had toured the British Isles. The series with
the All Blacks was drawn and Australia were beaten 3-2
in an extended series added to which was a grand slam
tour in which none of the four home nations was able
to contain an abrasive Springbok pack. But regardless
how successful the Springboks were during that five-
year period, lessons had been learnt which resulted in
South Africa adopting a new approach to the game,
one based on exciting back play, and at Auckland in
September 1937 such lessons helped the Springboks lay
a justifiable claim to being the best. The 17-6 victory
saw the visitors cross for five tries, the All Blacks
restricted to two penalty goals, all of which confirms
the dominance of a team reports suggest should have
won by a much greater margin, such was the strength
and superior technique of the Springbok pack and the
pace and craft of the backs.

Who were these men that time would come to
recognise as the 'Greatest Springboks'? The squad
of twenty-nine players contained many established
names and some who first made their mark in Australia
and New Zealand. Prominent among the forwards was
captain Philip Nel, Ferdie Bergh, Louis Strachan and
the front row trio of hooker Jan Lotz and the brothers
Boy and Fanie Louw at prop. These players formed the
nucleus of a formidable pack of forwards while behind
the scrum there was an equal array of talent: Gerry
Brand at full-back, Dai Williams, Louis Babrow and
Freddy Turner in the three-quarters alongside half-

backs Tony Harris and the inimitable Danie Craven. The 1937 Springboks were the first team to win a Test series in New Zealand, an achievement only the 1971 British Lions can claim to have matched, and the following year it would be visitors from the British Isles who would have the first opportunity to play these newly crowned 'world champions' in their own back yard.

Returning from New Zealand in October 1937 the Springboks could look forward to a long summer and some months away from rugby before the next season got under way but in the northern hemisphere the new season had kicked off on 1 September, the start of an eight-month period that would include the International Championship in the new year. This would be preceded by the trial matches which allowed the selectors of the four home unions the opportunity to assess players away from their club environment and at the end of another arduous campaign there would be a British Isles team to select to tour South Africa during the British summer and beyond. For some it would mean twelve months non-stop rugby, unpaid rugby, and it was little wonder that not all the first-choice players would be able to travel.

The 1937–38 season conformed to what had become a regular pattern, one only ever disrupted by the visit of an overseas touring party. There were the long-established fixtures: Oxford won the Varsity match; the Royal Navy became Service Champions; Lancashire won the County Championship; and St Mary's triumphed in the Hospitals Cup for a fifth successive year. The Barbarians completed their annual fixtures against Leicester and the East Midlands together with the four-match Easter tour of south Wales. With no league structure present among the four divisions in England it is difficult to identify the leading clubs but the records of Coventry, Gloucester, Percy Park and Wasps suggest these were the dominant forces in their respective regions.

In Scotland, Stewart's College Former Pupils were crowned champions for the first time and Selkirk won the Border League Cup. In Ireland it was University College, Dublin who won the Leinster Cup, Young Munster the Munster Cup and north of the border the Ulster Cup went to Instonians for the eighth time when, under the leadership of Sam Walker, they defeated North of Ireland 11-6 in the final. Cardiff and Aberavon were the most successful of the Welsh clubs, the blue and blacks heading an unofficial championship table after winning thirty-nine of the forty-seven matches played.

With France omitted since 1931 following doubts held by the four home unions concerning the way the game was being administered by the FFR, it was England, Ireland, Scotland and Wales who contested the International Championship in which Scotland proved to be the dominant force when beating the other three countries to secure an eighth Triple Crown. This was nothing less than the Scots deserved, the backs in particular lighting up a tournament that had become a rather dour affair in recent years. The 1938 Championship was particularly notable for producing the highest number of points and tries of any to date that had featured six matches – 176 and 35 respectively.

As the international season drew to a close it was time for the Tour Committee of the Four Home Unions under the chairmanship of James Baxter to convene and select the twenty-nine players to represent the British Isles in South Africa. Baxter knew what such an extensive tour entailed. He had managed the British team which had visited Australia and New Zealand in 1930, a tour that extended to six months and was not without its share of controversy. Issues regarding the interpretation of the Laws were frequently raised, not least New Zealand's use of a roving forward which the International Rugby Football Board (IRFB – now the IRB) had inadvertently encouraged by failing to identify the number of forwards required to make up the scrum.

An ex-president of the Rugby Football Union (RFU), James Baxter won three caps in 1900 and featured prominently on the Selection Committee for a number of years while his prowess as a yachtsman brought him a bronze medal in the 12-metre class at the 1908 Olympics. Together with his fellow selectors he now faced the responsibility of putting together a group of players equal to the task of competing with a South African team recognised as the best that country had produced.

Where the team selection would present the usual problems largely due to the unavailability of leading players, the choice of management was much more straightforward. Major Bernard Charles Hartley was a well-known figure in English rugby circles. A Cambridge blue, stalwart of the Blackheath club and winner of two international caps, he was currently the Army's representative on the RFU, making him ideally suited to the role of Honorary Manager. Likewise, his assistant H.A. Haigh Smith was also one of the game's leading administrators whose principal office was Honorary Secretary of the Barbarians. In the capable hands of these two individuals the demands and problems that would inevitably impact on a group of young men away from home for an extended period of time were certain to be competently dealt with.

If only the selection of the twenty-nine players were so straightforward. Rugby union being a strictly amateur sport there was little if any latitude available to men who relied totally on regular wages for their day to day existence. Conditions may have improved since the General Strike and the depressed economy of the twenties but employment was still a major cause for concern particularly in the industrial regions which often meant the parts of the country where the game was most prominent.

The selectors were obviously satisfied with what they had seen during the first five fixtures of the Championship as the squad of players to tour South Africa was announced on the eve of the final match. This saw Scotland defeat England 21-16 in front of 70,000 spectators at Twickenham, King George VI and Queen Elizabeth among them, and beyond the environs of Billy William's Cabbage Patch there was another audience watching events unfold as this was the first international rugby match to be broadcast live on television. But the selection process was over and those players performing in front of the King and Queen and the television audience already knew if they were included.

On Friday 18 March the secretary of the RFU, Engineer-Commander S.F. Cooper announced the twenty-nine man squad invited to tour South Africa. It was made up of seven players from England, eight from Ireland, five Scots and nine Welshmen and included three men yet to be capped by their country. Notable among those unable to travel were England centre Peter Cranmer, who captained his country against Wales and Ireland in the Championship; Hal Sever, an outstanding wing three-quarter who scored five tries in ten consecutive appearances for England, and Ray Longland, a loose forward with nineteen England caps to his credit. From Wales, captain and outside-half Cliff Jones and Wilf Wooler, an outstanding centre who would have thrived on the hard grounds in South Africa, had previously declared their unavailability. North of the border, Scotland captain Wilson Shaw was another brilliant outside-half who would be sorely missed, as would centre Charles Dick and loose forward W.H. Crawford. The Irish contribution was less noticeably affected and included the Ulster forward and current Ireland captain Sam Walker who would also lead the tourists.

Between 18 March and the scheduled departure date of 20 May five of those originally selected withdrew. After suitable replacements had been found the final party comprised nine Englishmen, eight players from both Ireland and Wales together with four Scots, and the number of uncapped players had increased to six, five of them found among the forwards where the outcome of the Test series would almost certainly be decided. The players were a mix of university students, local government officials, policemen, members of the armed forces, bank employees and self-employed businessmen – occupations which enabled employers to look favourably on an extended leave of absence. Others were not so fortunate, but with an average age of twenty-five and only two married men among the squad any potential financial worries appear to have been overcome.

For reasons which are not altogether clear the recognised composition of touring parties between the wars catered for twenty-nine players. Generally this broke down to fifteen forwards and fourteen backs but the 1938 Lions saw the balance reversed in favour of the extra back – two full-backs, eight three-quarters and five half-backs. The fourteen forwards included two specialist hookers but the remainder were all players who were equally comfortable in at least two positions, which would give those responsible for team selection various options to pursue.

The enforced changes saw the English representation increased from seven to nine but there was a definite lack of international experience with the players only having eighteen caps between them. The four forwards were all uncapped. A.H.G. Purchas, Gerald Dancer and W.G. Howard were late additions to the party replacing M. Inglis, D.T. Kemp and Eddie Watkins while Stanley Couchman, an original selection, had been an England reserve. Of the five backs, scrum-half Jimmy Giles was the most experienced with six caps to his name. Among the three-quarters, James Unwin had been capped twice as had Basil Nicholson while Roy Leyland and outside-half Jeff Reynolds had both played for England three times.

Such limited experience among what amounted to a third of the squad needed to be redressed by the Celtic nations. Ireland boasts a rugby tradition that has historically favoured age over beauty and with seventy-two international caps between them the Irish players certainly brought a wealth of experience to the table. Sam Walker was something of a veteran who had won fifteen caps since being introduced to the team in 1934.

Joining him in the forwards were fellow Ulstermen, Bob Alexander and Blair Mayne who had eight and three caps respectively and Charles Graves, a Dubliner and one of the two specialist hookers in the party who, like Walker, had played for Ireland fifteen times..

Behind the scrum, wing three-quarter Vesey Boyle returned to the side against Wales to win an eighth cap after missing the first two matches of the season. Centre Harry McKibbin won his first cap in the same match and outside-half George Cromey made six consecutive appearances during 1937 and 1938. Scrum-half George Morgan was the most experienced of the Irishmen with sixteen caps and, like Walker, had also captained his country. By modern standards not the most experienced group of players but seventy-one years ago international caps were hard to come by and most of these Irishmen knew all there was to know about the international game. Theirs was a wealth of experience that would shortly be put to the test in some of rugby's most demanding arenas and in front of equally demanding and knowledgeable spectators.

Championship and Triple Crown winners they may have been but Scotland provided the smallest representation of the four home unions, reduced from the original selection of five to four. This followed the withdrawal of George Roberts and William Inglis and the inclusion of Charles Grieve who had not played international rugby for two years. His two outings in a Scotland jersey were at outside-half but Grieve was now included as a full-back and what an inspired selection that would prove to be. Duncan Macrae had been a permanent fixture in the centre for the past two seasons, winning six consecutive caps, and much was expected of this exciting talent but it was disappointing that his colleagues in the Scottish midfield, R.C.S. Dick and Wilson Shaw, were unable to tour. Among the forwards, master butcher Jock Waters, at twenty-nine the elder statesman of the party, had not featured in the Championship but his sixteen consecutive caps won over the previous five seasons were certain to stand him in good stead when faced by the beef and brawn of the South African eight. Neither was five-times-capped Laurie Duff expected to shirk his responsibilities. Few in number they may have been but the Scottish representation would make their presence felt on tour, each of them playing Test match rugby.

The Welsh contingency was reduced to eight following the withdrawal of wing three-quarter F.J.V. Ford and forward Eddie Watkins, the uncapped Elvet Jones called up as Ford's replacement. Senior among them was full-back Vivian Jenkins, an outstanding goal kicker and a seasoned international with thirteen caps. Wing three-quarter Bill Clement had won six caps and at scrum-half Haydn Tanner, at twenty-one the baby of the squad, continued his meteoric rise having won ten consecutive caps after being introduced to the Welsh team against New Zealand in 1935, three weeks before his nineteenth birthday. Up front, loose forwards Russell Taylor and the uncapped Ivor Williams were joined by prop Eddie Morgan, present in the Welsh team throughout the Championship, and specialist hooker Bill Travers, first capped in 1937 since when he had become an indispensable member of the pack.

Most of the twenty-nine players played for the leading clubs of the day. Bedford, Coventry, the Harlequins, Rosslyn Park and to a lesser extent the Army all continue to play the game at the higher levels in England but Old Cranleighans and Old Birkonians are names which suggest rugby of a bygone era. Dublin University and Queen's University, Belfast are still very much associated with the game as is Clontarf but the fortunes of Instonians have seen the club enjoying less successful years than those when it could boast a British Lions captain among its ranks. St Andrew's University, Glasgow Academicals and Selkirk still play their part in Scottish club rugby as do Cardiff, Cross Keys, Newport, Llanelli and Swansea in Wales while London Welsh continue to entertain at Old Deer Park in south-west London.

Before looking at the tour in detail it is important to consider the way rugby union was played in 1938. The basics were much the same: there were fifteen players in a team; the ball was oval; and the size of the playing area was consistent other than the introduction of the metric system, meaning that references to the 25-yard line etc. will appear in the text. Rugby was a game of two halves. International matches were played over two periods of forty minutes but the duration of all other games was determined by the two captains. For the upcoming tour the respective unions had confirmed that all matches would be played over eighty minutes. Although not as technically advanced as seen today, players wore clothing and footwear of similar design and the game was controlled by a referee and two touch judges.

Scoring methods have changed several times over the game's long history but the values in place in 1938 had been unaltered since 1905. Three points were awarded for a try and a further two for a successful conversion. Penalty kicks were worth three points, the same value applying to place kicks or drop goal attempts following a mark or fair catch, but a drop goal from open play scored four points. For conversions and place kicks following a mark or fair catch the ball had to be held by a 'placer' and only when it made contact with the ground were the opposition allowed to advance. Laws concerning kicks at goal from a penalty were consistent with the modern game – the player kicking for goal allowed to place the ball and the opposition not allowed to charge.

The dominant feature of the game in the 1930s was the scrum. It was not unusual to see as many as fifty contested during the game and the team that gained the ascendancy in this area of play usually went on to take the spoils. The number of scrums was influenced by the Law stating that when the ball was kicked into touch the team with the put-in could elect to take a line-out or a scrum ten yards infield, the latter option usually the preferred choice of a dominant pack. The scrum also instigated the favoured attacking option that saw the forwards take the ball upfield at their feet – a foot rush or dribbling were the common terms for this passage of play. The scrum was wheeled with the ball held in the second row. The locks and loose forwards would break off and move forward with the ball at their feet and it took a brave man to bring this move to a stop by falling on the ball and taking the consequences.

Players could kick to touch from any part of the field, jumpers in the line-out could not be assisted, there were no substitutions or replacements allowed, the teams remained on the field at half-time and much else besides. Rugby union was a different game circa 1938 but it was also in essence the same as that played today. A sporting contest between teams made up of fifteen players who set out to win a match by scoring most points – tries and goal kicks still paramount in that objective.

Above all, in 1938 rugby was first and foremost a pastime, an opportunity to meet like-minded individuals, an opportunity to socialise and make friends, and when the game allowed all that to happen 6,000 miles from home life must have seemed very, very kind indeed.

CHAPTER ONE

DEPARTURES AND ARRIVALS

London – Southampton – the *Stirling Castle* – A committee is formed – Cape Town – A pressing encounter – Running on a full stomach – A luncheon and a training session – Onward to East London – The first win – The first train journey – The first defeat.

They arrived from the four corners of the land. By road, by rail and for some by ship, the journey starting with a trip across the Irish Sea. These were short hops compared to what lay ahead but for the twenty-eight players who met up in London they represented the start of the adventure – '... a journey of a thousand miles must begin with a single step'. The only absentee was England three-quarter Basil Nicholson who had to take his final engineering examinations and would travel at a later date and join up with the party in South Africa. Major Hartley and H.A. Haigh Smith were on hand to make the introductions. Most of the players knew each other from their encounters in the Championship but there were those with little or no international experience who may not have been so familiar to their new colleagues. That minor problem could be addressed over the coming months and in time many lifelong friendships would be forged.

The time spent in the capital was hectic but thankfully only extended to a couple of days.

There were official functions to attend where the players were introduced to a never ending number of anonymous faces, the important and sometimes less important dignitaries and officials who were all keen to make their acquaintance. The South African High Commissioner, the Hon. C de Water entertained the party at South Africa House and former England captain W.W. Wakefield, now the Conservative Member of Parliament for Swindon, hosted a dinner at the Houses of Parliament following which the guests listened to a debate on foreign policy. The players who had already been feted by their clubs and unions could be forgiven for thinking they were about to undertake a marathon of gourmet indulgence – in which respect time would prove them right.

Glad to leave London behind them the Lions arrived in Southampton on Saturday 21 May, a day later than originally scheduled. Here they boarded the *Stirling Castle* which would be their home for the next two weeks but before they could settle into the daily routine that is life at sea there was one final reception to attend. This was hosted by the Union-Castle Line on board ship with the company's assistant manager, Mr D. Storrar overseeing proceedings. Over lunch the good wishes of the King were read out. His Majesty's private secretary sent a telegram to Major Hartley that read – 'I am commanded by the King to thank you and the members of the British Rugby team for your loyal message which he greatly appreciates. His Majesty hopes that you will all have a pleasant and successful tour'. Wined and dined and with all non-travelling personnel safely deposited ashore, the Lions watched as the *Stirling Castle* moved away from her berth, the tugboats took over and at 4.00

p.m. precisely she set sail for Cape Town, a journey of 5,987 nautical miles.

The *Stirling Castle* was first introduced into service in January 1936 and soon broke the records for both the outward and return journeys between London and Cape Town. The *Stirling Castle* arrived in Cape Town in September 1936 after completing the outward journey in 13 days 6 hours and 30 minutes. The record for the return journey was improved later that month and a year later it had been reduced to 12 days 22 hours and 18 minutes. The time taken to complete the journey was critical as the Union-Castle Line had recently negotiated a ten-year contract with the South African Government stipulating that the weekly mail service from London be received within fourteen days. Some of the existing fleet needed to be upgraded to meet this requirement and the *Stirling Castle* and her sister ship the *Athlone Castle* were commissioned to be built to the higher specification at the Harland and Wolff yard in Belfast.

With 25,550 gross tonnage and 696 feet in length the *Stirling Castle* carried 784 passengers and for the first time these fell into two classes, first and cabin, unlike other vessels in the fleet which catered for first, second and third class accommodation. A high level of specification was maintained throughout the ship with passengers able to enjoy a swimming pool and gymnasium which were both put to good use by the tourists as a supplement to their ninety-minute daily training routine. Exercise could not be ignored and use of the pool and gym helped to work off the additional calories three full meals a day produced. From the long gallery dominated by a painting of the fifteenth century castle overlooking the Forth in Scotland's Central region after which the ship was named, through the lounge areas, dining room and cabins, the furnishings, fixtures and fittings were of the highest quality and travelling as first class passengers the party enjoyed every comfort.

With time of the essence, the voyage included just one scheduled stop at Madeira, 1,314 miles and some three days from Southampton. This presented the opportunity for the players to send home some early correspondence and among the mail left with Blandy Bros. & Co. Ltd, Union-Castle's agents at Funchal, was a letter to the secretary of the RFU. This advised that a committee had been elected comprising of Major Hartley, Jack Haigh Smith, Sam Walker, Vivian Jenkins, James Unwin and Jock Waters. The main responsibility of the six men would be team selection but they had already made one significant decision in appointing Vivian Jenkins as vice-captain.

With Madeira behind them, the party had time to reflect on the Europe they had left and the Union of South Africa that awaited them. The Spanish Civil War would shortly enter its third year and with the support of 50,000 enlisted men from Germany and Italy, General Franco and his National Party looked likely to succeed in their efforts to overthrow the Republican government. Germany's annexation of Austria had prompted Czechoslovakia to deploy 400,000 troops to the border shared with the new Austro-German alliance the day before the *Stirling Castle* sailed from Southampton. Despite earlier reassurances from Prime Minister, Neville Chamberlain that the Anglo-Italian Agreement signed in early May heralded a new start in relationships between the two countries, an opinion fiercely contested by the opposition, there was growing concern that Germany under Adolf Hitler's

Nazi Party, was intent on conflict. Chamberlain's 'peace in our time' reassurance was some months off but contrary to this optimism the defence budget had been increased. Mock wartime 'blackout' exercises would be carried out, people had to be measured for gas masks and an assessment of the nation's air defences was commissioned.

And South Africa? The Boer War may have ended thirty-six years earlier, but the wounds were far from healed and when the Great War of 1914–18 followed, loyalties to the Crown were divided. Recent happenings in Europe were being watched with interest from the Union and in the event of another major conflict the same loyalties would once again be put to the test. The United Party formed in 1934 by an alliance between a divided Nationalist Party and the South African Party was re-elected on 18 May 1938. Prime Minister Herzog and his deputy Jan Smuts continued to head the government but with Herzog's Nationalist background there were likely to be anti-British sympathies. Added to which 1938 would celebrate the centenary of the Great Trek, the most significant episode in Afrikaner history.

The *Stirling Castle* was due to arrive in Cape Town on the morning of Saturday 4 June but as was normal practice she dropped anchor in Table Bay the previous night. Come dawn the ship moved to her mooring in the Victoria Basin and the official welcoming party together with members of the press wasted no time in boarding to greet the tourists, who they found in good spirits after their journey. Already on-board was A.J. Pienaar, the President of the South African Rugby Board who had taken advantage of the opportunity to go out on one of the tugs, thereby stealing a march on the eager pressmen looking for that first scoop of the tour.

Among those on board to welcome the visitors were ex-Springbok captains Paul Roos, Billy Miller, Theo Pienaar, Boy Morkel and Phil Mostert. Roos was captain on the first overseas tour, to Britain and France in 1906, and Miller succeeded him when the Springboks returned to Europe in 1912. In Australia and New Zealand in 1921 the honour fell to Theo Pienaar with Morkel as his vice-captain and Mostert led the Springboks when New Zealand visited South Africa in 1928. Included among the representatives of the press was Willie Hook, a columnist for the *Cape Times*, whose light-hearted reporting style probably gave his readers a better introduction to the Lions than many of the more serious reports that found their way onto the sports pages of rival publications.

I had been told that I must get interviews with the individual players but I was not to let them know that I was interviewing them. It appears that if my gems of literature were published over in Britain the whole party would have to go home and play a team called the Northern Union because they would be professionals and the Sudeten Germans would be given land in Abyssinia, or am I getting a bit mixed?
Anyhow, disguising myself as a Minister Without Portfolio I made a list of the party and began my man to man interviews. I hunted out Vivian Jenkins and made him realise that I was not connected with the press by asking him if he would like to see the latest design in vacuum cleaners. Vivian, I Grieve to say, turned his full

back on me and that was that! Then I spoke to Unwin and Macrae and McKibbin and Clement and Boyle and Jones, but they would not even meet me at midfield so I passed along to the scrum halfs.

"Good morning Mr Morgan" I said to one of them, placing him entirely at his ease, "with a name like yours I know you probably play for Llantyphwelliphillanymadoc". "Sure now and its wrong entoirely ye are," replied Mr Morgan speaking with a delightful Irish brogue, "for tis for Old Belvedere I play". Noticing my eyebrows arched in surprise while my massive brain was detecting the flaw which I knew must be there, a charming, genial gentleman called Mr Giles came to my rescue. "It is a bit puzzling I admit," he said, "but it is easy to explain. Our friend here is a lost member of the tribe of Morgan". Mr Giles proved the perfect gentleman. To remove my embarrassment entirely he introduced me to a Mr Haydn, a tanner. I admit I did not quite catch the name but this is how it sounded. Then I was introduced to Mr Reynolds who, I was informed, was the "Hostler" of the team, although I must confess there was nothing the slightest bit horsey about him.

Ten minutes had elapsed before my next introduction. This was caused by the fact that they could not find 'Tiny' Cromie, the other stand off half. At last he was discovered hiding behind a deck quoit and I found he was not the least bit stand offish. This boy will be a great favourite but if the Springbok and Provincial flank forwards have as much difficulty in locating him as I had yesterday he will score many tries.

Before leaving the Light for the Heavy Brigade I counted up my original list and made it fifteen. Then I counted up my list of interviews and found it was fourteen. Checking up further by cross reference and the index filing system I discovered that Nicholson was absent from parade. I looked behind three other deck quoits and under the tarpaulin of a lifeboat but could not find him. "Where is Nicholson of the wavy hair?" I cried. "Oh, he is coming out on the *Athlone Castle* later," answered someone and somebody else added, "The final answer to the Maiden's Prayer!"

And so I came to the forwards. I began with Sam Walker the captain. He greeted me with a smile; he left me with a smile; he smiled at me throughout our interview. Somebody said he was a bank official. I don't believe it. He looks too good natured to mark a cheque RD. A host of others came up. Tall, strapping fellows. I felt as if I was lost in a beastly pine forest. A voice said "Crouch man" so I walked about doubled up for a couple of minutes until I found I was to meet the Old Cranleighans forward.

The last I met was another Mr Morgan. Remembering the remark made by Mr Giles I took the outstretched hand and murmured "Old Belvedere I presume." "No," came the answer, "Llanphthwheliphlly." All I can say is you never know where you are with these lost units!... As I was half way down the gangway someone shouted after me "What about Haig-Smith?" I

immediately rushed back. "I don't mind if I do,"
I said, "but my name is not Smith." (Reproduced
as printed in the *Cape Times*).

Following the initial introductions conducted aboard
ship, the party joined 200 guests at an official
luncheon held in the Banqueting Hall at the City
Hall. This was hosted by the Mayor, Mr William Foster
who in proposing a toast to the visitors said he was '...
convinced that the tour will prove of lasting benefit
to South African rugby and I am certain that the fare
provided will be enjoyed by all, whatever the result,
because we in South Africa have learned to associate
British sportsmen with the term sportsmanship in
all its implications...' Whether he dropped a faux pas
when suggesting that any of the players who won
renown on the playing field would receive '...almost
as much adulation as a Mussolini or a Hitler...' is
something which has to be considered in the context
of European politics vis-à-vis those prominent in the
Union but Major Hartley replied on behalf of the
party thanking their hosts for a '...most inspiring and
wonderful welcome...'

Hartley had been invited to tour with the British
team in 1903 but his father had insisted that he
decline the invitation and put his business interests
first. Now he was satisfying a long-standing ambition
and concluded by saying that '...we mean business...
we will do our utmost to win, and I think we shall
possibly do better than some think...' He presented
the mayor with a signed miniature rugby ball and the
mayoress with a Lion brooch. These were formalities
seen at every official function the Lions would attend
and in his first speech on foreign soil Sam Walker was

applauded when he concluded by confirming that '...
we have heard a lot about your players and we know
what we are up against but we have come here for a
purpose, and that is to do our best to beat you and
you may be certain that both on and off the field
every one of us will act like British sportsmen and
gentlemen...'

The first game was a week away and would be played in
East London, a further 569 miles by sea and the party
would return to the *Stirling Castle* and complete the
journey via Port Elizabeth. Following the luncheon at
the City Hall there was sufficient time for the players
to enjoy a training session at the Green Point Track
and break out of the regimes they had been restricted
to at sea. There was an opportunity for the backs
to go through their paces in front of an impressed
gathering of spectators while the forwards took on
board the principles of the 3-4-1 scrum they were
largely unfamiliar with but which was favoured in the
southern hemisphere. Wales had adopted the system
during the Championship but the 3-2-3 formation
was more familiar to the majority of the forwards and
likely to be preferred on the tour.

By learning the different techniques required
to pack down with a middle row consisting of four
players and an eighth man behind, the tourists would
be able to adapt as and when circumstances dictated.
Boy Morkel, Phil Mostert and A.H. de Villiers were
invited to assist the forwards in the new formation
which involved different body angles and foot
placement to those which they were accustomed to.
After a few scrums the Lions appeared to have got to
grips with the basic principles but there was a lot of

work to be done if they were to use the formation with any success against the Springboks.

Onlookers at the training session were undoubtedly confused as the players represented a real mismatch of colour in their various jerseys and socks. The Lions had no official training kit, as illustrated by Sam Walker who wore an England jersey. The only official kit was that which would be worn on match days. Early touring sides from the British Isles had worn hooped jerseys which represented the red, white and blue of the Union Jack but following the First World War it was decided by the Four Home Unions committee that a blue jersey, white shorts and red stockings would be the order of the day and it was in this combination that the Lions took to the field in South Africa in 1938.

Having briefly sampled the delights of South Africa's Mother City to which they would return in two weeks, the party set off on the final leg of their journey. Rounding Cape Point, the *Stirling Castle* crossed the line where two oceans meet; where the cold waters of the Atlantic give way to the more inviting temperatures associated with the Indian Ocean. Then it was Port Elizabeth and finally East London where the tourists disembarked after seventeen days at sea. The next four days would give the players time enough to get their land legs back before the serious part of the tour got under way.

East London lies at the mouth of the Buffalo River and it was into this estuary that the *Stirling Castle* sailed on the morning of 7 June. For the first time since leaving Southampton the baggage and players' personal luggage could be put ashore and placed into the care of the Thomas Cook baggage master John 'Mac' Strachan who would accompany the party throughout the tour. It would be Strachan's responsibility to liaise with the railway company and hotels to ensure that the luggage arrived in the right place at the right time, a not insignificant task that would entail looking after trunks and bags which numbered around 150.

Also joining the party was Richard Luyt, who the South African Rugby Union had appointed to accompany the party as its representative. Luyt, an ex-Springbok centre, had played in two Tests against the 1910 tourists and the five Tests on the 1912–13 tour to the British Isles and France. Accompanying him on that tour were brothers John, an outside-half, and Freddie, a loose forward and the three brothers had the unique distinction of playing together against England, Scotland and Wales. In 1938 Richard Luyt's principal function would be to handle all the ground arrangements and to ensure that all media and social engagements ran smoothly. He was also responsible for the day to day expenses of the party and the payment of the weekly allowances.

On disembarking, the party was taken to the King's Court Hotel where it would be based for the next six nights. Other than the few hours spent ashore in Cape Town, East London was the first chance for the tourists to experience the country where they would spend the next four months.

Not as well known as some of the bigger cities in South Africa, East London nevertheless played an important part in the infrastructure of the country by virtue of its geographical location, midway between the two major ports on the route to Asia – Cape Town and Durban. Founded on the west bank of the Buffalo River in 1846, by 1938 the city had expanded to both sides of the river which were now linked by a double-deck bridge opened in 1935 and the only one of its kind in South Africa. Major oil companies opened depots on the west bank allowing easy access to the west quay where more than 3,000 ft of berthing facilities was available. The east of the town benefited from a breakwater helping the miles of sandy beaches to be fully utilised. Freshwater and seawater swimming pools catered for the thousands of holidaymakers attracted to this popular resort during the summer months.

The opening match of the tour was against Border and would be played at the Recreation Ground located in the eastern suburb of Arcadia. Following the Lions' arrival in the town interest in the fixture grew to such a degree that a full house was expected. When the team was announced on Thursday it included both captain Sam Walker and vice-captain Vivian Jenkins and was made up of four players from England, Ireland and Wales together with three Scots.

The forwards had a mix of Celtic muscle with Bill Travers and Charles Graves joining Walker in the front row, Russell Taylor, Blair Mayne, Jock Waters, Bob Alexander and Laurie Duff behind. The backs included Jeff Reynolds and Jimmy Giles at half-back, Duncan Macrae and Roy Leyland in the centre, James Unwin and Bill Clement on the wings with Jenkins at full-back. Border were not expected to unduly trouble the tourists as the 5-1 odds on offer for a home victory confirmed. That this was the first match and the Lions were still trying to shake off the after effects of the long journey counted for little but there were those who predicted a much closer contest than such lengthy odds suggested.

Match day brought typical South African winter weather not dissimilar to that of a normal British summer. As was the usual practice at such matches there were two curtain raisers to keep the crowd entertained. An under-15 schools' match preceded an encounter between two of the region's top colleges, Dale and Queen's, both recognised as leading breeding grounds for players of the future. Then it was the turn of the British Isles team to strut their stuff.

Match 1, Border, Saturday 11 June, East London

At 3.30 Sam Walker led his players onto the field where a record crowd of 10,000 eagerly awaited them. Border were captained by centre James White who had toured Britain in 1931 and appeared in two of the Tests against New Zealand in 1937. Joining him in the team were fellow internationals Bernard Reid at full-back and Cecil Jennings among the forwards.

From the kick-off the tourists showed their intent, running the ball at every opportunity with Jeff Reynolds quick to catch the eye. The opposing forwards and half-backs struggled to contain his darting runs which benefited from Giles' accurate passing from the base of the scrum. This in turn allowed Macrae to carve up the midfield and create many opportunities for the men out wide. The Lions' forwards won the early exchanges and firstly Laurie Duff and then Macrae touched down but both players were recalled for technical infringements. To add to the frustration Jenkins missed two straightforward penalties and as so often happens in such circumstances it was the home side who scored first after Walker wandered offside in front of the posts in the fifteenth minute.

Finding themselves trailing by three points, the Lions responded well. A long touch finder from Jenkins took play deep into Border territory and from the line-out Giles broke before releasing the three-quarters who each handled well to create an overlap for Unwin to cross midway between the posts and the corner flag for the first try of the tour. Walker took over the place kicking duties but failed with the conversion attempt. With half-time approaching the Lions forwards were beginning to assert their authority on the game and the backs were receiving good-quality possession in the right parts of the field. From a scrum it was Reynolds who created space for the centres and following some crisp handling Macrae put Unwin clear for his second try which this time Jenkins made no mistake in converting to give the tourists an 8-3 lead. A third try should have followed when Reid had a clearance kick charged down leaving three Lions in the clear with only the full-back to beat but a wayward pass to Roy Leyland was knocked on and a clear-cut opportunity went begging.

As half-time approached Border were camped inside Lions' territory and following a missed penalty attempt by Kopke, Jeff Reynolds failed to find touch with what should have been the last play of the half. His loose effort was gathered by Jennings and, with the Lions' defence in disarray, the forward executed a perfect cross-kick which scrum-half Gordon latched on to with several players lined up outside him. Swift, accurate passing caught the Lions' defence flat-footed and Evans finished off an excellent move touching down in the corner. Kopke converted from the touchline and the half ended with the scores level at 8-8.

Founded in 1891, Border was one of the oldest provincial teams in South Africa but it was still looking for a first victory against a touring side. Recent encounters had witnessed comprehensive defeats, Border losing twice to both the 1933 Australians and the 1928 New Zealanders. The 1924 Lions had also beaten the province 12-3 but in 1910 despite comfortably winning 30-10 in East London, four days later Tom Smyth's team was held to a 13-13 draw at King William's Town. Now, with the scores level after the first forty minutes there was everything to play for. The Lions may have entertained the crowd with their open, running rugby but this was a match that had to be won if the tour was to get under way as expected. Within ten minutes of the restart the Lions crossed for what proved to be the decisive score of the match. Following an expansive move and forward rush, Unwin was caught in possession but he managed to release the ball which was hacked on by the Lions' forwards allowing Duncan Macrae to gather and score. Once again the extra points went begging, this time Jenkins failing to convert and in the weeks that followed the Lions would pay dearly for the lack of a consistent goal kicker. Fortunately they were not alone in this basic requirement as Kopke missed four penalties in succession, a great disappointment for the home forwards who played superbly throughout. It was in this first match of the tour that the Lions adopted the 3-4-1 formation in response to a reorganised home pack. They coped well with the unfamiliar formation and ended the game the stronger of the two units, winning sufficient ball to provide the backs with plenty of scoring opportunities but the finishing was poor, notably when Roy Leyland knocked on under the posts with the line at his mercy.

The score remained at 11-8 but at the final whistle there was no doubt those present had been impressed by the exciting and adventurous way in which the tourists approached the game. The first match of any tour is always going to be difficult as the players try to adapt to each other and the Lions had overcome the problems with great success, the backs in particular catching the eye despite putting down half a dozen try-scoring opportunities. The press were particularly generous in their coverage of the encounter with one paper claiming '...it is probably no exaggeration to say that South Africa today has no back line to match, for sheer brilliance and speed, that fielded by the British tourists on Saturday...'

There is no doubt that in today's climate the game would have been examined frame by frame, analysed to excess and the many lost opportunities highlighted. There would be recriminations on the wayward passing and the poor handling that undoubtedly cost the Lions a more emphatic victory but this was not the way in 1938.

The game had been won, the players had avoided injury and the Lions could look forward to the next match with confidence while the home side had been far from disgraced. Everyone was happy. It was time to celebrate.

British Lions – V.G.J. Jenkins, E.J. Unwin, R. Leyland, D.J. Macrae, W.H. Clement, F.J. Reynolds, J.L. Giles, S. Walker, captain, W.H. Travers, C.R. Graves, R.B. Mayne, J.A. Waters, R. Alexander, P.L. Duff, A.R. Taylor.
Scorers – Unwin 2T, Macrae T, Jenkins C
Border – B.C. Reid, A. Willmers, S.C Reid, J. White, captain, M. Moore, R.J. Evans, R. Gordon, C.B. Jennings, F. Brownlee, L. Kopke, J. Lewis, C. Woodford, J. Maartens, M. Petzer, N. Robertson.
Scorers – Evans T, Kopke C,P
Final score – British Lions 11, Border 8 (half-time 8-8)
Referee – A.H. Cook

Following the match the management and players were entertained at a gala ball held at the newly opened Colosseum Tea Room and Restaurant which was attended by 1,000 local dignitaries and leaders of industry and commerce. At this early point in the tour it had been reported that only Gerald Dancer and Elvet Jones were married men, something that would not have escaped the notice of the young ladies who attended such functions or met the players at other social engagements, and there would be many a broken heart left in the tourists' wake as they made their way around the country.

Similarly reported but perhaps with a degree of inaccuracy was that sixteen of the party were teetotal and the remainder only imbibed on the rarest of occasions – time would tell.

Sunday was a day of rest. Monday the party breakfasted early and their packed cases were passed into the care of 'Mac' Strachan. Trams were laid on to take the group to the railway station for a 10.15 a.m. departure and a journey that would begin to put in perspective the size of the country they were visiting. The Lions were due in Kimberley at 12.50 p.m. the next day, a journey of more than twenty-six hours and the first of many of similar duration to be completed in the coming months.

Such was the daunting prospect of these interminable rail journeys that a Mr Jenneson Taylor, who had accompanied the tourists on the journey from Southampton with the intention of following them throughout the tour, packed his bags and returned home. There was another version of the story that led to his rapid departure, one which suggested that while he was accepted as one of the party on the outward journey and had been allowed to sit in on an unofficial team photograph taken on the *Stirling Castle*, he was not allowed to be part of the official photograph taken on arrival in South Africa. Taylor apparently took umbrage at this, hence his premature return home. Jenneson Taylor appears to be something of an enigma as on arrival in Cape Town he was interviewed by the press and reports suggested that he was an ex-international player but there appears to be some doubt concerning this as none of the standard reference works on the game identify him.

All land arrangements were handled by Thomas Cook & Son and the management were issued with books of concession tickets which covered all the railway journeys to be undertaken and vouchers to be used for meals when in transit. 'Mac' Strachan was given labels that helped identify pieces of luggage to be stored in the luggage van and those destined for the two twenty-six-seater compartments South African Railways had reserved for the party on every journey. The voucher system accommodated the unavoidable situations when players would be unable to travel with the main party as a result of injury and enabled them to travel independently at a later date without incurring expenses over and above those catered for in the initial tour budget. One additional expense expected to rear its head at some stage was the penalty for carrying excess luggage. Despite an allowance of 100lbs per person it was expected this would not prove sufficient as the team and management began to collect the mementoes and souvenirs sure to come their way.

Train travel in South Africa was hardly in its infancy in 1938. Railways had opened as far back as the 1860s when Cape Town and Durban were the first cities to benefit. Initially the network had conformed with the European 4ft 8½in gauge but as the system extended so did the cost become prohibitive and the gauge was narrowed to 3ft 6in which explains why journeys took so long and explains why East London to Kimberley by rail, a journey of little more than 500 miles, took twenty-six hours – the train travelling at an average speed of 20 mph!

Even at this early stage a cursory glance at the itinerary told the tourists that little thought had been given to minimising the travelling as many cities would be visited more than once, an issue raised in the press. From Kimberley the party would return to Cape Town and then move on to Oudtshoorn before once again returning to Cape Town and then heading north to the Transvaal. Logically, the first two matches could have been played in Cape Town followed by the visit to Oudtshoorn and then on to East London via Port Elizabeth before heading to Bloemfontein and Kimberley. All of which would have saved two days' travelling.

Time consuming it may well have been but one of the big advantages of rail travel is that it allows the passenger plenty of opportunity to see the landscape and in South Africa there is plenty of variety to please the eye. After leaving East London, the train wound its way in a circuitous route north of the city on its way to Queenstown, 155 miles into the journey. This is farming country and cattle, sheep and fields of maize dominate the scenery, a vista which remained unchanged as the train made its way into the Orange Free State.

The border with Eastern Cape Province is marked by the Orange River that flows through Aliwal North, the halfway point of the journey. This is where those suffering from rheumatic and associated complaints came to enjoy the therapeutic benefits offered by the sulphur springs found in the area which are likened to those at Aix-la-Chapelle in France. On arrival in Bloemfontein, the capital of the Free State and to which the party would later return, it was all change for the last leg of the journey, the 100 miles to Kimberley where Griqualand West would provide the opposition in the second match of the tour.

The Griquas had some experience of playing sides from the British Isles, having met the tourists nine times and winning four. In 1891 Griqualand West were presented with a cup on behalf of Donald Currie, the proprietor of the Currie Shipping Line which

45

would later merge with the Castle Line to form Union-Castle. The intention was that the cup be awarded to the first provincial team to beat the tourists but the British team won all nineteen matches and in the event it was decided to award the trophy to the team that had fared best against the visitors and in losing 3-0 the recipients were the men from Kimberley. In compliance with Donald Currie's instructions it was then passed to the South African Union and from 1892 onwards has been presented to the winners of an inter-provincial competition which commenced in 1889. The Currie Cup is South Africa's main domestic tournament. Initially contested at irregular intervals, in 1968 it gained a permanent place in the fixture list and remains a much sought after trophy.

Kimberley was once the diamond capital of the world and despite the industry still suffering the effects of the depression that had impacted on the major economies of the western world in the 1920s the town remained in the forefront of the industry. From a rugby point of view the playing surface at the local stadium would be as hard as the minerals the area was famous for – a sure recipe for injury. After their long journey the tourists arrived at Kimberley on schedule and were transferred to the Queen's Hotel, their base for the next two days, but there was little more than twenty-four hours' preparation time before they were due to take the field for the second time.

When the team was announced there were starts for Elvet Jones on the wing and Harry McKibbin in the centre. Stanley Couchman, Eddie Morgan, Bill Howard and Ivor Williams were included among the forwards and the experienced Irish pair George Morgan and George Cromey were selected at half-back. Sam Walker continued to lead the side with vice-captain Jenkins again included at full-back.

Ten of the Griquas team including captain E. Billing were drawn from local clubs – Kimberley, the Pirates, Beaconsfield and De Beers. The remainder of the team came from the outlying districts and included two schoolboys from the Vryburg club:, David van der Merwe in the centre and Jannie Englebrecht on the wing.

Match 2, Griqualand West, Wednesday 15 June, Kimberley

Glorious sunshine and 6,000 spectators welcomed the teams when they took the field at the stadium and it was the home side who started the more promisingly. From a penalty inside their own half Wilson made fifty yards and aided by a fumble by Jenkins the Griquas found themselves inside the Lions' 25 for the first time. From the resultant line-out scrum-half Koen elected to work the narrow blind side and fed the ball to Englebrecht who despite stumbling recovered well, escaped the clutches of the Lions forwards and made for the line where a desperate tackle appeared to force him out of play as he made to ground the ball. The touch judge indicated the player had failed to score but his decision was overruled by the referee who awarded the try which went unconverted, Wilson missing the difficult kick.

The home side was not showing any signs of being overawed by their illustrious opponents but their defence was stretched on several occasions, two of

47

which saw Clement brought to ground short of the line by some fine tackling. The lighter home forwards were manfully containing the Lions' bigger pack but midway through the half the visitors began to take control which in turn led to long periods camped inside home territory. Vivian Jenkins missed two penalties and must have started to wonder if he had left his kicking boots at home, so uncharacteristic was his continuing failure to hit the target. Despite these missed opportunities the Lions had taken control of the game and following a line-out George Morgan broke and opted to take the ball back to his forwards where he found Walker up in support. The captain latched on to the scrum-half's pass to run thirty yards though a disorganised defence and score in the corner, Jenkins once again unable to hit the target with his conversion attempt.

With the scores tied players on both sides were guilty of poor, speculative out of hand kicking. As the half entered its final minutes, rather than attempting to play any constructive rugby the teams appeared content to wait for any unforced error to break the deadlock. When Du Plessis at full-back failed to field a high ball such negative tactics looked like paying off. Ivor Williams was quickly up and kicked the loose ball on into the 25. With the ball bobbing about in front of him the Welshman appeared to be in two minds, undecided whether to attempt to pick the ball up or simply hack it on. Fortunately he favoured the latter and fell on the ball as it crossed the goal line near the posts for a well-taken try which Jenkins was pleased to convert on the stroke of half-time.

There could be little doubting that the Lions had dominated the first period territorially. Superior at both the scrum and line-out there had been no shortage of good possession for the backs to use and yet the tourists had only scored two tries, both by forwards. Applauded for their adventurous, open rugby they may have been but whether this would serve them well against stronger opponents only time would tell. Similarly, the foot rushes so favoured by British teams during the less than hospitable weather conditions of the domestic season were unlikely to play such a prominent part in the games on tour. The Lions were going to have to adapt but for the time being it was sufficient to win the opening games during that difficult period when players drawn from four countries endeavour to come together as a team.

Griqualand West had no such concerns. On the resumption of play they continued to defy the odds stacked against them. Prolonged periods spent defending and minimal possession seemed to count for nought and just as they had done in the first half so did the home side open the scoring in the second. Following a penalty which took play deep into Lions' territory van der Merwe broke clear and found Wilson in space outside him on the touchline, the wing making twenty yards before passing back inside where Hay was on hand to receive the final pass, the hooker crossing for a try that went unconverted.

The Irish half-backs Morgan and Cromey were familiar with each others game and this was proving to be of some significance as they worked together to try and break the defensive line and create some space for the three-quarters to exploit. The pair were proving difficult to contain and on one occasion they linked well to take play deep into home territory. Supported by the forwards play moved on towards the line and the Griquas conceded a penalty wide out which Sam Walker goaled to restore a five-point advantage.

Continually seeking to move the ball, the next Lions' attack saw Jenkins enter the line at pace and release McKibbin. The centre made ground before handing on to Morgan who in turn found Cromey. Missing out Leyland the outside-half threw a well-judged lob pass to Bill Clement on the wing, who gathered the ball at pace to beat the stretched defence and race over in the corner. Walker failed with the difficult conversion but there now seemed to be more urgency about the Lions' play and it was not long before the lead was improved, Morgan once again creating trouble for the Griqua loose forwards with another of his penetrating breaks from a line-out. This time it was Bob Alexander who had anticipated the scrum-half's action and got himself in position to take the scoring pass and cross beneath the posts. Harry McKibbin converted and at 19-6 down the Griquas looked a beaten team.

With the game all but over it was time for the Lions to throw caution to the wind and they began to go through their paces. Attack after attack swept down the field but for all their enterprise a try by Elvet Jones was the only addition to their score and it was the home side who finished the match on a high when full-back du Plessis latched on to a loose ball and ran fully 60 yards up the touchline before sending a perfectly timed inside pass to the supporting Koen who scored unopposed. Wilson again failed to add the points with what proved to be the final kick of the game.

After two matches it was difficult to assess exactly how good the Lions were. That both games were won was good news but it was far too early for any in-depth analysis of the performances. This did not stop the local press enthusing over the style of play which the tourists had adopted and the general feeling was that come the harder provincial games and the Test matches the Lions would have developed into a strong outfit, one capable of causing a major upset.

British Lions – V.G.J. Jenkins, W.H. Clement, R. Leyland, H.R. McKibbin, E.L. Jones, G.E. Cromey, G.J. Morgan, S. Walker, captain, W.H. Travers, M.E. Morgan, R.B. Mayne, S.R. Couchman, R. Alexander, W.G. Howard, I. Williams.
Scorers – Walker PT, Jenkins C, Jones T, McKibbin C, Alexander T, Couchman T, Clement T.
Griqualand West – P. du Plessis, W. Engelbrecht, L. Louw, D. van der Merwe, R. Williams, S. Smith, G. Koen, F. Moult, W Hay, E. Kelley, G. Snyders, A. van der Merwe, E.R. Hammond, E Billing, captain, A. Wilson.
Scorers – Engelbrecht T, Koen T, Hay T.
British Lions 22, Griqualand West 9 (half-time 8-3)
Referee – N. McCurrie

What better way to follow a second impressive win than with a second, equally impressive gala ball, this held at the City Hall with 400 guests in attendance. Organised by the joint committees of Kimberley's four clubs the function proved to be another great success with the revellers carrying on into the early hours but unfortunately the tourists had another appointment with South African Railways, a 9.35 a.m. departure for the twenty-four-hour journey to Cape Town which prevented any risk of the celebrations getting out of hand. Such functions were funded by the respective unions or, as was the case in Kimberley, jointly funded by local clubs. There would be no cost to the tourists, who were always lavishly entertained in the manner appropriate, but the players had to be careful not to cross what was a very fine line. Board and lodging, food and drink and general everyday expenditure were all perfectly acceptable but anything that could in any way be misconstrued as a form of payment and the alarm bells would start ringing, the amateur ethos always guarded with great propriety.

It was Richard Luyt's responsibility to ensure that all financial matters were accurately recorded and his attention to detail is seen in the exhaustive handwritten expenses journal that he kept. He was accountable to the South African Rugby Board for every penny spent and his records were broken down into sections detailing the expenditure. Gratuities, laundry bills, taxi fares, medical expenses, telegrams, entertainment – these were all legitimate expenses but had to be recorded and the appropriate receipts produced. The voucher system covering train travel and meals taken in transit which fell into Strachan's remit had been paid for in advance, as had all hotel accommodation with meals billed direct, but all other incidental expenditure had to be accounted for, hence Richard Luyt's meticulous records.

Weekly cash withdrawals were made by cheques drawn on a special account in the name of the South African Rugby Board. From this cash float the players and management received their personal allowance which was intended to cover any out of pocket expenses that did not fall within the accepted categories; beer money, tobacco etc. To cover these costs the players received the sum of one guinea per week, while Major

Hartley and H.A. Haigh Smith enjoyed a weekly stipend of seven pounds each.

It was the individual's responsibility to ensure that any additional out of pocket expenses incurred were supported by a receipt. If a player became detached from the party through injury he was likely to incur some legitimate bills but throughout the expenses ledger there are very few examples of Luyt making recompense to a player without the necessary paperwork being produced. With the strict amateur code having to be respected at all times, these controls were in place not only to accurately record the cost of the tour but also as a form of protection for the players. If any payment seemed unnecessary or was unaccounted for it could impact on their status as amateurs and their eligibility to play the game.

The Friday morning arrival in Cape Town once again left the Lions with little more than twenty-four hours to prepare for what promised to be the toughest encounter to date against a Western Province Town and Country XV that included eight Springboks. The team would be captained by Gerry Brand, an outstanding Springbok full-back now in his thirty-second year and nearing the end of a glittering career. Brand was part of the welcoming committee that met the tourists on their arrival at the railway terminus in Adderley Street and together with representatives of the Western Province Union he accompanied the party to the Arthur's Seat Hotel in Seapoint in a cavalcade of cars provided by local supporters of the province.

Situated a short distance from the city centre, Seapoint fronts the Atlantic Ocean making out of season bathing an unattractive proposition, the cold waters sufficient deterrent for the hardiest of swimmers. Its out of town location coupled with a resort atmosphere made it a most suitable base for the tourists and they would use the Arthur's Seat whenever they were in the city. The hotel was also ideally located for the Green Point Track where the Lions would hold training sessions and with time at a premium it was here that the players headed in the afternoon.

The team for the third game was selected on the journey from Kimberley and showed six changes from that which had defeated the Griquas. A late change saw Charles Grieve introduced at full-back in place of Jenkins who was forced to withdraw with an injury picked up training. The local press paid particular attention to the team, seeing it as the strongest selected to date, and although it was another seven weeks before the first Test there had already been sufficient evidence to suggest that several of the players now included would face the Springboks.

Jimmy Giles and Jeff Reynolds were at half-back with Duncan Macrae and Harry McKibbin in the centre. Sam Walker and Bunner Travers continued in the front row with Blair Mayne behind them and a new combination of Alexander, Howard and Taylor was chosen in the back row, the selectors still to be convinced of any advantages the 3-4-1 formation offered. Walker, Travers, Mayne, Alexander and Clement were included for the third time.

There was little doubt that the home side was going to provide stronger opposition than either Borders or Griqualand West and their forwards were expected to get the better of the Lions' eight. Behind the scrum it was a different matter and although Johnny Bester in the centre, Dai Williams on the wing, Daniel Van de Vyver at outside-half and Brand at full-back had all toured with the Springboks the previous year the Lions had already demonstrated that this was where their strength lay and the backs were expected to be the more dangerous if their forwards could lay a suitable platform for them to play off. Among what locals saw as an ageing pack were two players who had also toured New Zealand. Matthys 'Boy' Louw first played for South Africa in 1928 and had toured Britain in 1931–32 and Mauritz van den Berg played in the three Tests in New Zealand. A mighty clash of contrasting styles of play was a mouth-watering prospect and come match day almost 15,000 spectators made their way to one of South African rugby's spiritual homes.

On Thursday 9 July 1891 the first representative team from the British Isles to visit South Africa had played their opening match at Newlands. In fact the first three matches of that particular tour were played at the famous ground, those responsible for organising the twenty-match itinerary much more sympathetic to the demands touring a country the size of South Africa put on players. Newlands lies some four or five miles from the city centre meaning that the Lions made the short journey from their hotel by coach. Their arrival at Newlands coincided with one of the curtain raisers but this did not prevent the crowd giving them a tremendous ovation. When the Lions took to the field it was to an equally rapturous reception, matched when Brand led the home side out, and the stage was set for what proved to be an enthralling encounter.

Match 3, Western Province Town and Country, Saturday, 18 June, Newlands, Cape Town

From the start the Lions surprised their hosts by adopting the 3-4-1 scrum formation which they had almost reluctantly introduced in the second half of the previous matches. Travers was beginning to make his mark at hooker and ended the game winning the set scrums 21-12. Blair Mayne was always prominent in the line-out and made a general nuisance of himself in the loose exchanges. At half-back Giles was well marshalled by van Reenan and Apsey but still managed to give Jeff Reynolds sufficient good ball enabling the outside-half to make several telling breaks. Territorially the game was finely balanced during the first quarter, both teams having opportunities to score but failing to do so with final passes going to ground but the tourists should have secured early points only for Alexander, Howard and McKibbin to miss four penalty kicks. The deadlock was finally broken following a scything break by Reynolds that led to a scrum inside the 25 from which the outside-half again made ground. Howard was up in support and continued the move before passing to Couchman who crossed near the posts for McKibbin to convert.

Town and Country were forced to make some changes behind the scrum when van der Vyver received a knock forcing him to leave the field, not to return until the second half. Gerry Brand took over at outside-half and Ackermann was drafted from the scrum to take over at full-back. Brand immediately kicked the visitors back to their goal line. The Lions secured the ball from the line-out but rather than play safe and relieve the situation with a kick to touch McKibbin was caught in possession under the posts after some over speculative play and Brand converted a penalty that could easily have been avoided to bring the first half to an end with the score 5-3 in the Lions' favour.

The crowd was very much taken with the Lions' adventurous play behind the scrum during the opening forty minutes but on occasion safety-first measures should have been the order of the day. With scant regard for such a policy, the Lions began the second half in similar style and were soon rewarded when Clement on the left wing swooped on a cross-kick from Macrae following an enterprising attack on the right of the field to score in the corner for his second try of the tour. This time it was Howard who failed with the touchline conversion.

The Lions could take comfort from their general superiority but with only five points separating them the scoreboard suggested there was little between the sides as the game entered the final quarter. The home forwards upped the tempo, allowing the half-backs to work the touchline effectively and take play into the Lions' half. Brand was just wide with a drop goal attempt and failed with two penalty kicks, one which saw the ball rebound off the posts. For the first time in the game the Lions' line was under serious threat. Sensing some uncertainty among their ranks the Western Province players threw the ball about at every opportunity and when Meiring, Bester and Williams worked well together to create some space in the middle of the field van der Spuy was on hand to pick up a loose ball and score beneath the posts, giving Brand the easiest of kicks to level the scores.

Desperate to maintain their unbeaten record the Lions now threw caution to the wind with Reynolds spinning the ball wide at every opportunity. On more than one occasion the tourists looked like scoring the winning try but each time the home defence held firm and on their final foray into Lions' territory the home side were awarded a penalty wide out which Brand stepped up to convert with the last kick of the match. The Lions were the better side on the day but the scoreboard rarely lies and with the result 11-8 in their favour, Western Province Town and Country were the first team to claim their scalp.

British Lions – C.F. Grieve, E.J. Unwin, D.J. Macrae, H.R. McKibbin, W.H. Clement, F.J. Reynolds, J.L. Giles, S. Walker, captain, W.H. Travers, C.R.A. Graves, R.B. Mayne, S.R. Couchman, R. Alexander, W.G. Howard, A.R. Taylor.
Scorers – Couchman T, Clement T, McKibbin C.
W.P. Town and Country – G. Brand, captain, D.O. Williams, H. Meiring, J. Bester, J. Louw, D. van der Vyver, S.J. van der Spuy, M.M. Louw, P. Louw, G. Englebrecht, J. Apsey, M.A. van den Berg, W. Heinrichsen, G. van Reenen, G.J. Ackermann.
Scorers – Brand 2P.C, van der Spuy T
British Lions 8, W.P. Town and Country 11 (half-time 5-3)
Referee – P.D. Tunbridge

It is not unusual for home supporters to want to see a touring team do well and there was a sense of disappointment at Newlands, disappointment that such enterprising and entertaining play had not been rewarded. For the Lions a first defeat proved there were lessons to be taken on board before they could face the stronger opponents that lay in wait with any degree of confidence. Naive best summed up the Lions' approach and if games were to be won rather than simply provide a stage on which their undoubted skill and flair could be showcased things would have to change. But that was not about to happen; Sam Walker and his men were intent on entertaining at every given opportunity.

CHAPTER TWO

LOST AND FOUND

A trip underground – A hat-trick to celebrate
– Back to the Cape – Another defeat – The
injuries arrive – To and fro up country –
More injuries – The cavalry arrives – Back
on track.

S *truthio camelus* – the ostrich. If members of the
party were not familiar with this large, flightless
bird then their next destination would certainly
rectify the matter. Another twenty-four-hour journey
took the tourists east from Cape Town up into the Little
Karoo, a stretch of land bordered on the north-west
by the Swartberg mountains and to the south-east by
the Langeberg-Outeniqua range. By being positioned
between these two mountainous regions the area
benefits from the rain that falls on the higher ground
and eventually finds its way into the valley, enabling a
carpet of vegetation to thrive and the ostrich to enjoy
an ideal habitat.

In 1938 there were approximately 40,000
domesticated or farmed ostriches in South Africa,
ninety per cent of which were to be found in the
Western Cape, predominantly in the Little Karoo.
When Dr Cove-Smith's British team visited the area
in 1924 there were many more of the birds domiciled
there with the figure approaching 250,000 and if
the 1910 tourists had ventured onto the Little Karoo
they would have been overwhelmed by something
approaching a million. The reason for the boom and

subsequent decline in numbers – fashion. What at the turn of the century had become South Africa's third major export behind gold and diamonds was no longer de rigueur. The demand for ostrich feathers had fallen off since the First World War, most noticeably in the millinery trade coupled with the move away from art nouveau-influenced costume wear. But 40,000 birds is still a lot and several of our intrepid travellers bought ostrich-related items during their three-day stay at Oudtshoorn during which they were based at the Queen's Hotel located on the main street of this popular country town.

The day after their arrival was the first since East London that the players were not involved in either travelling or playing. Training was held at the local ground, a short walk from the hotel, and later in the day the party were taken to one of the area's great tourist attractions, the Cango Caves, a network of passages and chambers which contain fine examples of stalactite and stalagmite formations not dissimilar to those found in Somerset. Once inside the caves a guide gave a potted history, beginning with their discovery in 1780 when a herdsman followed a wounded buck into the entrance, before going on to explain how rock paintings suggested the caves were occupied 15,000 years earlier. All of which proved to be very interesting – then the lights went out.

Bringing up the rear of the party were Duncan Macrae and Eddie Morgan. After taking a wrong turning in the darkened labyrinth the stragglers became detached from the main group and an element of panic quickly unsettled the situation. In a section of the caves known as Lumbago Walk because of the low ceilings and narrow passageways the pair soon realised that they couldn't hear any of the noise which had previously accompanied the party. There was an absence of laughter, joking and even footsteps – they were alone. H. du P. Steytler, a journalist from Cape Town, was with the main body of tourists in the cave and reported '... a series of heartrending Welsh and Scotch (sic) howls coming in unison from the depths of the darkness behind us, two real brothers by this time yelling for succour. The succour arrived in the person of Alexander, the Irish policeman who, to the great joy of Sammy Walker, went back and saved a Welsh policeman.'

With the party now reunited there was an impromptu rendition of the team song, 'A Credit to Ould Ireland is MacNamara's Band' which sounded '...strange and eerie in that high vaulted chamber in almost total darkness'. Eddie Morgan was particularly pleased to have come through his ordeal with little more than a few bumps and bruises and he celebrated by '... buying his first pipe which he smoked with so much gusto that his tongue was sore and burning before an hour was out. I hope it will stop him singing...' continued Steytler; '...he is one Welshman who can't'. The trip to the Cango Caves was memorable for all the wrong reasons. To add to the misery caused by the light failure and the temporary loss of two players, before they exited the caves Ivor Williams, who was celebrating his birthday, stumbled in the almost total darkness and landed awkwardly on his knee. An unfortunate accident but one which resulted in an injury that would make him unavailable for selection in the next four matches.

A month since the *Stirling Castle* set sail from

Southampton the period of acclimatisation during which players from four countries strived to become one group with a common purpose had long since passed. This was in no small way thanks to the leadership qualities of Sam Walker who was proving to be an inspired and most popular choice as captain. Before the International Championship had started, the likely candidates for this most prestigious of roles were almost certainly the incumbent leaders of their respective countries. England's Phil Cranmer together with Wilson Shaw from Scotland and Wales's Cliff Jones all declared their unavailability, which left George Morgan of Ireland. When the men in green suffered heavy defeats against England and Scotland, Sam Walker took over as captain, leading Ireland against Wales and in so doing became a leading candidate to captain the Lions in the summer.

Following in the footsteps of Tom Smyth, who captained the 1910 tourists, Walker became the second Irishman to lead a British side overseas and the first of four consecutive captains from Ireland. Karl Mullen, Robin Thompson and Ronnie Dawson led the first three post-war tours and like Sam Walker, all three were forwards. As did Walker so too did Thompson hail from the famous Instonians club, the name by which the Royal Belfast Academical Institution, perhaps the most famous public school in Ulster, is better known in rugby-playing circles. Captain of his club and more recently Ireland, Sam Walker was used to the responsibilities that came with the role. He won his first cap when he was introduced to the side against England in 1934 and was an absentee from the team only once in the following five seasons. Extremely popular with the players and South African hosts alike, the only disparaging remarks heard regarding Walker came from his fellow forwards who bemoaned the fact that in the heat of battle he would rally his men by calling 'Come on Ireland!' And if things really did begin to boil over it would be to cries of 'On Insts, on!' that his fellow Lions were expected to respond.

Spectators at Oudtshoorn were to be denied hearing the Ulsterman's exhortations. The South Western Districts were not expected to mount a strong challenge, allowing the selection committee the opportunity to rest several players who had played prominent roles in the first three matches, genial Sam Walker among them. Also consigned to the touchlines were forwards Bill Travers, Blair Mayne and Bob Alexander with Jimmy Giles, Jeff Reynolds, Harry McKibbin and Bill Clement among the backs not considered for selection. The four players yet to start a game were all included in the line-up; Vesey Boyle on the wing, Haydn Tanner at scrum-half with Gerald 'Beef' Dancer and A.G. Purchas among the forwards. Vivian Jenkins captained the team for the first time and Charles Graves was handed the responsibility of leading the pack.

Match 4, South West Districts, Wednesday 22 June, Oudtshoorn

A crowd of 3,500 saw a disappointing match in which the home side, as if aware of their limitations, set out to disrupt the tourists at every opportunity, never allowing them to break into their established brand of open, attacking rugby. That there were new combinations in key areas of the Lions' line-up certainly did not help the flow of the game and it was well into the first half before the forwards started to play as a unit and assert their authority on the home pack. This in turn enabled Tanner at scrum-half to settle into his normal rhythm and begin to work in tandem with Cromey outside him.

Despite their negative tactics, it was the home side that took the lead from a penalty in front of the posts which full-back Manfeldt goaled. The District XV continued to keep the Lions penned deep in their half with Jenkins being called upon to provide some sterling work in defence and prevent any further early scoring. With a long relieving kick the captain took play into opposition territory and from the ensuing line-out the Lions' backs had a first chance to show their class, spreading the ball to Boyle on the left wing who was brought down short of the line. The forwards were in support and claimed the ball which was quickly moved to Elvet Jones on the opposite wing, who ran around a stretched defence to touch down under the posts for a try which Jenkins duly converted.

Macrae was beginning to find the form he had produced to help Scotland win the Triple Crown and he set up the second and third tries with decisive breaks. The first saw him burst through the midfield defence before taking the ball back to his forwards where he found Purchas and Dancer in support for the latter to give the scoring pass to Taylor who crossed in the corner for an unconverted try. Minutes later a second break by the centre left the defence flat-footed and with only the full-back to beat the ball was moved to Leyland and out to Jones for the wing to score his second try which also went unconverted. The Lions were now firmly in control and held a comfortable 11-3 lead at the interval.

The second half began as the first had ended with the tourists moving the ball among the backs at every opportunity and the home side seemingly content to rely on a massive defensive effort in which loose forward Semon van der Riet was outstanding. No effort was made to use the little possession that came their way to attack the Lions' midfield through Snyders and Gildenhuys, two centres with glowing reputations. This in turn meant that the pacy Louw on the wing hardly touched the ball throughout the eighty minutes, unlike his opposite number Elvet Jones who was given a wealth of possession and it was not long before he completed the first hat-trick of the tour, running in a simple try after more good work in the centre, this time Roy Leyland the protagonist who created the opening. Vivian Jenkins kicked a fine touchline conversion and at 16-3 the Lions were coasting to a comfortable victory.

A penalty brought the home team some respite but it was not long before the Lions were running in a fifth try, this by Duncan Macrae, whose earlier efforts deserved to be rewarded. A cross kick by Elvet Jones eluded Purchas but Tanner collected the ball and flung out a long pass to the centre who crossed unopposed for a score that again went unconverted. As they had opened the scoring so did the home team have the final word, when the outstanding van der Riet, finding no supporting player following a burst through a ruck, elected to drop for goal and sent the ball sailing high above the crossbar much to the obvious delight of the home crowd.

The 19-10 final score was more than welcome after the disappointment at Newlands. In addition to a comfortable victory the Lions had the added satisfaction of keeping their line intact and the four players who made their first appearances all looked comfortable once the inevitable rustiness was shaken off. Dancer and Purchas in particular caught the eye with their contrasting forward strengths: Dancer's tight play and Purchas's good work in the loose. Tanner was an obvious talent and Boyle although failing to get on the score sheet came close on three occasions. For one player in particular the afternoon was of special significance. Elvet Jones was yet to be capped by Wales but against South West Districts the twenty-six-year-old Llanelli wing joined a select band of players to have scored hat-tricks for the British Lions. All twenty-eight members of the party now had at least one experience of South African rugby and the selectors could begin to explore the various options available to them in their search for the combination which they would select for the first Test.

British Lions – V.G.J. Jenkins, captain, E.L. Jones, D.J. Macrae, R. Leyland, C.V. Boyle, G.E. Cromey, H. Tanner, M.E. Morgan, C.R.A. Graves, G.T. Dancer, S.R. Couchman, A.H.G. Purchas, P.L. Duff, W.G. Howard, A.R. Taylor.
Scorers – Jones 3T, Macrae T, Taylor T, Jenkins 2C.
South West Districts – S. Manefeldt, J.H. Louw, E. Snyders, J. Gildenhuys, M. Jackson, M. Eksteen, B. Perry, T. Gouws, D. Marais, H. Taljaard, S. Segall, L. Roberts, S. van der Riet, captain, B. de Klerk, W. Myers.
Scorers – Manefeldt P, van der Riet P, DG.
British Lions 19, South West Districts 10 (half-time 11-3)
Referee – P.K. Albertyn

On their return to Cape Town the party was greeted

by weather which could be likened to a hot British summer rather than the South African winter that was almost upon them. The Friday afternoon arrival and the shortening daylight hours left little opportunity to shake off another lengthy journey after they had settled in at the Arthur's Seat Hotel which would once again act as their base for the next three days. Saturday's match against Western Province would be the biggest test to date and as the team had been announced earlier in the week, the selectors were able to assess its strengths, particularly as it contained many familiar names. Eight of the W.P. Town and Country side were included. Gerry Brand, Dai Williams, Johnny Bester, Boy Louw and John Apsey were certain to figure in the Springbok selectors' plans and the seven new faces were all seasoned provincial players with Currie Cup experience. Western Province had dominated the Currie Cup competition since its inception. The province had been crowned champions fifteen times and shared the title twice. For some years Western Province had been the leading force in South African rugby and Donald Currie's silverware currently occupied pride of place in the trophy room at Newlands. It was going to be a big ask but if the Lions could secure a victory then the tour would be firmly back on track.

Realising the enormity of the challenge, for the first time on tour the British team trained behind closed doors at the Green Point Stadium in their all too brief Friday afternoon session. The team was finalised earlier in the day with Ivor Williams and Jock Waters not considered, both players suffering with knee injuries but problems picked up in very different circumstances. Sam Walker returned to lead the team and Travers, Mayne and Alexander joined him in a strong pack that included Graves, Couchman, Duff and Howard, who retained their places following the midweek match. Jenkins continued at full-back, Unwin and Clement returned on the wing and McKibbin joined Macrae in the centre but it was at half-back that the tourists hoped to gain an advantage with the selection of Giles and Reynolds for their third match in tandem. There was an eleventh-hour setback when shortly before kick-off Walker had to withdraw after bruising his hip in training. Eddie Morgan was brought in to replace him and the captaincy reverted once again to Jenkins.

Vivian Jenkins' lasting claim to fame came playing for Wales against Ireland at Swansea in 1934 when he became the first full-back to score an international try. Copybook tackling, safe hands and an expert kicker of the ball out of hand were the main attributes needed to play full-back and Jenkins was adept in all departments, making his selection for the Lions a formality. Captain of his club London Welsh in the 1936–37 season, Jenkins was about to lead the British Lions for the second time and in a match they were desperate to win.

Match 5, Western Province, Saturday 25 June, Cape Town

There were the usual curtain raisers, the sun shone and when Vivian Jenkins led the visitors on to the field 19,796 spectators were crammed into Newlands. The crowd had started to gather hours before kick-off and when the gates opened there was a rush for the best vantage points. The Malay stand was a sea of red fezzes and the standing areas in front of the Railway and mountain side grandstands were packed, many spectators preferring to take their positions on the ramps that led down to the field. Western Province were also forced into a last-minute change. Pierre Louw was called up in place of Rutter who was badly burnt when disposing of some rubbish on the morning of the game. Louw's inclusion bringing to nine the number of players who had been on the winning side seven days earlier.

From the start Western Province elected to play an open game which was no small tribute to the style of play that the tourists had become associated with. They ran the ball with great adventure and intent and were rewarded early on when Travers was penalised for foot up at a scrum in front of the posts, Brand stepping up to kick the simple penalty. The Lions did not look at all comfortable during the early exchanges. The forwards in particular clearly were not displaying their usual commitment, something onlookers attributed to the absence of Walker, who was a major influence even if his rallying calls were of a parochial nature. With their forwards well on top, the Western Province backs had plenty of opportunities to threaten with Bester and Williams only denied tries by some fine tackling. McKibbin was concussed bringing Williams down and left the field with Unwin brought into the centre and Alexander withdrawn from an already struggling pack to take his place on the wing.

A try was inevitable but it did not come from a constructive phase of play as the home side took advantage of the extra man, rather a wonderful piece of individual skill which saw Williams break through a poor tackle by Macrae and go on to beat several despairing efforts for a try which Brand converted. The Lions desperately needed a score to bring them back into the game and restore some confidence and when a kick ahead by Reynolds caused some confusion in the defence Western Province were forced to concede a penalty which Jenkins goaled to give the visitors a much-needed boost. The seven forwards responded magnificently and for the final ten minutes the Lions played their best rugby of the half. Jenkins missed two penalty attempts before a golden opportunity went begging. Reynolds followed a break through midfield with a kick ahead which Macrae and Clement dribbled on towards the goal line with no defenders in sight. When a try seemed certain Bester appeared from nowhere to touch the ball down just as it crossed the line with the two Lions apparently deciding who should claim the score. This brought the half to an end and despite their unproductive late rally the Lions were happy to be only five points behind. Unfortunately, any thoughts they may have had of winning the game would soon be dramatically laid to rest.

It took ten minutes. Ten minutes during which the home side produced some individual and combined skills to leave the tourists clutching at thin air, chasing shadows and on occasion totally exposed in defence. From the restart Morkel sent the ball high into Lions' territory where Howard prepared to collect and make a mark only for Bester to claim the ball and run unopposed under the posts for a try which Brand had no difficulty converting. From the restart the ball was knocked on but the Lions failed to win the resultant scrum and de Wet was quickly into his stride and released Williams who made ground into the 25 before being forced into touch by Clement. One of the differences in the Laws as they were in 1938 gave the team whose player was forced out of play the throw-in. Williams reacted quickly to the situation, throwing the ball to Boy Louw supporting in the middle of the field. The prop linked with Morkel for the centre to release Bester on the opposite wing to cross unopposed in the corner for an unconverted try. For the first time on tour the Lions were in complete disarray and there was to be no respite as the home forwards gathered from the restart and took play immediately back into the visitors' half. Williams was unable to collect a pass from de Wet, the ball going into touch and from the resultant line-out the home forwards knocked-on to give the Lions a relieving scrum. But reduced to seven forwards the Lions were unable to win the ball and when it popped out in front of Apie de Villiers the Province scrum-half gratefully latched on to it and dived over in the corner for a try which the consistent Brand converted from the touchline.

What was 8-3 now stood at 21-3 and all the Lions had left to play for was their pride. Surprisingly, the seven forwards began to dominate proceedings as the remainder of the game unfolded. Boy Louw appears to have assisted the visitors' cause by changing the Province scrum. He dropped himself into the back row in place of van der Berg, who he moved to lock, allowing Classens to replace the captain at prop. The reason was never explained but from then on the home pack struggled in the tight and it was during this period that Bunner Travers confirmed what an outstanding hooker he was. Many already appreciated this and the South African press would soon refer to Travers as 'The Prince of Hookers', a title that would stay with him for the remainder of his playing career. Although playing in a weakened pack, Travers took ten of the fifteen scrums in the second half after sharing the honours with his opposite number in the first period. This area of superiority enabled the visitors to assert some authority on a game which was certainly lost but from the solid platform established by the forwards late on Giles was able to feed Reynolds some good ball and the outside-half delighted the crowd with his elusive running off the mark. From one such break Reynolds created space for Macrae and a perfectly timed pass put the centre in at the posts for a try which Jenkins converted.

Reynolds was playing his best rugby of the tour and another of his decisive breaks set up a further scoring opportunity only for Unwin to be tackled short of the line. Then it was the turn of Clement who found himself in space following another break by the outside-half but the wing's clever kick ahead was knocked on by Couchman who had the line at his mercy. Alexander, Mayne and Duff were all on hand following another well-placed kick ahead but none of the players managed to get a hand on the ball as it bounced around in the in-goal area. The Lions did manage one final score, a 45-yard penalty goal by Jenkins which reduced the deficit to ten points but, outscored by four tries to one, there were no complaints. It was not to be and neither should it have been, the Lions being outplayed for most of the game, but they had created several try-scoring opportunities when the odds were stacked so much against them following McKibbin's early departure. That at least allowed them to take something from the game. The large crowd were clearly delighted with their team's performance but never showed anything less than the highest respect and appreciation for the tourists' efforts, a fact highlighted by an incident in the Railway Stand from where a spectator heckled Jenkins as he was preparing to take a kick at goal. Irate spectators chastised the individual and the police were soon in attendance to evict the culprit from the ground.

As was to be expected, this game generated the most interest and post-match analysis of any to date. Accepting that Walker's late withdrawal exposed a lack of leadership among the forwards and the early departure of McKibbin left the Lions having to play much of the match with fourteen men there was still much that needed to be addressed. The opening ten minutes of the second half highlighted many frailties in the Lions' defence that were not entirely due to having to play much of the match a man short. Also there was a general feeling that the backs were going to have to play a more organised game rather than relying totally on their individual flair and pace. In particular it was felt that the good work Reynolds was doing in creating openings often went to waste through the centres not linking up with him. The Lions were still very much playing as individuals behind the scrum and needed to introduce more cohesion and unity into their three-quarter play, something that was going to be difficult to achieve in the immediate future.

Following his injury, McKibbin was taken to Woodstock Hospital where he was detained overnight and advised not to play for two weeks. With Basil Nicholson still to join the party this effectively meant that Macrae and Leyland were the only experienced centres the selection committee could call on for the next three matches. This would necessitate selecting players out of position, something hardly conducive to preparing a back division to take on the Springboks.

British Lions – V.G.J. Jenkins, captain, E.J. Unwin, D. Macrae, H.R. McKibbin, W.H. Clement, F.J. Reynolds, J.R. Giles, M.E. Morgan, W.H. Travers, C.R. Graves, R.B. Mayne, S.R. Couchman, P.L. Duff, W.G. Howard, R. Alexander.
Scorers – Macrae T, Jenkins 2P, C.
Western Province – G.H. Brand, captain, D.O. Williams, H. Meiring, P. de Wet, J.L.A. Bester, J. Morkel, A.C. de Villiers, M.M. Louw, P. Louw, J. Oberholster, J.Apsey, J. Smit, B. Claassens, G. van Reenen, M. van der Berg.
Scorers – Brand 3C.P, Bester 2T, Williams T, de Villiers T.
British Lions 11, Western Province 21 (half-time 3-8)
Referee – J.J. Strasheim

They never complained but when the party boarded the train at 7.15 p.m. on the evening of Monday 27 June the players must have already grown tired of the sight of the maroon and yellow livery of the coaches that would on this occasion be their home for the best part of the next thirty-six hours. The journey took them north to Potchefstroom where they arrived at 4.00 a.m. on Wednesday morning, giving the selected team less than twelve hours before they were due at Olen Field to play Western Transvaal.

Potchefstroom, which celebrated its centenary in 1938, is a town of no little importance in the history of South Africa. It was here that a band of Voortrekkers led by Hendrik Potgieter established the first town north of the Vaal River and Potchefstroom in due course became the first capital of the South African Republic. Early indications of the enormous gold deposits to be found in the Transvaal were seen when a collection of mineral specimens was displayed at an agricultural show in 1867 and later in the same year it was the Potchefstroom-based *Transvaal Argus* that announced to the world the potential of the gold seams in the area.

Fully recovered, Sam Walker was able to lead the team and took his place in the front row alongside Travers and Dancer. Mayne and Duff formed a new second row partnership and Purchas, Taylor and Howard completed a pack which averaged less than 15 stone a man. Haydn Tanner was partnered by Reynolds, necessity saw Leyland and Macrae paired in the centre with Boyle and Unwin on the wings and Jenkins at full-back. For Boyle, Tanner, Dancer and Purchas it was a second outing contrasted with Jenkins, Macrae, Travers, Mayne and Howard who would all be playing their fifth game of the tour.

Little was known of the Western Transvaal team. Formed in 1920, the province was included in the itinerary for the 1924 British tour and contested a close encounter, the tourists hanging on to win 8-7 but by 1938 Western Transvaal could only lay claim to three Springboks, Hans Aucamp, Willem 'Champion' Myburg and Nic du Plessis.

All three played Test rugby in 1924 but since those heady days there had been no further international representation. With the Lions expected to record an easy victory, Western Transvaal, led from the wing by P.J. Joubert, had nothing to lose and with ten minutes of the game remaining, and to the great surprise and satisfaction of their supporters, the home side was still very much in contention.

Match 6, Western Transvaal, Wednesday 29 June, Potchefstroom

The weather was good, the ground in excellent condition and there was a crowd in excess of 6,000 to welcome the Lions on to the field for a game which would be long remembered for the outstanding play of Jeff Reynolds. The outside-half struck an immediate rapport with Tanner and revelled in the freedom he enjoyed at the end of the scrum-half's outstanding service. Quick, long passes are all an outside-half asks of his partner and Tanner provided them in abundance. Unlike many other exponents of the position who preferred the dive pass to gain greater distance, Haydn Tanner quite simply flicked his wrists and sent the ball out, not only with unerring accuracy but further than any of his contemporaries were capable of doing.

Suffice to say, those who played alongside him benefited greatly from the extra space he created and at Potchefstroom it was Reynolds who claimed the headlines following a sparkling display that saw him create havoc, leaving loose forwards in his wake and his midfield opponents flat-footed as he effortlessly glided past would-be tacklers. He created many opportunities for those around him and three of the four tries scored by the tourists came as a direct result of Reynolds' brilliance but not the first, a result of some indecisive play by the home forwards.

From the base of a scrum inside the 25, the No. 8 took it upon himself to pick up the ball and throw a loose pass to his outside-half. This was well read by Russell Taylor who intercepted and ran directly at the full-back before releasing a perfectly timed pass to Boyle for the wing to score and Jenkins convert. Reynolds was unlucky not to be credited with a try after a darting run saw him brought down on the line, the referee deciding he had not grounded the ball. But he was not to be denied and following another break made ground before handing on to Leyland, who had a clear run to the posts for a try which Jenkins again converted.

Half-time arrived with the score 10-0 in the Lions' favour but ten minutes into the second period two penalties by Grobler and Rivers brought the home side back into contention before Jenkins responded with his third successful kick of the afternoon to take the score to 13-6. Western Transvaal took the game deep into Lions' territory, the result of some sterling work by the home forwards and from a line-out Grobler broke through before linking with du Preez who was brought to ground short of the line. Prop forward Ritter was first up to claim the loose ball and touched down for an unconverted try that reduced the Lions' lead to four points.

With ten minutes remaining the Lions should have been in control and comfortably ahead on the scoreboard. Realising the urgency of the situation there was a marked increase in tempo which led to a Jenkins penalty and two tries, both instigated by Reynolds. Duff was the beneficiary of a scoring pass from the outside-half before Reynolds completed an outstanding performance with a brilliant individual effort. Both tries were scored under the posts and Jenkins had no difficulty in converting to bring his personal tally for the afternoon to fourteen points and the final score to 26-9.

For the first time the tourists did not find favour with

the local press. Despite a convincing victory, onlookers felt that the forwards in particular went about their task in a disinterested fashion which was born out by the first-half statistics that confirmed they had only edged the scrums 10-9 and were behind 13-6 on the line-out count. The scrum may have improved after the interval but the line-out was still a cause for concern with a final statistic of 22-20 in favour of the home side.

The suggestion that the forwards in particular looked out of condition can perhaps be put down to the excessive entertaining to which they were subjected and the lack of quality time on the training paddock. Neither could the fact that they were spending so many hours in the confines of a railway carriage be overlooked, but how much of this was taken on board is debatable. Were the Lions paying any attention to the press they were receiving? They would probably have preferred to distance themselves from any adverse comment, particularly as one correspondent continually referred to them as England in his match report! On the plus side, Vivian Jenkins had at last found his true goal-kicking form, converting the four tries and adding two penalties, but this upturn in fortune was dampened when it was revealed that a pulled thigh muscle picked up in the early stages of the game would keep him sidelined for the next two weeks.

British Lions – V.G.J. Jenkins, E.J. Unwin, R. Leyland, D.J. Macrae, C.V. Boyle, F.J. Reynolds, H. Tanner, S. Walker, captain, W.H. Travers, G.T. Dancer, P.L. Duff, R.B. Mayne, A.H.G. Purchas, W.G. Howard, A.R. Taylor. Scorers – Jenkins 4C, 2P, Boyle T, Leyland T, Duff T, Reynolds T.

Western Transvaal – R.H. Rivers, P.Snyman, D. Talmud, L.H. van Rensburg, P. Joubert, captain, A. Dietrich, J. Steenekamp, J. Badenhorst, G. van Niekerk, G. Ritter, J. du Preez, F.du Plooy, H. van Heerden, A. Jacobson, H. Grobler.
Scorers – Rivers P, Grobler P, Ritter T.
British Lions 26, Western Transvaal 9 (half-time 10-0)
Referee – C.W. Wright

Short the stay may have been but their hosts went to great lengths to ensure that for the tourists it would be one of the more memorable. An official dinner was held at the King's Hotel following which the party moved on to the Town Hall where the local rugby club had organised a dance in their honour. Among those to speak at the dinner was the Lady Mayor who thanked the tourists and suggested that while Western Transvaal were expected to be trounced it was essential for visiting teams if they were to get to know the real South Africa to visit country towns like Potchefstroom. This theme was taken up by Mr J.P. Pretorius, President of the Western Transvaal Union, who stressed that it was equally important for touring teams to visit the country towns because the game had been in decline in the area until the announcement that the tourists would be playing at Potchefstroom. Major Hartley, in thanking the hosts on behalf of what he was now referring to as '...his twenty-nine sons...' (Nicholson was yet to arrive) presented Councillor Nel with a ball signed by the party which she confirmed would be put on prominent display in the town together with a Lions brooch, a much sought after item of tour memorabilia.

With a casual look at the map suggesting life would have been much easier for the tourists if the match at Potchefstroom had followed those at Bloemfontein and Kroonstad rather than preceding them it was a return journey south into the Orange Free State (OFS) that now faced the Lions with matches against OFS at Bloemfontein on Saturday and then an OFS Country side at Kroonstad the following Wednesday next on the itinerary.

A late departure from Potchefstroom meant an early morning arrival in Kimberley, where there was a six-hour wait for the connection to Bloemfontein. Having breakfasted on the train at two shillings and sixpence per head the Lions made their way to the Queen's Hotel where they could while away the hours before taking lunch and returning to the station to resume the journey. Absent at this stage were Vivian Jenkins, Roy Leyland and Jock Waters, who had travelled to Johannesburg to receive specialist treatment for their respective injuries, something not always readily available with the team constantly on the move.

Bloemfontein had played host to three British touring sides. In 1903 and 1910 matches were played against the Orange River Colony at the Ramblers Club, both ending in victory for the visitors, but in 1924 things were very different. Following the introduction of the newly formed OFS Union to Currie Cup football in 1911, the province was granted two fixtures with the 1924 British team. Both OFS and OFS Country defeated the tourists, part of a consecutive run of eight matches that saw the visitors suffer six defeats with two matches drawn. Not only the lowest point of the 1924 tour but of all those which had preceded it and the many that would follow.

In the early years of international rugby in South Africa the majority of players came from Griqualand West, Transvaal or Western Province. Following the First World War, the Griquas' representation fell away and Natal began to provide Springboks, but elsewhere the representation was minimal. By 1938 OFS could boast five players who had represented South Africa. Most recently Louis Hattingh and Jack Gore had played against Australia in 1933. Before them Murray 'Tiny' Francis toured the British Isles in 1931–32 but took no part in any of the Tests and Hennie Potgieter won two caps against the 1928 All Blacks. However, it was on the 1912–13 tour of the British Isles and France that the Free State's favourite son made his name. Boetie McHardy was a flying wing who scored twenty tries in his seventeen appearances on tour. He played in the five Tests, all of which were won, and scored six tries including a hat-trick against Ireland. Inside him at centre in eleven of the games including the five Tests was Richard Luyt, who was now the SARB representative with the tourists. Of the current Free State players thirty-one-year-old outside-half 'Tiny' Francis was in outstanding form and many saw him as a serious contender for inclusion in the first Test.

As inevitable as it was unfortunate, injuries had started to impact on the tourists. For what was only the seventh match of the tour there were six players who were unavailable for selection. The worst of the situation was among the backs with both full-backs and two centres ruled out of contention. Of the forwards only Jock Waters and Ivor Williams were temporarily out of action with Williams expected to be fit for selection within the week. It was very much a case of needs must and the team selected to face the Free State included players in unfamiliar positions.

Irish scrum-half George Morgan was included at full-back, English scrum-half Jimmy Giles was chosen to partner Duncan Macrae in the centre, leaving Welsh scrum-half Haydn Tanner to continue his successful partnership with Jeff Reynolds. Injuries had necessitated the inclusion of the three scrum-halves but with Clement and Unwin on the wings, a confident pair of half-backs and Macrae's steadying influence in the middle of the field the unusual mix could work. There were no such problems up front where Walker, Travers and Dancer continued where they had left off against Western Transvaal. Couchman was back in harness with Mayne, and Alexander Taylor and Duff were reunited as the loose trio for the first time since the opening match of the tour.

Match 7, Orange Free State, Saturday 2 July, Bloemfontein

In front of a record crowd at Springbok Park the Lions produced their best display of the tour to date, the team looking confident and in control throughout. Nowhere was this more noticeable than among the backs where the handling and passing was assured and accurate. Less reliant on individual flair, the backs looked a complete unit and consequently became a threat every time the ball was moved wide. It cannot be denied that the loss of centre van Coller late in the first half hampered the home side, who played out the game with seven forwards, but the assured performance by the Lions' backs was apparent long before his unfortunate departure.

Jeff Reynolds' outstanding performance at Potchefst-room had obviously not gone unnoticed in the Free State and from the start he was hounded by loose forward de Bruyn and barely five minutes into the game Reynolds felt the weight of a thundering tackle as he made a clearance kick to touch. Caught off balance, the outside-half landed awkwardly on his ankle and though remaining on the field he was unable to contribute much other than to act as a link between Tanner and the three-quarters.

On the receiving end of Tanner's long passes, Reynolds was still able to bring the centres into play with Macrae in particular benefiting from the quicker ball. The Scottish centre assumed control of the midfield and played his best game of the tour. It was Macrae who was in support of his forwards as they dribbled the ball into the home 25 and when it came to hand he threw a scoring pass to Russell Taylor, who scored wide out. The Free State struck back immediately, 'Tiny' Francis showed why he was still a contender for a Test place with a wonderful individual try following a break down the blindside that saw him outpace the defence with only George Morgan able to get a hand to him. But the full-back's tackle came too late to prevent Francis diving over in the corner.

Rather bizarrely, Reynolds' injury had worked to the visitors' advantage with the ball reaching the midfield seconds after Tanner had flung out his accurate passes from the set piece. Reynolds simply moved the ball on instantly which opened up room for Macrae to exploit and immediately following Francis' effort the Lions centre lobbed the ball out to Clement, who made ground before returning it back infield to Macrae who crossed unopposed. It was during this particular passage of play that van Coller was injured and left the field. Hefer was taken out of the pack to play on the wing but as the half-time whistle approached the visitors were clearly in control, something the 6-3 score certainly did not confirm.

Their numerical superiority enabled the Lions to take control in the second half and further tries were scored out wide by the wings where Hefer's lack of pace was exposed by Clement who crossed twice, Unwin adding a third on the other side of the field. Both Clement's tries came from good centre play, Macrae and Giles working well together to create the overlap, while it was Unwin's pace that took him past a tired defence late in the game. George Morgan could convert only one of the five tries but made amends with a well-taken drop goal. Going into the final minutes the Lions were ahead 21-6 only for a lapse of concentration by Bill Clement to gift the home side a consolation try scored by Hefer, who hacked on a dropped pass. It had not been a day for the goal kickers and Francis completed a poor afternoon with the boot when his conversion attempt rebounded from the crossbar.

This was another victory that should have been much more comprehensive. Four tries had gone unconverted, together with several penalties, and there were numerous opportunities to attempt field goals which had to be passed up because of the obvious shortcomings in this department. When it came to the harder provincial matches and the Tests in particular one could not see the Lions running in four or five tries and goal kicking would become critical. Vivian Jenkins had found some form with the boot against Western Transvaal but his earlier inconsistency suggested that another player likely to play in the

Tests should be given some responsibility with the goal-kicking duties. Several would be tried but when one finally put his hand up, surprisingly, he was found not among the backs but in the depths of the scrum.

British Lions – G. Morgan, W.H. Clement, D.J. Macrae, J.L. Giles, E.J. Unwin, F.J. Reynolds, H. Tanner, S. Walker, captain, W.H. Travers, G.T. Dancer, R.B. Mayne, S.R. Couchman, A.R. Taylor, P.L. Duff, R. Alexander.
Scorers – Morgan DG, C, Clement 2T, Unwin T, Macrae T, Unwin T.
Orange Free State – B. van der Walt, H. Lamprecht, N. de Bruine, C. van Coller, A. Thorburn, M.G. Francis, C. Botma, P. Lurie, J. Louw, captain, J. van Schalkwyk, B. de Bruyn, G. van Rensburg, A.T. Taute, H. Hefer, J. King.
Scorers – Francis T, Hefer T.
British Lions 21, Orange Free State 6 (half-time 6-3)
Referee – A.M. Horak

The comparatively short five-hour journey to Kroonstad on Monday left the players with time on their hands, Sunday bringing one of those rare luxuries – a free day. The golfers in the party had three local clubs to choose from, twelve players visited the cinema and for those with an eye for local history and culture the National Museum opened its doors between 2.00 p.m. and 5.00 p.m. on the day of rest.

When the party boarded the train the following morning they were greeted by Basil Nicholson, who had arrived in Cape Town on the *Athlone Castle* on Friday and made his way north by rail. With Jeff Reynolds added to the list of injured players Nicholson immediately found himself included in the team to play at Kroonstad. The selectors were hopeful the rest would allow Reynolds' ankle time to recover before Saturday's game against Transvaal. Also pencilled in for duty in Johannesburg was Duncan Macrae and he was grateful for a well-earned rest after appearing in six of the seven games played. The team selected to play OFS Country saw Nicholson paired in the centre with Giles and with both full-backs still unavailable Morgan was once again asked to fill the role. This meant Tanner would play a third consecutive game at scrum-half, now partnered by George Cromey, and it was all change on the wings with Jones and Boyle taking over from Clement and Unwin.

Ivor Williams, now fully recovered from his fall at the caves, was brought in for his second game alongside Duff and Charles Graves in a new back row combination. Like Macrae, Blair Mayne was also rested after six appearances, which allowed Couchman and Purchas to pair up in the second row and Morgan joined the captain and the almost ever present Travers in the front rank. Seven of the team had played against the Free State and five of their opponents in that match were included in the Country XV.

Match 8, Orange Free State Country, Wednesday 6 July, Kroonstad

Kroonstad is a farming town and the local community was prominently represented among the 4,000 spectators who filled the recreation ground on the banks of the Valsh River. Many had travelled as much as 400 miles to attend the match and they were not disappointed, the Lions giving another entertaining display of fast, open, attacking rugby in stark contrast to the local side, who were intent on keeping the ball among the forwards and closing the game down at every opportunity. As experienced elsewhere the home tackling was uncompromising, Cromey in particular coming in for some heavy knocks but it was the outside-half who opened the scoring when he touched down under the posts following a searing break that left the opposition stranded. Giles added the points with the simplest of conversions. The Lions were clearly missing the controlling influence of Macrae in the centre, where Nicholson was understandably finding it difficult to settle after his long journey, which left Elvet Jones and Ves Boyle on the wings spending much of the half as spectators. The Lions had enjoyed most of the play in the first half but could not add to Cromey's converted try and the half ended with the visitors holding an unimpressive 5-0 lead.

George Cromey had asked questions of the home defence and the Country loose forwards were now firmly focused on the outside-half which in turn presented Tanner with some room which the scrum-half was only too eager to exploit. From the base of a scrum the young Welshman darted through the inside channel and was clear and under the posts before the opposition realised Cromey was not about to receive man and ball. Minutes later Stanley Couchman latched on to a pass from Travers to add a third try, again scored under the posts, and Jimmy Giles, as elected place kicker, must have started to wonder what all the fuss was about as he calmly slotted his third conversion to put the visitors 15-0 ahead.

There were signs late in the game that Nicholson was beginning to settle, the player twice involved in an exciting move that took play deep into the Country

25. From an orthodox three-quarter attack Nicholson looped outside Jones to make ground up the touchline and when the home full-back threatened to put him out of play he found his wing in support to take a well-timed pass and cross for a fourth try which Giles narrowly failed to convert from wide out. At 18-0 the game was effectively over but the expected final flurry of scoring from the Lions did not materialise and it was the home side who ended proceedings when Ivor Williams was found guilty of handling the ball on the ground for Kruger to kick a penalty.

British Lions – G.J. Morgan, E.L. Jones, J.L. Giles, B.E. Nicholson, C.V. Boyle, G.E. Cromey, H. Tanner, S. Walker, captain, W.H. Travers, M.E. Morgan, S.R. Couchman, A.H.G. Purchas, I. Williams, P.L. Duff, C.R.A. Graves.
Scorers – Giles 3C, Cromey T, Tanner T, Couchman T, Jones T.
Orange Free State Country – A. Kruger, P. Jacobs, R. Bishop, J.C. Symington, A. Thorburn, W. Brotherton, J. Armour, D. Schnetler, B. de Bruin, J. van Schalkwyk, P. du Plessis, A.T. Taute, J. Louw, captain, P. Brotherton, J. King.
Scorers – Kruger P
British Lions 18, Orange Free State Country 3 (half-time 5-0)
Referee – S. Wessels

All things considered the 18-3 victory was a good result. The Lions had put together three victories following the second defeat in Cape Town and could adopt a degree of satisfaction with the tour back on track. There were still a lot of rough edges that needed attention but the forwards were winning the ball and the backs were getting used to crossing the try line, scoring ten of the thirteen tries registered in the past week. Six of the eight games played had been won, producing a total of 136 points which included twenty-nine tries – an average of over three per match. This Lions team were entertaining the crowds with their enterprising brand of open rugby, proving to be hugely popular visitors wherever they went. At every opportunity Major Hartley and Sam Walker would remind listeners that it was the manner in which the game was played that mattered, not the result. While not exactly preaching to the converted the comments did not fall on deaf ears. The 1938 Lions were worth the entrance money and that could only be good.

CHAPTER THREE

ALTITUDE SICKNESS

There's gold in them there hills – Transvaal
take no prisoners – Among the jacaranda
– The Lions get it together – Back to the
diamonds – The longest journey.

The city of Johannesburg came into being for one
very simple reason – gold. There are records of gold
deposits being worked along the Witwatersrand
during the second half of the nineteenth century but it
was not until 1886 that George Harrison, a prospector
helping a farmer to build a house, used his spare time
to search for minerals and came upon an outcrop on
the Main Reef. Word quickly spread and in a short time
the area became a sea of hastily put together shanty
towns as thousands of prospectors arrived in search of
their fortune.

With such chaos abounding in a stretch of land
previously deemed of little or no value and where
large tracts had changed hands for trivial amounts,
State President, Paul Kruger sent his private secretary
Jan Eloff to select a focal point around which a town
should be based. Eloff selected a seemingly worthless
stretch of land that the government had no interest
in and it was here that the first building, a corrugated
shed that became the mining commissioner's office,
was erected. The town developed around this focal
point, forming a triangle with Commissioner Street at
the base and Hillbrow at the apex, both still part of
downtown Johannesburg. From an area of land that

once held no economic value, building plots of 2,500 sq. ft began to realise in excess of £50,000 – £20 per square foot.

Bisecting Commissioner Street is Eloff Street, named after Kruger's secretary and the location of the Carlton Hotel, the Lions' next temporary home. The city's newly opened railway station extended to some sixteen acres and boasted more than two miles of platform and it was here the Lions arrived at 6.15 p.m. on Thursday 7 July and were driven the short distance to their hotel by motor cavalcade. An official dinner was first on the agenda and included on the guest list alongside the usual city officials and union representatives were members of the Transvaal team who the Lions would play on Saturday.

When the itinerary was first announced, the matches due to take place at this stage of the tour were against Reef in Johannesburg and, on the following Wednesday, Combined Country at Pretoria. At the start of the 1938 season the Northern Transvaal Union was formed which meant that those players who were based north of Johannesburg would now be included under the auspices of the new union. Therefore, for Reef read Transvaal and in place of Combined Country a first-ever fixture against overseas opposition for what in time would become one of South Africa's strongest provinces – Northern Transvaal. That the original itinerary included Transvaal later in the tour had no bearing on the matter as there were several precedents of touring sides meeting the same provincial opponents on more than one occasion and any suggestions that the fixtures had been strengthened by the changes were dismissed out of hand by the organisers, who insisted that Reef would have been a stronger combination than either of the provinces could now hope to field.

There was much evidence to contradict this. Other than the missionary teams of the 1880s, British tourists had met with little success against Transvaal. In 1903 Mark Morrison's team were beaten 14-4 and 12-3 and in 1910 Dr Tom Smyth's men fared little better, losing 27-8 and 13-6. Of the Lions only Cove-Smith's team in 1924 could claim any success against the province, a 12-12 draw preventing the home team continuing a remarkable run of success that also included victories over the 1928 New Zealanders and the 1933 Australians. Only the All Blacks had defeated Transvaal in one of the two matches played in 1928. More recently a combined Reef and Country XV did play the 1933 Australians in a game won by the visitors but what this sequence of results suggests is that the new fixtures would provide the Lions with two harder encounters than originally scheduled. This was something no number of reassurances to the contrary could hide and which events over the next seven days would only confirm.

What the revised itinerary did mean was that some familiar names would not be among the Transvaal players who greeted the tourists at their hotel. There was no Ben du Toit, Ferdie Bergh, Roger Sherriff or Louis Strachan, forwards who were all expected to feature in the Springbok team. Also absent was Danie Craven, who many thought would lead South Africa but who now also found himself drafted into the newly formed province. It would be another week before faces could be put to these well-known names but in the meantime the dinner gave the visitors an opportunity to meet Tony Harris, expected to partner Craven at half-back despite the challenge of the in-form Tiny

Francis, and the versatile Freddy Turner who had tormented the Australians and New Zealanders from the centre, wing and full-back positions twelve months earlier. Forwards Fanie Louw, brother of Boy, and Jan Lotz, whose hooking dual with Bunner Travers was eagerly anticipated, remained attached to Transvaal and with wing Morris Zimerman and loose forward Fred Smollan, both experienced Springboks, also in the ranks, the home side were still expected to provide stiff opposition, despite losing so many players to Northern Transvaal.

On arrival at the Carlton, the main party were reunited with Jenkins, Leyland and Waters who had travelled ahead from Potchefstroom in the hope that a week's rest coupled with regular treatment would speed their recovery, but unfortunately none of the three were available for selection. With Basil Nicholson now on board it was decided he should get another game under his belt, allowing Harry McKibbin more time to complete his recovery from the head injury he suffered against Western Province. Jeff Reynolds was another player the selectors decided had not sufficiently recovered from injury to warrant inclusion in the team but neither were they keen to expose George Cromey to further punishment following the game at Kroonstad in which he had taken a fearful battering. More of the same was certain to be handed out by the Transvaal loose forwards. Difficult choices had to be made and it was with some reluctance that the selectors finally accepted that Cromey would have to play.

Announced on Friday, the team included George Morgan at full-back, the Llanelli pair Elvet Jones and Bill Clement on the wings, Macrae in the centre with Nicholson and Giles and Cromey at half-back.

Sam Walker was chosen alongside Blair Mayne in the second row, allowing Charles Graves and Beef Dancer to be included with Travers in the front row. The loose forwards Alexander, Taylor and Duff were selected together for the third time, which suggested this was the preferred combination of those tried to date.

Recent matches between the two teams had been played at the Wanderers Ground but in 1937 the Transvaal Union's lease had expired and the opportunity was taken to move to Ellis Park, located in the east of the city and little more than a mile from the Lions' hotel. The ground had opened in 1928 and hosted the second Test against the All Blacks which was played in front of 38,000 spectators, at the time the biggest attendance for any sporting event in South Africa. Judging by the interest shown in the Transvaal game, this figure was likely to be threatened when the Lions arrived back in the city for the first Test.

The winter months on the Transvaal see temperatures fall, particularly at night, but they remain largely dry and the sun is usually in attendance to make conditions for playing rugby almost perfect. The hard grounds can be a problem as the tourists were beginning to realise with their ever growing list of injuries but because of its location there was another factor that would now have to be taken into consideration. At 6,000 ft above sea level the air is much thinner and until a period of acclimatisation has been completed it would have a tiring effect on players not used to the rarefied conditions and this debilitating factor would be particularly noticeable in the latter stages of a match. On a more positive note the thin atmosphere allowed the ball to be kicked farther than at lower altitudes, enabling players kicking out of hand to gain better field positions but more importantly, goal kickers could afford to be more speculative with their place kicks, greater distances than those normally achieved now within reach.

Match 9, Transvaal, Saturday 9 July, Johannesburg

On Saturday morning it appeared all roads led to Johannesburg. Supporters arrived in their thousands by road and rail and at 7.00 a.m. the first queues started to form at Ellis Park. Eight-year-old Sonnie van Wezel stood proudly at the front and when asked what had brought him to the ground at such an early hour he replied that he wanted to get a good vantage point '...to see Mr Zimerman play...' All seats were taken up an hour before kick-off but spectators continued to pour into the standing areas, leaving estimates as to the match attendance suggesting that a crowd approaching 30,000 had turned out, a record for a provincial game.

Among the spectators were several ex-Springboks, including Chubb Vigne, a centre who had played his rugby for Main Reef RFC and Transvaal before being included in the South African team which met the first British Tourists at the Port Elizabeth Cricket Club Ground on 30 July 1891, the first Test match played by the Springboks. Also in attendance were the Springbok selectors, A.F. Markotter, W.P. Shreiner, G. St Leger Devenish, W. Zeller and Frank Mellish.

'Long George' Devenish, Bill Zeller and Frank Mellish had each played Test match rugby. Mellish had the distinction of not only appearing in six Tests for South Africa but also winning six caps for England during 1920 and 1921. A.F. Markotter was recognised as one of the game's great thinkers and long before such things would become the norm he doubled up his duties as a selector by carrying out those now more associated with a coach. At twenty-six, chairman of selectors Bill Schreiner was the youngest person ever invited to join the selection committee and was still playing first-class rugby.

There was some good news for the Lions' camp. Following treatment on his injured ankle Jeff Reynolds declared himself fit to play if needed. Whether this was a rash decision taken by the player at the eleventh hour or whether it was always in the plan to include him in the team if fully recovered is uncertain but on arrival at the ground his inclusion was confirmed to the crowd, who were eager to see the outside-half in action after word of his exploits elsewhere had preceded the Lions' arrival in Johannesburg. For George Cromey, nicknamed 'The Little Minister' after being ordained into the Presbyterian Church of Ireland the night before the Lions departed from Southampton, being replaced was a disappointment but at barely five feet tall and weighing little more than 10 stone, common sense suggested he needed time to recover from the battering he had received on Wednesday. More of the same on such hard playing surfaces could put his tour in serious jeopardy.

From the whistle both teams immediately put into practice tactics which they hoped would swing the early stages of the contest in their favour. The visitors kicked high and long in the hope of exposing Basson at full-back while Transvaal captain Fanie Louw elected to take a scrum at every opportunity in the hope of wearing down the Lions' forwards. Neither tactic had any immediate effect and after obstruction on Taylor it was Duncan Macrae who had the first chance to open the scoring but his penalty attempt sailed just right of the upright. Both sides produced good attacking moves only to be denied by a handling error as the line beckoned, but from a scrum in the visitors' 25 it was Tony Harris who made a decisive break that took him inside the despairing reach of Bob Alexander before linking with Freddie Turner to put the centre over wide out.

Reputations counted for nothing in the early exchanges as Fanie Louw and his much vaunted pack of forwards were more than contained by the Lions' eight. Travers benefited from this, taking five consecutive heels to gain an early edge over Jan Lotz in a personal duel that would become one of the most keenly contested of the tour. Behind the scrum it was a different but all too familiar story as the Lions produced some wonderful individual touches only for the collective effort to contrive to disappoint. This was perfectly illustrated when Giles broke from a scrum, threw dummies left and right to totally confuse the defence and crossed for a wonderful solo try which levelled the scores, the scrum-half failing with the conversion attempt.

On twenty minutes the first of several injuries occurred. Morris Zimerman was cut down by a Blair Mayne tackle that left him a virtual passenger. Zimerman was unable to continue on the wing but gamely joined the forward effort, his place out wide taken by Smit. There were scoring opportunities aplenty as the half drew to a close. Twice the Lions created opportunities that would have given them the lead at the interval. After running the ball from deep in their own half firstly Nicholson and then Morgan were held up on the line before referee Nick Pretorius blew his whistle with the teams tied at 3-3.

On the resumption of play the Lions immediately found themselves having to defend their line. Lotz took two scrums, the second giving scrum-half Segal a chance to exploit the space on the blind side and link up with Collin. The wing put in a short kick ahead which Clement retrieved only to be enveloped by the Transvaal forwards and concede a penalty that Turner converted. Clement was again in the thick of the action following a foot rush led by Walker and Mayne but it was clear that the wing had twisted awkwardly in the tackle and would take no further part in the match. A knee cartilage had become detached and though the player decided to continue after receiving attention, Sam Walker eventually led him from the field and his place on the wing was taken by Alexander. What was not appreciated at the time was that Bill Clement's tour was over.

It is often the case that a team reduced to fourteen men will take the initiative, even gain some advantage regardless that the odds are now firmly stacked against it, and, following Clement's departure, the Lions mounted a concerted effort to get back on level terms. The seven forwards raised their game and took play into the Transvaal half where a good bout of inter-passing saw Walker and Giles prominent before the ball was moved to Alexander on the wing to score a well-taken try. Walker failed with the difficult conversion but the teams were now level at 6-6.

The Lions were then subjected to a period of intense pressure largely instigated by the Transvaal forwards who kept play inside the visitors' half. The backs were unable to take advantage of this territorial dominance until Tony Harris finally broke the deadlock with a sparkling individual try to match Giles' first-half effort. Taking the ball at pace from a set scrum he beat Reynolds on the outside before wrong-footing Morgan to score under the posts. Turner had no trouble with the easy conversion and in such a closely contested encounter the Lions were faced with a mountain to climb. They were not to reach the summit. Any glimmer of hope disappeared when Reynolds suffered a recurrence of the ankle injury that had kept him out of the original selection and was forced to leave the field. This saw Giles take over at outside-half, Morgan replace him at scrum-half and Taylor drafted from the forwards to fill in at full-back.

Though reduced to thirteen, and having to chase the game, the Lions refused to throw in the towel, opting to run the ball at every opportunity. They deserved some reward for the competitive spirit shown in the final quarter but an inside pass from Elvet Jones after a thrilling 50-yard dash down the touchline was intercepted. Then followed a glorious handling move between Giles, Macrae, Nicholson and Alexander. This stretched the defence but broke down when the replacement wing was tackled short of the line. Fourteen men may be able to raise their game sufficiently to make light of the handicap but when the number is reduced to thirteen gaps will appear, the open spaces prove impossible to fill and it was only a matter of time before the home side exploited their advantage to release Smollan in space for the second row to cross near the posts and Turner complete the conversion to take the game away from the Lions.

It was obvious that Clement and Reynolds had picked up serious injuries and when Basil Nicholson went to ground awkwardly after trying to hand off Fred Turner it looked as if three names would be added to the list of injured players. Nicholson refused to leave the field despite being led to the touchline with what was later diagnosed as mild concussion. This necessitated taking Duff out of the pack to cover in the centre, which left five forwards to contest the forward battle for the remainder of the match. Despite this disparity up front it was the Lions who had the final word. Travers secured the next scrum and an infringement saw Sam Walker hand the ball to Russell Taylor, who converted the penalty with a well-struck kick. This brought the match to a close and Transvaal were the third team to inflict defeat on the Lions. It was a hard day at the office for the tourists, who were clearly affected by the altitude in the last quarter of the game, but more importantly, the injuries picked up by Clement and Reynolds looked long term and likely to keep them of action for some weeks.

The match statistics confirmed that the Lions were beaten in the scrum and line-out but had more than held their own in both departments until the last quarter of the match when they were depleted up front and the altitude factor started to kick in. The scrums were lost 25-19, the line-outs 22-20 and ten penalties had been conceded against eight by the home side. At 6-6 midway through the second half there was little to choose between the teams and with a second meeting between the sides scheduled in three weeks there would be an opportunity to redress the balance.

British Lions – G.J. Morgan, W.H. Clement, D.J. Macrae, B.E. Nicholson, E.L. Jones, F.J. Reynolds, J.L.

Giles, G.T. Dancer, W.H. Travers, C.R.A. Graves, S. Walker, captain, R.B. Mayne, R. Alexander, A.R. Taylor, P.L. Duff.
Scorers – Giles T, Alexander T, Taylor P.
Transvaal – C. Basson, M. Zimerman, J. Roux, F.G. Turner, R. Collins, T.A. Harris, J. Segal, S.C. Louw, captain, J.W. Lotz, S. Neville, F.C. Smollan, W. Pretorius, R. Farndell, J. Smit, J. Klopper.
Scorers – Turner T,P, 2C, Harris T, Smollan T,
British Lions 9, Transvaal 16 (half-time 3-3)
Referee – N.F. Pretorius

The Lions could now enjoy two days in Johannesburg in the knowledge that their next journey was the shortest of the tour, the forty-mile trip north to Pretoria. The golfers among them played golf, the cinema goers caught up with the latest films while the injured players took advantage of as much treatment as possible in an effort to get their tour back where it should be, out on the field of play. The news that Nicholson's concussion would not prevent his inclusion in the next match if selected was a boost and Harry McKibbin was also declared ready for action. Nor would the altitude be as draining in Pretoria, which lay some 1,500 ft lower than Johannesburg – although going down, things were looking up.

Pretoria is named after Andries Pretorius, one of the leaders of the Voortrekker movement which brought to the region in the late 1830s thousands of Dutch settlers, desperate to get away from British rule on the Western Cape. Pretorius also led a body of 464 men who fought the Battle of Blood River on 16 December 1838, wreaking savage retribution for the death of Piet

Retief by claiming the lives of 3,000 Zulus without loss. It would not have escaped the tourists' attention that their visit coincided with the centenary of this major event in Afrikaner history and as they approached the city they would have seen the site on top of a hill to the south-west of Pretoria which was earmarked for a monument to commemorate the arrival in the Transvaal of the Great Trek and the events which took place at Blood River.

Only forty miles separated Pretoria from Johannesburg but the contrast between the two cities could not have been more marked. Where Johannesburg was fast becoming a city based on commerce and industry Pretoria, which had been made the administrative capital of South Africa after the formation of the Union in 1910, still prided itself as a rural development with an abundance of tree-lined avenues prominent in an attractive and well-laid-out centre. The jacaranda was introduced from South America in the late nineteenth century and thousands of samples of this colourful tree are to be found in Pretoria which now holds a carnival in October when the trees are in blossom turning the city into a sea of lilac and blue.

Polley's Hotel would play host to the party for two nights. Situated on the busy Pretorius Street, Polley's Hotel was two blocks away from the State Model School located on the corner of Van der Walt and Skinner Streets. It was here that Winston Churchill was held prisoner during the Boer War.

On 15 November 1899 the armoured train carrying Churchill and a platoon of British soldiers was derailed and the company taken as prisoners of war. Churchill's argument that he was a war correspondent fell on deaf ears. Churchill finally offered a pledge that if he was granted parole he would not join forces against the Republicans. General Joubert finally acceded to this promise and on 12 December issued the instruction that Churchill be released but it was too late; the future British Prime Minister had gone over the fence.

The newly formed Northern Transvaal Union played home matches at the Caledonian Ground, a central location on the banks of the Aapies River. New union it may have been, but Northern Transvaal included eight Springboks in its line-up. Among the forwards Bergh, Strachan, Sherriff and Harry Martin had toured in Australia and New Zealand in 1937 and Nic Bierman toured with the 1931–32 Springboks in the British Isles. In the three-quarters were two experienced Springbok wings, Floors Venter, who had played in three Tests in 1931–32 and scored eight tries in fourteen appearances, and Tallie Broodryk, who crossed six times in six matches in 1937. At scrum-half and captain was Danie Craven. Craven had moved to Pretoria from Grahamstown in the Eastern Province to take up a position as director of physical education for the South African Army. He had represented South Africa thirty-five times including thirteen Test matches, and, in addition to his favoured position of scrum-half, had also appeared at outside-half, centre, full-back and No. 8. Craven brought a wealth of experience to the team and, following the result at Ellis Park Northern Transvaal, under his leadership, were expected to inflict another defeat on the tourists.

With Jenkins and Grieve still unavailable, George Morgan started at full-back for a fourth consecutive game, Unwin and Boyle were chosen on the wings and Macrae was joined in the centre by a fit again

McKibbin. Nicholson formed what looked to be an exciting half-back partnership with Tanner. In the front row Morgan and Dancer were included alongside Travers, Walker and Mayne continued in the second row and the adaptable Charles Graves dropped back to complete the loose trio with Taylor and Ivor Williams. A new front row, back row and half-back pairing and a player out of position at full-back confirmed the ongoing injury problem which also forced the selectors to include some players who were much in need of a break.

Against Northern Transvaal, in what was the tenth match of the tour, Travers would make his ninth appearance with Macrae, Mayne and Walker all turning out for the eighth time. These four players were almost certain to be selected for the first Test but any thoughts of giving them a rest was proving to be nigh on impossible. With five games remaining before that first encounter with the Springboks it was essential that there was an immediate return to winning ways, one which then needed to be maintained over the coming weeks, and there was little doubt that the principal players were going to be involved in most of the matches, with the selectors keeping everything crossed in the hope that the backbone of the team remained injury free.

Match 10, Northern Transvaal, Wednesday 13 July, Pretoria

Another big crowd welcomed the Lions on to the field but any hopes the spectators may have had of seeing their team emulate Transvaal were quickly forgotten when the visitors scored eleven unanswered points in an impressive ten-minute spell at the start of the game. From the kick-off, a scrum on the home 25 resulted in a penalty which gave Russell Taylor the opportunity to continue where he had left off in the last minute at Ellis Park. He made no mistake and from the restart the Lions quickly returned to the opposition half of the field where they pressurised the defence into several unforced errors, outside-half du Toit looking particularly uncomfortable. Taylor missed an opportunity to increase the lead following a line-out infringement and a clever piece of play by McKibbin to create an overlap went to waste, Macrae guilty of throwing a poor pass to Boyle who had the line at his mercy. With Northern Transvaal unable to take play out of their half, de Wet was caught offside at a scrum and this time Taylor made no mistake with the kick and the Lions were six points to the good in as many minutes.

Against all predictions the home team were playing second fiddle to a Lions side which looked full of purpose and intent, keen to put memories of Saturday's defeat behind them. From a scrum Tanner flung a long pass to Nicholson, the outside-half and centres handled crisply before passing the ball to Unwin on the wing. There is no substitute for pace, and, well into his stride when receiving the ball, the wing accelerated around the stretched defence to score behind the posts. Taylor made sure of the extra points, the loose forward looking comfortable in his new goal-kicking role.

At 11-0 the Lions were firmly in control and it was fifteen minutes before Northern Transvaal threatened, only to be met by a good defensive effort that held firm. As the game settled into a pattern so too did the experienced trio of Strachan, de Wet and Sheriff begin to control the loose ball which in turn gave Craven a better platform off which to operate. The Northern Transvaal backs tried every trick in the book to open the Lions' defence but to no avail and in desperation the captain elected to launch a succession of speculative drop kicks in an attempt to get his team off the mark. After three failed attempts he struck a well-judged kick from midfield to reduce the deficit to seven points.

This gave Northern Transvaal the confidence needed after the early setbacks and the players now set about their task with a new found determination that put the visitors under intense pressure during the final minutes of the half. The home side were finally rewarded for their efforts when on the stroke of half-time Giles broke through the middle of the field and linked up with Broodryk, the Springbok wing needing no encouragement to finish off a good move that brought the half to an end with the score 11-7 in the Lions' favour and all to play for in the second period.

Immediately following the restart an unforced error behind his goal line by home full-back Colenbrander presented the Lions with a 5-yard scrum. The backs cleverly drew their opposite numbers to create space for Macrae to take Tanner's deep pass and ease the pressure with a drop goal. Travers was not getting his own way in the scrums, which helped Craven to keep his side going forward and a sequence of well-placed kicks kept the Lions pinned back in their own half for extended periods. The pressure instigated the return of some bad habits. Desperate to get out of their own territory, the three-quarters reverted to the adventurous, speculative rugby that had made them so many friends but a poor pass from Macrae to McKibbin was intercepted by Broodryk, who side-stepped Morgan at full-back with some ease to score near the posts, leaving du Toit with the simplest of conversions to reduce the deficit to three points.

After appearing to tire badly earlier in the half, as the game entered the final quarter it was the Lions who seemed to find a second wind and finish the stronger. Craven had to leave the field for running repairs but was quickly back among the action though unable to inspire his team to a final score that may well have won the game. As the clock counted down it was the Lions who confirmed their victory with a move started by Tanner at the base of the scrum and finished by Boyle after the ball had been quickly and efficiently moved along the three-quarter line. Taylor's splendid touchline conversion took the score to 20-12 and minutes later the referee blew his whistle for full time – the Lions had bounced back from their disappointment at Johannesburg with some style.

British Lions – G.J. Morgan, E.J. Unwin, D.J. Macrae, H.R. McKibbin, C.V. Boyle, B.E. Nicholson, H. Tanner, M.E. Morgan, W.H. Travers, G.T. Dancer, S. Walker, captain, R.B. Mayne, C.R.A. Graves, I. Williams, A.R. Taylor.
Scorers – Taylor 2P, 2C, Unwin T, Boyle T, Macrae DG.
Northern Transvaal – A. Colenbrander, J. Broodryk, J. Giles, W.L. Kriel, A.H. Venter, D.A. du Toit, D.H. Craven, captain, H.J. Martin, H. Tindale, P. de Wet, L.C. Strachan, F. Bergh, R. Sheriff, G.P.Uys, J.N. Bierman.
Scorers – Broodryk 2T, du Toit C, Craven DG.
British Lions 20, Northern Transvaal 12 (half-time 11-7)
Referee – N. Bosman

The Lions' twenty-three match itinerary included a visit to Rhodesia, where two games were to be played against the national team. Before setting off for pastures new there was one match outstanding that would bring the first half of the tour to an end. Once again the Lions headed to the Queen's Hotel in Kimberley for a game against Cape Province, a combination drawn from the Western and Eastern Provinces, Border and Griqualand West. Ten of the team had appeared in the earlier matches and for the Western Province trio of Johnny Bester, Piet de Wet and Jan Smit it was a final chance to impress the Springbok selectors who were expected at the game before announcing a squad of players to attend a training camp in Johannesburg, following which the team to face the Lions would be selected.

Sammy Walker had twisted an ankle in training but his absence was offset by a timely return to action for Vivian Jenkins after a break of four games which also avoided the need to appoint a new captain. Jones and Unwin took their places on the wing with the Macrae and McKibbin partnership given another outing in the centre. The selectors would monitor this pairing closely as it had been expected to appear against the Springboks since the squad was first announced but McKibbin's injury had restricted their appearances together and time was running out. There was an interesting half-back partnership, Giles playing outside Tanner, two scrum-halves in tandem. For Tanner it was a fifth appearance in the last six games which had given him every opportunity to stake a claim for a Test place but with the established English and Irish pairings both available it was doubtful if the selectors would break up an international combination for the first Test unless injury dictated otherwise. Up front there were returns to duty for Couchman, Duff and Purchas while Dancer, Morgan and Taylor continued – the latter expected to carry on with the place-kicking duties.

Making up the numbers at forward were the apparently indispensable Bunner Travers and Blair Mayne. Travers was a coal trimmer and Mayne apprenticed to a solicitor and it is difficult to imagine two more diverse occupations. This did not prevent the pair developing a great friendship, one based on a mutual respect formed in the heat of battle but which strengthened away from the playing field. The two players represented the extremes of what being a rugby tourist meant. To take his place in the party Travers had to leave his job and hope it would be there when he returned and, perhaps more importantly, postpone an eagerly awaited wedding. Blair Mayne, on the other hand, was from a prosperous family with a thriving wine and grocery business in Newtownards and there was no difficulty in putting the completion of his articles on hold.

The two had first met on a rugby field in the Ireland –Wales match played at Ravenhill, Belfast in March 1937. Mayne was not slow in coming forward when it came to the physical aspect of the game and reports indicate that he was involved in some serious bouts of fisticuffs in what was his first international appearance. Neither was Travers one to take a backward step. The son of George Travers, who had hooked for Wales during the first Golden Era at the start of the century, Bunner Travers was a fine athletic specimen. Throughout the tour both players were consistently identified as essential components of the Lions scrum and general forward effort. When the Lions first arrived in Cape Town it was suggested in the local press that many of the players were abstainers or only partook of the occasional drink at social gatherings. Even seventy years on such comment raises the eyebrows of those who know better. Bunner Travers and Blair Mayne were perfect examples of what being on a British Lions tour meant – nobody played the game harder on the field and equally so there is much evidence to suggest that nobody played harder off it.

Match 11, Cape Province, Saturday 16 July, Kimberley

The Lions' second appearance at the De Beers Stadium attracted another good crowd of 5,000 spectators. That the tourists were keen to secure another important victory in the rebuilding process was apparent from the off with the backs not giving their opposite numbers any opportunity to create space from which to attack. Macrae and McKibbin in particular were causing the Western Province centres de Wet and Meiring all sorts of problems in both defence and attack and after twenty minutes they carved an opening for the first try. Harry McKibbin ghosted through a gap and with Macrae acting as a dummy runner he fed the ball directly to Unwin for the wing to finish off a thrilling move, crossing in the corner.

The game was producing exciting end to end rugby and both sides had scoring opportunities that went begging but any suggestion that the combination team was not equal to the task in hand was clearly mistaken. The scrum was again proving to be an area of concern for the Lions, the home forwards proving more than competent in this facet of play. Bester was injured in the final minutes of the half and van der Westhuizen was taken out of the pack to replace him but even with their numerical advantage the Lions were glad to hear the half-time whistle.

On the resumption of play Taylor narrowly missed a speculative drop goal attempt from fully forty yards. If any player was laying a claim for inclusion in the Test team it was Haydn Tanner who produced another outstanding performance. He regularly released the backs with long, accurate passing from the base of the scrum, rarely opting to make a break himself, but occasionally an opportunity would present itself that was too good to pass up on. The opposing loose forwards, confident the ball would be moved wide, were committing themselves early in their desire to get among the midfield players and from a scrum deep in the 25 Tanner exploited this only to lose the ball in the tackle with the line at his mercy.

The scrum-half could only look on as the ball was punted downfield with twenty-eight players giving chase. From such loose kicking some of the best scoring opportunities arrive and such was the case now. First back was Unwin, who gathered the ball and launched a sweeping counter-attack. An arcing run took him across the field towards the waiting Elvet Jones who continued the move, making his way deep into the 25 before passing to Dancer, only for the forward to drop the ball as he fell over the line. The Lions were back where they had started thirty seconds earlier.

Coetzee had to leave the field with a broken collarbone and it looked as if Cape Province would have to play out the remainder of the game with thirteen men but the welcome sight of Johnny Bester returning to action limited the Lions' numerical advantage to one. Tanner and Giles were both denied before the Lions were rewarded with a penalty which Taylor made no mistake in converting but at 6-0 the Lions could not afford any lapses of concentration – this was a game they simply had to win. Any hopes of the home team making a dramatic comeback were forgotten when Bester was once again led from the field. To their credit the thirteen Province players made life difficult for the Lions but Giles dropped a goal from a scrum in front of the posts to take the score to 10-0 and effectively beyond them. It had been another difficult afternoon for the Lions and it was no less than the home side deserved when following a sustained period in the opponents' 25 outside-half Parent crossed unopposed for an unconverted try.

British Lions – V.G.J. Jenkins, captain, E.J. Unwin, D.J. Macrae, H.R. McKibbin, E.L. Jones, J.L. Giles, H. Tanner, M.E. Morgan, W.H. Travers, G.T. Dancer, R.B. Mayne, S.R. Couchman, P.L. Duff, A.H.G. Purchas, A.R. Taylor.
Scorers – Unwin T, Giles DG, Taylor P.
Cape Province – B. Reid, J. Bester, captain, H. Meiring, P. de Wet, W. Coetzee, N.D. Parent, R. Evans, H. van der Westhuizen, E. Rutter, J. Oberholzer, J.N. Smit, L. du Plessis, B. Classens, A. Wilson, F. Billing.
Scorers – Parent T.
British Lions 10, Cape Province 3 (half-time 3-0)
Referee – N. McCurrie

The first phase of the tour had come to an end with the record showing eight matches won and three lost. Three more games were scheduled in the three weeks leading up to the first Test but the players knew that opportunities to impress the selectors were running out. Happily there were no further injuries reported and if the leading players managed to avoid any problems in the run-up to the Test then it could be assumed that most of the team was pencilled in.

Among the backs Vivian Jenkins, Duncan Macrae, Harry McKibbin and Jeff Reynolds all looked certain to play with Jimmy Giles likely to get the nod ahead of an unlucky Haydn Tanner. Sam Walker, Beef Dancer, Bunner Travers, Blair Mayne and Bob Alexander were all certain to take their places in the pack, leaving five positions up for grabs. The wing berths were still very much open and would be decided over the coming weeks, as would Mayne's partner in the second row. This left the make-up of the loose forwards and with the Lions likely to adopt a 3-4-1 formation the selectors had to get it right.

The Lions were now headed for Rhodesia, where the intensity of the rugby was not expected to be at the levels experienced in South Africa. Two comfortable victories were predicted and there would be a brief period of R&R to enjoy before they returned to Johannesburg to play the eagerly anticipated first Test. The only drawback to the diversion was that it involved the longest rail journey the party would undertake. Leaving little time to celebrate and socialise with their hosts the Lions left Kimberley at 9.25 p.m. on Saturday and were not scheduled to arrive in Salisbury until 7.30 a.m. the following Tuesday.

CHAPTER FOUR

A DIVERSION

The train takes the blame – The Lions take
the strain – Two matches and a bonanza
of tries – Following in Dr Livingstone's
footsteps – A wonder of the world.

The 1,000-mile rail journey to distant Salisbury
meant two and a half days in transit whiling
away the hours watching the ever changing
landscape pass by. The train headed due north from
Kimberley into the Protectorate of Bechuanaland before
continuing north-east into Southern Rhodesia and on
to Salisbury via Bulawayo. Among the first stops were
Vryburg and Mafeking, the scene of a major incident
in the Boer War when 800 troops under the leadership
of Col. Robert Baden-Powell held the besieged town for
271 days before relief finally arrived. From Mafeking
the train crossed the border into Bechuanaland and
made its way through Pisani and the capital Gaberones
before taking a more easterly route to Francistown,
eventually crossing the border into Southern Rhodesia
at the Ramaquabane River. The Monday morning
arrival in Bulawayo saw the party with time to kill
before the early evening departure to Salisbury and the
final leg of an exhausting journey. The Grand Hotel
provided lunch and there was sufficient time to hold
a training session at the Hartsfield ground, which
the Lions would officially open when they returned
at the end of the week. The players were particularly
impressed with the lush playing surface which looked

inviting after the hard, almost grassless pitches they had played on in the Transvaal.

The 1938 Lions were not the first to have undertaken the journey from Kimberley to Rhodesia. In 1910 Southern Rhodesia were beaten 24-11 and the 1924 tourists defeated a full Rhodesian side 16-3. The story of Rhodesian rugby football can be traced back to the 1890s when it was introduced by an expeditionary force led by Frank Johnson that travelled to the region at the instigation of Cecil Rhodes. The settlers set up base in Mashonaland, establishing what in time would become Salisbury, but it was in the more accessible Matabeleland that Rhodes was especially interested. This was where he believed the mineral wealth found in the Transvaal extended and a base in the region was also essential if the proposed Cairo to Cape Town railway line was to be completed.

Rugby clubs were established in Salisbury and Bulawayo and by 1895 there was sufficient interest in the game to justify the formation of the Rhodesian Rugby Union. In 1901 the first inter-provincial match between Matabeleland and Mashonaland was played and when in 1928 these two regions were sub-divided to form the Midlands and Manicaland the rugby-playing base expanded and competition between the four provinces began to thrive.

In 1898 Rhodesia was invited to take part in the Currie Cup for the first time. A team travelled to Cape Town and en route played Griqualand West at Kimberley. This first official match ended in a 13-8 defeat but the visitors acquitted themselves well in the remaining four fixtures, beating Eastern Province and OFS and claiming a creditable draw with Transvaal. The involvement in the Currie Cup continued into the new century and come the visit of the 1910 British team it was decided to include Rhodesia in the itinerary, where it remained until 1980 when the need for shorter tours meant the journeys north, despite the much shorter flying time, could no longer be accommodated.

All of which was a long way off in 1938 and Sam Walker and his team were given a heroes' welcome when they arrived at Salisbury on the morning of Tuesday 19 July.

Other than the fact that they were not expected to provide strong opposition, little was known about the Rhodesian team. The general consensus of local opinion suggested that the home side were going into the match with scant hope of containing the Lions, whose forwards would weigh in at a stone heavier per man, but such pessimism failed to dampen the interest the arrival of the Lions had generated throughout the country. On match day the local radio station transmitted the first live commentary of a sporting event to the nation and it was later reported that crowds in Bulawayo and the outlying districts had gathered around wireless sets positioned in public areas to listen as the game unfolded.

Rhodesia were led by W 'Trods' Hards and the team contained eight players who had learned their rugby at South African public schools and universities, where standards were never less than high. The Lions had twenty-four fit and able bodies from which to select the team. Unavailable were Jock Waters, who had not played since the opening match but was back in training and expected to play at Bulawayo; Roy Leyland, still recovering from the injury he sustained against Western Transvaal; and Charles Grieve, who had not played since the third match but would more than make up for this in the second half of the tour.

Jeff Reynolds could perhaps have played but the selectors wisely decided not to risk his ankle unnecessarily; and then there was the unfortunate Bill Clement, whose knee was not responding to treatment but who was yet to be confirmed as unlikely to take any further part in the tour.

Recent Lions tours have all too often fallen into a pattern where two teams are very quickly identified – one to play the weaker midweek games and the other to contest the Saturday fixtures which include the Tests and the stronger provincial sides. In 1938 there was never any suggestion that the squad would fall into this undesirable pattern and to the end every player was in with a chance of playing Test match rugby. Testament to this is the fact that twenty-four of the twenty-nine players appeared in one or more of the Tests, and even allowing for the inevitable injuries when success finally came, the starting line-up bore little resemblance to what was earlier perceived to be the best fifteen.

The team to face Rhodesia included a new centre pairing in Nicholson and McKibbin and the Irish partnership of Cromey and Morgan at half-back. Jenkins, Unwin and Boyle completed the backs and among the forwards Ivor Williams was chosen for his fourth appearance alongside Purchas, Couchman, Howard and Duff. Walker, Eddie Morgan and Graves made up the front row. There was no Travers or Mayne, both players at last given a long overdue day off.

Match 12, Rhodesia, Wednesday 20 July, Salisbury

On the morning of the game Salisbury Sports Ground was covered with a host of locusts several inches deep in places and hundreds of children were encouraged to help clear the area before the expected 5,000 spectators began to arrive. Those fortunate enough to be there would long remember the great defensive effort the home team produced. How the forwards, admirably led by Hards, played themselves into the ground with their never say die attitude against bigger and more experienced opponents. Nor did the backs shirk their responsibilities, putting in many fearless tackles that kept the visitors in check for much of the game.

Whatever the Lions tried there was always a green and white jersey lying in wait and for the first time the Lions backs were forced to forget their adventurous style of play, preferring the safety first tactic of a kick to touch, allowing the forwards to take charge whenever possible. By keeping the ball among the forwards for extended passages of play the Lions slowly exerted their authority on the game and when the opportunities to move the ball presented themselves firstly Boyle and then Unwin were on hand to touch down, Jenkins converting one of the tries to add to an earlier penalty. Right wing Gordon had also kicked a penalty for the home team and at the half-time interval the Lions were leading 11-3. The opposition may not have been the strongest team played but they had given the Lions plenty to think about and it was good to see the tourists playing a more structured game, getting the basics right before throwing caution to the wind.

An early second-half try by Boyle increased the lead but for the next twenty minutes it was Rhodesia who took control. A lapse of concentration between McKibbin and Jenkins saw a loose pass picked up by du Plessis, who got the ball out wide for Johnny Owen to score a try converted by outside-half Ted Jacklin. This was quickly followed by a penalty and with the score now standing at 14-11 all thoughts of the predicted rout were dismissed.

As the game entered its closing stages it became clear that the home players had given all they had to offer and were starting to struggle. Fitness began to play a significant part in proceedings and the last ten minutes saw the tourists run in three more tries through Unwin, Graves and Duff, one of which Jenkins converted for a final score of 25-11. Rhodesia may have suffered yet another defeat at the hands of a touring side but the score flattered the Lions and with the teams due to meet again in three days' time there was every cause for optimism among the local rugby fraternity that an upset could be on the cards.

British Lions – V.G.J Jenkins, C.V. Boyle, H.R. McKibbin, B.E. Nicholson, E.J. Unwin, G.E. Cromey, G.J. Morgan, S. Walker, captain, C.R.A. Graves, M.E. Morgan, S.R. Couchman, P.L. Duff, A.H.G. Purchas, W.G. Howard, I. Williams.
Scorers – Jenkins 2C,P, Unwin 2T, Boyle 2T, Graves T, Duff T.
Rhodesia – D.H. Gau, N.A. Shackleton, P. Brunton, S.L. Wolffe, L.R. Gordon, F.E. Jacklin, L.A.W. Parker, W.H. Hards, captain, W.A. Pringlewood, M. Stokes, G.M. Moir, T. Watson, P. du Plessis, R.S. Parker, J. Owen.
Scorers – Gordon P, Stokes P, Owen T, Jacklin C.
British Lions 25, Rhodesia 11 (half-time 11-3)
Referee – F. Jameson

Before the Lions arrived in South Africa they were presented with a mascot that took the form of a lion cut from a flat piece of wood attached to a pole. It was

The 1938 British Lions.
Back row, left to right - R. Alexander, M.E. Morgan, G.T. Dancer, I Williams, A.H.G. Purchas, R.B. Mayne, S.R. Couchman, P.L. Duff, W.G. Howard, F.J. Reynolds, D.J. Macrae. Middle row - J. 'Mac' Strachan (baggage master), C.V. Boyle, E.L. Jones, H. Tanner, J.L. Giles, W.H. Clement, B.E. Nicholson, A.R. Taylor, H.R.McKibbin, C.F. Grieve, G.E. Cromey. Seated - W.H. Travers, E.J. Unwin, J.A. Waters, S. Walker (captain), Major B.C. Hartley (manager), H.A. Haigh Smith (assistant-manager), V.G.J. Jenkins (vice-captain), G.J. Morgan, R. Leyland, C.R.A. Graves.

Cigarette cards were particularly popular during the 1920s and 1930s. Many subjects were covered including sport and, in 1938, United Tobacco (South Africa) issued a set celebrating the Lions tour. A total of 62 cards were issued, 31 Lions including Major Hartley and Jack Haigh Smith, and 31 depicting the leading South African players. Despite this blanket coverage it is disappointing that neither Pieter de Wet nor George Smith are included.

On this page, top left is Dai Williams, top right Gerry Brand, above left Jan Lotz, above right Dannie Craven.

Opposite, a random selection of the Lions shows top left Sam Walker, top right Harry McKibbin, middle left Jeff Reynolds, middle right Bunner Travers, bottom left Vivian Jenkins, bottom right Charles Grieve.

Over the years the match programme has evolved into the glossy, magazine style production. In 1938 it was a much simpler product but still provided the essential information relating to the match. The programme here is that of the first match against Transvaal which ended in defeat tor the Lions. The Transvaal team is named and the 3-4-1 scrum formation clearly identified but the programme obviously went to the printers before the Lions' team was announced.

The full Lions' squad is given together with the jersey numbers they wore throughout the tour which meant they were never numbered 1-15. Captain Sam Walker referred to his number 14 jersey being one of his proudest possessions and it is interesting to note that Vivian Jenkins' jersey was number 30 - no Lion wore number 13 on his back.

THE TRANSVAAL TEAM AVERAGES 13 STONE ODD
WEIGHT LIKE THAT IS NOT BUILT UP ON PEANUTS AND LENTILS. IT IS DUE TO THE BODY-BUILDING QUALITIES OF
CHANDLERS' STOUT

CURTAIN RAISERS.
1.20 p.m. — CENTRAL RAND Under 19 vs. EAST RAND Under 19.   2.20 p.m. — CENTRAL RAND JUNIORS vs. EAST RAND JUNIORS.

GREAT BRITAIN
Selected from

V. G. J. Jenkins (30)
C. F. Grieve (29)

W. H. Clement (27)   R. Leyland (24)
D. J. Macrae (23)   E. L. W. Jones (26)
C. V. Boyle (25)   B. E. Nicholson (21)
H. R. McKibbin (22)   E. J. Unwin (28)

H. Tanner (16)
G. J. Morgan (17)   E. J. Reynolds (20)
J. C. Giles (18)   G. E. Cromey (19)

R. Alexander (1) A. R. Taylor (2) I. Williams (3)
P. L. Duff (4) J. A. Waters (5) A. H. G. Purchas (6)
S. R. Couchman (7) G. T. Dancer (8) R. B. Mayne (9)
C. R. Graves (10) W. H. Travers (11) W. G. Howard (12)
S. Walker (14) M. E. Morgan (15)
(Capt.)

KICK-OFF ON

THE SAVING SPIRIT

TRANSVAAL

C. J. K. Basson (1)

M. Zimmerman (2) J. Roux (4) F. G. Turner (3) R. L. Collins (5)

T. A. Harris (6)   J. Segal (7)

J. F. Kloppers (15)

J. Smit (14) W. Farndell (13) W. J. J. Pretorius (12)
F. C. Smollan (11)

S. B. D. Neville (10)   J. Lotz (9)   S. C. Louw (8)
(Capt.)

Reserves: C. Scrooby (21) E. King (22) J. Harmse (23)
F. S. Kriel (24) S. Delaporte (25) N. Gordon (19)
C. Newham (20) F. W. Waring (18) F. R. Williams (17)
J. Hirst (16)

THE TRANSVAAL TEAM AVERAGES 13 STONE ODD
WEIGHT LIKE THAT IS NOT BUILT UP ON PEANUTS AND LENTILS. IT IS DUE TO THE BODY-BUILDING QUALITIES OF
CHANDLERS' STOUT

Match day Rhodesia style circa 1938. Above, 'Trods' Hards leads Rhodesia out at Bulawayo for the second match. The press are seated pitch-side while Major Hartley can be seen standing to the left of the players. Should refreshments be required during the match, waiter service would appear to be on hand. The opponents meet (left). This is not the customary congratulatory gathering at the end of the match, rather a discussion about the first forty minutes. British Lion, Charles Graves takes the opportunity to meet the opposition in the short half-time interval during which the players remained on the field.

Above left – The Natal Rugby Union made a financial loss in 1937 and perhaps it was with this in mind that a programme was printed which covered the games against Northern Province and Natal. The Lions' strip of blue jersey, white shorts and red socks failed to recognise the green of Ireland and so did the artist who omitted the island from the design.

Above right – Eight Irishmen were included in the party. It is just as well they were not forgotten as each played a significant part in the tour and all appeared in the Third Test. Not least among the Irish contingent was Blair Mayne, between Duncan Macrae and former Springbok and England international Frank Mellish.

Three players led the Lions in South Africa. Tour captain Sam Walker led them in twenty matches; vice-captain Vivian Jenkins took over the duty three times; and against North East Districts Irish scrum-half George Morgan (below right) assumed the responsibility.

No stranger to the role of captain, Morgan had previously led Ireland and would do so again in the 1939 Championship.

The might of the front row. Boy Louw (left) and brother Fanie proudly wear their Springbok blazers. They played major roles in the defeat of the Lions in the first and second Tests before having to accept second best in the third. Boy won eighteen caps and Fanie twelve, appearing together in five Tests.

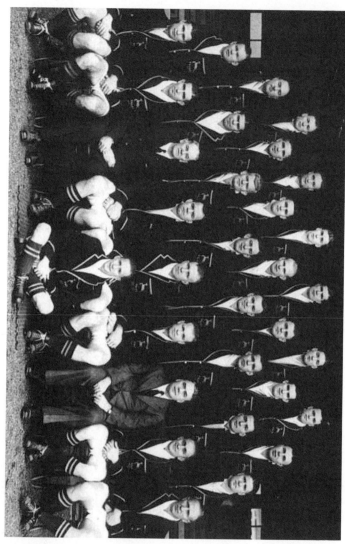

The South African party that toured Australia and New Zealand in 1937. This squad won a first series in New Zealand to become unofficial 'world champions' and earn the accolade of 'Greatest Springboks'. Back row left to right – T.A. Harris, D.F. van der Vyver, S.R. Hofmeyr, J. White, A.D. Lawton, L. Babrow. Third row - W.E. Bastard, J.W. Lotz, J.L.A. Bester, G.P. Lochner, H.J. Martin, D.O. Williams, J.A. Broodryk. Second row - C.B. Jennings, S.C. Louw, M.A. van den Berg, W.F. Bergh, G.L. van Reenen, A.R. Sherriff, B.A. du Toit, H.H. Watt. Seated - F.J. Turner, P.J. Lyster, P.W. Day (manager), M.M. Louw, P.J. Nel (captain), D.H. Craven (vice-captain), A. de Villiers (assistant-manager), G.H. Brand, L.C. Strachan. In front - P. du P. de Villiers.

the duty of one of the non-playing members of the party to carry this at pitchside when the team took the field. By the time the party arrived in Southern Rhodesia this unprecedented novelty had become an indispensable part of the proceedings. Bunner Travers took responsibility for the mascot at Salisbury and as the game became a much more closely contested affair than predicted and the excitement of the occasion took over two of the lion's legs were broken off. It was ironic that this should happen in Salisbury because the mascot had been presented to the Lions by the Rhodesian ladies' hockey team, who it would appear met up with them either before they departed from Southampton or, more probably, on the journey to South Africa. A carpenter was needed!

Bulawayo – 'the place of the killing' – and indeed there were many who died before Cecil Rhodes could finally lay claim to the area. Hopes of another rich seam of gold had not materialised but another mineral was found to be in plentiful supply and Bulawayo's proximity to the Wankie Coal Fields to the north was sufficient for the Rhodesian railways to be centred on the town, ensuring it a prosperous future. The overnight journey from Salisbury saw the party arrive at midday on Friday, allowing time to visit Rhodes' grave in the hills outside Bulawayo and have another practice at the Hartsfield ground in preparation for the second encounter with Rhodesia.

When the team was announced it was no surprise that it included several changes. Only five players had featured in Salisbury. Vivian Jenkins, George Cromey and Eddie Morgan retained their positions while Basil Nicholson was selected on the wing and Sam Walker dropped back into the second row. The inclusion of ten fresh players, including Jock Waters, meant that all the fit members of the party played against Rhodesia. With the selectors likely to field a shadow Test team against Transvaal a week later this was a final chance for players to remind the selectors what they were capable of. In particular Elvet Jones, Haydn Tanner and Russell Taylor would have known they were in with a good chance of being selected and were especially keen to make an impression. There was much to play for. Fewer changes in the Rhodesian team saw the half-backs replaced, Napier and Phillips taking over from Jacklin and Parker and among the forwards, Potgieter came in for Watson.

Match 13, Rhodesia, Saturday 23 July, Bulawayo

The match marked the official opening of the new ground and among the 4,000 spectators was the Rhodesian prime minister, the Hon. G.M. Huggins, who was introduced to the teams before kick-off. Any thoughts of an improved performance by Rhodesia giving them the chance of a major upset were quickly forgotten as the Lions immediately set about their task in earnest. Tries by Jones, Alexander and Morgan in the first ten minutes were soon followed by a brace from Nicholson and the visitors were 21-0 up in as many minutes. Unfortunately Rhodesia's captain 'Trods' Hards had to leave the field with a badly cut head and although he returned was not the inspiration he had been at Salisbury. Next to score was Taylor following a break by Tanner and the half-time whistle went with the score standing at 26-3 to the Lions, a late penalty by Phillips getting the home side off the mark.

The second half saw more of the same with Jones

opening the scoring before Nicholson was forced off with an ankle injury, Alexander replacing him on the wing. Waters celebrated his return with the next try and then it was the turn of the home side to enjoy a period of dominance during which the outside-half created space to cross for a try which Gordon converted before scrum-half Phillips added his second penalty to bring the score to 34-11. In the last ten minutes Jones completed his second hat-trick of the tour and Alexander and Waters both crossed for their second tries of the match to make the final score 45-11. The Lions had scored eleven tries, six of which had been converted; Jenkins, Giles, Macrae and Taylor sharing the kicking duties.

British Lions – V.G.J. Jenkins, B.E. Nicholson, D.J. Macrae, J.L. Giles, E.L. Jones, G.E. Cromey, H. Tanner, M.E. Morgan, W.H. Travers, G.T. Dancer, S. Walker, captain, R.B. Mayne, R. Alexander, J.A. Waters, A.R. Taylor.
Scorers – Taylor T, 3C, Jones 3T, Waters 2T, Nicholson 2T, Alexander 2T, Morgan T, Giles C, Macrae C, Jenkins C.
Rhodesia – D.H. Gau, N.A. Shackleton, P. Brunton, S.L. Wolffe, L.R. Gordon, E.M. Napier, O.D. Phillips, W.H. Hards, captain, W.A. Pringlewood, M. Stokes, G.M. Moir, I.P. Potgieter, P. du Plessis, R.S. Parker, J. Owen.
Scorers – Phillips 2P, Napier T, Gordon C.
British Lions 45, Rhodesia 11 (half-time 26-3)
Referee – A.L. Reynolds

Rhodesia had been unable to raise their game a second time, but even allowing for the clear difference in ability between the two teams this latest performance by the Lions was the most confident and assured of the tour to date. The handling was first class and that six of the tries were claimed by forwards again confirmed how comfortable they were ball in hand as all the scores had come from adventurous, open play. There can be no doubt that the Lions were more than happy with the playing surface, a fact Haigh Smith alluded to in his speech at the after match banquet held in the Crystal Court at the Grand Hotel when he confirmed it was the best the tourists had played on.

With thirteen matches consigned to the record books the log now made much better reading. Ten games had been won and an impressive 245 points scored including fifty-one tries. Against this the Lions had conceded 138 points and twenty tries. The two matches against Rhodesia had been timely. The first had tested the Lions and forced them to adapt to a more sensible approach than that often shown in the past and the second had allowed them to fully express themselves as a unit, the players visibly gaining in confidence.

The following Saturday would see the return match with Transvaal. That would give a good indication of any progress made in Rhodesia and seven days later it was the Springboks who would line up against the Lions in a packed Ellis Park. Then there would be nowhere to hide. However, before thinking about the return to Johannesburg there were four days in which the players would be able to relax, recharge the batteries and give their battered bodies some well-deserved rest.

There were many subsequent claims but it is universally accepted that in 1855 Dr David Livingstone was the first white man to cast eyes on the Victoria Falls. Located to the north of the Wankie Coal Field and some 280 miles from Bulawayo, the falls are found on the upper reaches of the Zambesi River, which acted as the border between Northern and Southern Rhodesia. More than a mile across and some 300 ft deep they are one of the world's most spectacular natural sights and it was inevitable that efforts would be made to allow visitors to enjoy the spectacle. At the turn of the century a railway spur from the main line north was constructed, taking passengers to within a mile of the falls. This was eventually extended to continue north crossing the river via a cantilever bridge spanning the Zambesi a short distance from the falls at a point where the gorge narrows to 500 ft. At more than 300 ft high the bridge was for many years the tallest in the world and in 1932 the railway line and bridge were modified to allow the passage of motor vehicles.

The 2.00 p.m. Sunday departure from Bulawayo is worth recording because in an effort to ensure that the Lions got to the falls with sufficient time at their disposal to fully enjoy the experience the Rhodesian Railways authorised two carriages to be attached to a goods train scheduled to arrive at Victoria Falls Station at 6.30 a.m. the following day. When the line first opened in 1904 the need for a hotel to accommodate the expected influx of visitors saw the Victoria Falls Hotel open its doors in the same year. From the railway station a covered walkway took visitors directly into the hotel which is situated a mile from the falls and it was here that the party checked in for one night before an evening departure for Johannesburg on Tuesday.

One of the world's great hotels in 1938, no expense had been spared by its owners to ensure that the

Victoria Falls Hotel met the highest standards of accommodation and cuisine for what would have initially been a particularly discerning clientele. It was a first class, five-star facility and with two full days now at their disposal the tourists set about putting the time to good use and making the most of what would certainly be a once in a lifetime experience.

The hotel held the franchise for the many activities that focused on the river and the surrounding area. There was a trolley car service to take residents from the hotel to the various vantage points above the falls and there were also several options available for passengers wishing to negotiate the Zambesi River. From the boat house located at the end of the trolley line, launches took passengers further upriver to Kandahar Island, a round trip of sixteen miles that offered sightings of crocodile, hippopotamus, elephant, antelope and buck. The entire party took advantage of the host union's generosity, the Rhodesian RFU picking up the tab which at 7/6d per head included the customary afternoon teas. Another option would have been the slower canoes manned by local natives and costing between 1/0d and 2/6d dependent on both the size of the canoe and the number of men employed, but these were known to venture much nearer to the top of the falls than many would have liked.

The stopover also provided an opportunity to enter Northern Rhodesia and the party took the bus over the cantilever bridge and continued the seven miles north to the first port of call for visitors to the northern colony. Livingstone was founded in 1905 and had been the capital of Northern Rhodesia until 1935 when the mantle was handed to Lusaka. This journey allowed a different perspective on the area, the chance to view the falls from the elevation offered by the bridge and the opportunity to visit a town with a name that was a reminder of the days of the great Victorian adventurers and explorers.

The excursion to Victoria Falls had taken the party out of its way but the 600-mile round trip was undoubtedly well worth any additional inconvenience it may have entailed. Besides, these were now seasoned travellers and the two train journeys would not have been a problem, but the next one they faced was a harsh reminder of the size and extent of the country they were visiting. From Victoria Falls on the 8.05 p.m. Tuesday departure the party arrived at Bulawayo the following morning and after a four-hour wait for their connection set off on the thirty-hour journey that would get them into Johannesburg early Thursday evening, allowing them a full day to prepare for Saturday's game. Regardless of the many inconveniences that rail travel in South Africa produced there was no alternative but the knowledge that the next two matches would both be played in Johannesburg did at least mean there would be no travelling for the next ten days, the longest period of stability since the Lions had arrived in South Africa almost two months earlier.

CHAPTER FIVE

REVENGE AND REALITY

Court is adjourned for the day – Transvaal
beaten – A serious blow as the 'Prince' is laid
low – What's in fashion? – The Springboks
prepare – All roads lead to Ellis Park – The
first Test.

The return to Johannesburg began a ten-day
period during which the progress made since
the opening match in East London would be
measured. The Lions knew that the outcome of the
next two encounters would also be significant when
it came to assessing the success or otherwise of the
tour as a whole. Defeat against both Transvaal and the
Springboks would be a major setback and at least one
of the matches had to be won. If the Test was lost the
Lions would have two further opportunities to save the
series but a second loss to Transvaal was not an option.

That the 1938 British Lions were proving to be the
most popular tourists to visit South Africa was never
questioned. They were the most approachable bunch
of individuals off the field and the locals had taken
to them wherever they appeared. Many had become
household names in the relatively short time they had
been in the country and some of their number were
regularly singled out for favourable comparison with
the leading Springboks of the day. In rattling up ten
victories the tourists had won over the support of those
fortunate enough to watch them play and while there
could be no questioning where local allegiances would

lie when the Springboks took the field the visitors had unquestionably made a lot of friends with their cavalier approach to the game. This was in stark contrast to much of the fare South Africa had produced in the years leading up to their triumph in New Zealand which home supporters would only have read about and they were keen to witness for themselves the open brand of rugby the Springboks had adopted in 1937.

News of the try fest in Rhodesia would have reached the Transvaal and whetted the appetites of those who would again make their way to Ellis Park but as no British tourists had enjoyed success against Transvaal since 1896, a statistic that now included the current Lions, the omens for Sam Walker and his men were not good. With no midweek match arranged between the second encounter with Transvaal and the first Test it was important that the Lions took this final opportunity to field a shadow Test team. This would give the players a last chance to not only prove themselves against strong opposition and hopefully gain the confidence generated by winning but it would also present another opportunity to acclimatise, adjust to the extra demands that eighty minutes' rugby on the high veldt place on the body. When it came to the final analysis thirteen of the team originally chosen to face Transvaal would also appear in the first Test but two late changes and a most unfortunate injury meant twelve players would line up in both games.

Following the late withdrawal of Duncan Macrae, Roy Leyland was given the chance to stake a claim for a place in the Test team. Leyland had not played for a month and it was more than three years since his previous appearance on the international stage, the three-times-capped England centre having been ignored by the national selectors since the 1935 Championship. Regardless of his time spent in the international wilderness, there was little doubt that Leyland possessed all the qualities required at the highest level and if Macrae was unavailable for selection in a week's time it was felt that Leyland could be relied upon to step up to the mark.

The second late change saw Ves Boyle called up to replace Bas Nicholson who was selected on the wing against Transvaal but had failed to recover from an ankle injury picked up at Bulawayo, giving Boyle, another yet to show his true potential, the chance to impress. Vivian Jenkins, James Unwin and Harry McKibbin only had to avoid injury to ensure their places in the Test and it also looked as if Jimmy Giles and Jeff Reynolds would get the nod at half-back if Reynolds experienced no further ankle problems.

The forwards were almost certain to continue en bloc, the preferred eight now virtually finalised with the inclusion of Beef Dancer in the front row alongside Eddie Morgan and Bunner Travers. Sam Walker and Blair Mayne were settled in the second row, where they would feature in most of the remaining matches, and Russell Taylor, Bill Howard and Bob Alexander had each looked likely Test players. The forwards had adjusted to the different demands posed by using the 3-4-1 scrum formation favoured by the Springboks and it appeared that the only positions waiting to be pencilled in were on the wing and in the centre.

Meanwhile, the Springbok selectors had been taking their responsibilities seriously. A squad of players met in Johannesburg and the selectors conducted a series of trial matches giving all those in contention a final chance to impress. The selectors would have been only too aware of the expectation surrounding the Springboks and there could be no room for complacency on their part. Having stolen a march on their greatest rivals twelve months earlier, the Springboks would not want to be knocked off their pedestal by a team from the northern hemisphere. There was much at stake and the ever demanding South African public would settle for nothing less than a resounding victory from their team. The fifteen men on whose shoulders the responsibility would rest were to be named on the Thursday before the Test.

For the second meeting with the Lions, the Transvaal team showed five changes from the side that had triumphed three weeks earlier. Fred Turner scored ten points in the first meeting between the teams but with his likely inclusion in the Test it was decided he should rest a minor injury and sit out the game. Fred Waring replaced him alongside Roux in the centre and Williams came in on the wing in place of Collins. Among the forwards Pretorius, Farndell and Klopper were replaced by Scrooby, Badenhorst and Delaporte but the solid front row of Louw, Lotz and Neville remained intact with Smollan and John Smit, outstanding in the first game, also included. The match would be watched by the South African selectors and the Lions were sure to come under as much scrutiny from the learned gentlemen as any potential Springbok included in the Transvaal team.

Match 14, Transvaal, Saturday 30 July, Johannesburg

For the second time in three weeks all roads led to Ellis Park, the city again caught up in the grip of rugby fever. The magistrates' courts which regularly sat on

Saturday mornings largely completed the judicial
business of the day by 10.00 a.m., allowing judges,
barristers and clerks alike to make an early start for
the ground, although there was growing concern in B
Court where the party acting for the defence went to
great length with his address to the bench, oblivious
to the interests of those seeking an early conclusion
and quick getaway. Neither did the prosecuting
lawyer help matters by outdoing his learned friend in
the time spent on his feet despite obvious indications
from above that matters should be moved along. At
the adjacent registry office there was also concern
as bookings had been taken through to 1.00 p.m.,
leaving little time for the registrar and his staff to make
their way to the ground for the 3.30 kick-off.

Estimates varied but there were certainly in excess of
20,000 spectators in the ground to see the Mayor of
Johannesburg Mr J.S. Fotheringham introduced to
the teams. Walker lost the toss and Louw elected to
make the tourists play into the sun in the first half.
Harry McKibbin got the match under way and it was
immediately noticeable that the Lions were more
focused than on their first visit to the ground and in
every department the players set about the task with
a greater commitment than shown in most of the
previous matches. The forwards dominated the early
exchanges, which set the pattern for what would
follow. This was to go down as the game in which the
pack began to look like the finished article. The eight
played as a complete unit not only in the set pieces
but also in the loose exchanges where the proverbial
blanket could have covered them, such was their
united work ethic. As one they took the game to their
opposite numbers, preferring the close contact to any

temptation to release the ball to the backs. Pretty it may not have been but with Walker leading his men by example, the home side were often found on the back foot, unable to do anything against the dribbling game which the Lions forwards adopted.

Press reviews summed up the match by commenting that it was both won and lost in the critical first twenty minutes, during which Leyland scored a try converted by Jenkins and Taylor put over a fine penalty from forty yards for an 8-0 lead. Later in the half, Basson kicked a penalty for the home side to reduce the deficit but on the stroke of half-time Unwin dropped a goal, giving the visitors a 12-3 lead to take into the second half. The first period had been a brutal affair with no quarter given or asked for by either set of forwards but in the Lions' camp there was a concern that Bunner Travers may have done some serious damage to his neck. The hooker was clattered to the ground by an all-embracing tackle and his unprotected head bounced off the rock-hard surface. Although clearly dazed, Travers refused to leave the field, saw out the half and after the short break took his place in the line-up when play recommenced.

The Transvaal forwards were clearly outplayed in the first half, prompting captain Fanie Louw to fine tune the pack during the half-time break, Scrooby moving into the front row in place of Neville, who dropped to the back of the scrum. This immediately had the desired effect, the home side much more competitive in the first scrums of the second half. Travers was clearly not himself and without any shadow of doubt should not have been on the field but it was a revitalised Transvaal who now threatened to take control of the match. Early pressure led to an infringement inside the

Lions' 25 and Basson stepped up to kick the penalty, and immediately following the restart the Transvaal forwards took play back into Lions' territory only for Louw to knock on with the line at his mercy. Lotz won the strike against the head at the resultant scrum and a passage of crisp handling by the backs put Zimerman over in the corner, Basson narrowly failing with the conversion. But the score now stood at 12-9.

Transvaal had gained the upper hand largely due to an improved performance from the forwards. Up front the contest had been hard but always fair but as the game moved into the final quarter tempers began to fray and matters started to get out of control. There were several exchanges of blows, making life difficult for the referee, who had his work cut out in trying to keep the big men in order, but the Lions held firm both within and outside the Laws of the game. With only three points separating the sides, the match was heading towards an exciting conclusion with the home side looking the most likely winners.

After a prolonged period of pressure during which the Lions' defence was subjected to the closest scrutiny it was very much against the run of play when Giles broke away from a scrum and made inroads into home territory. The scrum-half linked with Reynolds who in turn found McKibbin in support. The ball was transferred smoothly along the line to Unwin, who made his way back infield leaving several would-be tacklers in his wake. With only full-back Basson standing in his way welcome support arrived in the shape of Sam Walker and the captain readily accepted the scoring pass to touch down near the posts, giving Jenkins an easy conversion to take the score to 17-9 with ten minutes remaining on the clock. At last the game opened up with both teams creating try-scoring opportunities following good passages of play but a combination of bad handling and poor judgement prevented any further score.

While some press reports claimed that the match was won and lost in the first twenty minutes during which the Lions opened up an eight-point lead, J.G. Kneen highlighted Walker's try as the game's defining moment, writing '...it seemed "all London to a Chinese orange" that Transvaal would win the day...' and that in Smollan '...it seemed that Transvaal had (only) one forward who knew that tackling did not mean grabbing a man's eyebrows.' Descriptive journalism of a unique and quite incomprehensible variety.

If Sam Walker's try had been the seminal moment of the game for the Lions, it was a second thumping tackle on the already dazed and confused Travers that detracted from a resounding victory. Midway through the second half Fanie Louw collared the Lion with another crunching tackle and Travers' head again met the ground with some force. The hooker got to his feet but was clearly concussed and was led from the field to great applause and although he somehow contrived to return for the last moments it was obvious that the injury cast grave doubts over his inclusion in the Test team.

The second encounter with Transvaal had first and foremost been a forward-dominated game that had seen both packs enjoy prolonged periods of superiority but at the end there were no dissenting voices heard when it was suggested that the Lions had held the upper hand overall. This was a victory that sent reverberations throughout the land and any thoughts that the Springboks would be in for an easy ride were soon forgotten. For the Lions there were more injury concerns. Blair 'Paddy' Mayne had been magnificent in the type of encounter the big Ulsterman relished but he made his way through the thousands of spectators who invaded the pitch at the final whistle limping badly in obvious discomfort. Giles and Leyland both required attention in the latter stages of the game but were able to continue. Reynolds had come through the match unscathed but showed none of the confidence he had displayed earlier in the tour, perhaps aware that a further problem with his ankle would effectively put an end to any hopes he had of making the Test team. And of course there was the almost certain loss of Travers.

British Lions – V.G.J. Jenkins, E.J. Unwin, R. Leyland, H.R. McKibbin, C.V. Boyle, F.J. Reynolds, J.L. Giles, M.E. Morgan, W.H. Travers, G.T. Dancer, S. Walker, captain, R.B. Mayne, R. Alexander, W.G. Howard, A.R. Taylor.
Scorers – Jenkins C, Unwin DG, Leyland T, Walker T, Taylor P, C.
Transvaal – C. Basson, M. Zimerman, F.W. Waring, J. Roux, F.R. Williams, T.A. Harris, J. Segal, S.C. Louw, captain, W.J. Lotz, S.B.D. Neville, C.W. Scrooby, C.J. Badenhorst, C. Delaporte, J. Smit, F.C. Smollan.
Scorers – Basson 2P, Zimerman T.
British Lions 17, Transvaal 9 (half-time 12-3)
Referee – N.F. Pretorius

With no midweek match or long-distance travelling to worry about it was time for the players to let their hair down and where better to let off some steam than at the biggest function of the tour. Held at the Wanderers

Club, the annual ball was always a highlight of Johannesburg's social calendar and it had long been arranged that the 1938 bash would coincide with the visit of the Lions. Eight hundred people attended, making the ball the biggest the club had ever hosted and the ballroom was decked out in the red, yellow and black club colours while the lounge and tables were decorated in the red, white and blue of the principal guests. The mayor and lady mayoress, leading figures from the worlds of industry and commerce, guests from several of the local unions and clubs together with many club players were in attendance and part of the entertainment was supplied by Miss Poppy Frames' troupe who '...gave an excellent tap dancing display and an amusing skit on rugby football which was heartily applauded.'

The fashion columnists reported on what was in favour with the social set that season. Among the outfits to draw attention '...Mrs W. Green was strikingly dressed in black velvet with deep amber roses. Miss Joan Attwell's champagne lace frock was ashed with pink, with a spray of matching pink flowers. Mrs Morgan Evans' gossamer lace frock had blue flowers trailing over it and Miss Gloris Beck's fluttering chiffon gown was shaded from palest pink to deepest scarlet... Royal blue taffeta suited Mrs B. Sieff. Miss Daisy Durie's black dress was trimmed with a yoke of bugle beads and Mrs A.B. Inglis wore an attractive shade of blue faille... Mrs R.G. Denny topped a vivid turquoise dress with an ostrich feather cape to match...' And so it went on. Descriptions of finery that would have graced any function – now the Lions knew why they had been asked to bring their 'tuxedoes' with them!

The week leading up to the Test saw a mix of training and leisure activities. Most popular among the options available, the Royal Johannesburg Golf Club had extended honorary membership to the party for the duration of their stay and rounds were played on Tuesday, Wednesday and Friday. Those players still carrying injuries were closely monitored but immediately following the Transvaal match it was clear that Travers would not be available for selection. He had suffered a bad concussion which necessitated his being kept under twenty-four-hour supervision. This meant checking into a nursing home and it seemed unlikely that he would be released in time to attend the match. This was a bitter blow as the popular hooker had been one of the outstanding successes of the tour and his absence was a huge loss. Although he had appeared in eight matches, Charles Graves had hooked on only two occasions and would have very little time to adjust to the middle of the front row with the new formation behind. This would cause problems at any time but when one considers the strength of the Springbok front line forwards it looked a monumental task.

The Springbok selectors had watched the Lions at every opportunity, which gave them the advantage of knowing what to expect; where the strengths and weaknesses lay and how to counter and expose them. This was in marked contrast to the Lions' selectors who had very little on which to base their preparation. There was no television footage to study, neither had there been any opportunity to see their opponents play as a team. The Lions had come across most of the players in contention for places during the provincial matches but the collective was going to present a much greater challenge.

Following a final trial held on Thursday, the South African team was announced and there were very few surprises. Twelve of those selected had played in the third Test in New Zealand, the Springboks' last competitive match, and two others had been on the tour. There were suggestions among the media that the team included too many players who were a bit long in the tooth for Test match rugby, certainly in the pack where the average age was twenty-nine. Many felt that the selectors should have included some of the younger men who were starting to make their mark but it had to be remembered that the Springboks had not played at home for five years, not since the visit of the Australians in 1933, and the way the team had conquered the All Blacks on their own patch less than twelve months earlier gave every justification for the inclusion of those players still available for selection.

Gone were forward and tour captain Philip Nel, who had led the team in Australia and New Zealand. Nel had announced his retirement from the game by ceremoniously throwing his boots overboard on the sea journey home. Also unavailable was centre Louis Babrow, who had travelled to England to continue his medical studies at Guy's Hospital where he continued playing the game, leading the hospital team with distinction and making several appearances for the Barbarians. The other omission from the final Test of 1937 was Mauritz van den Berg, who had been prominent when playing against the Lions for Western Province Town and Country and Western Province but who now found himself out of favour.

As expected, Danie Craven was appointed captain. First capped against Wales in 1931, Craven had been Nel's vice-captain in 1937. When Nel was surprisingly dropped, Craven led the Springboks against the All Blacks in the first Test but from outside-half. He was also included as a loose forward against Australia on the same tour but it was as a scrum-half that his undoubted talents were best seen and his trademark dive passing from the base of the scrum was particularly innovative. Aged twenty-eight, Craven had announced he would be leaving South Africa at the end of the series to take up an eighteen-month physical culture education course in Europe and it was almost certain that the Tests against the Lions would be his last in a Springbok jersey.

Even at what in rugby circles was seen as an advanced age, thirty-one-year-old Gerry Brand was still far and away the best full-back in South Africa and probably in the world game. Brand had played in fifteen Tests during an international career that stretched back to the 1928 New Zealand tour to South Africa and also included the tours to the British Isles in 1931 and Australia and New Zealand in 1937. Gerry Brand was another expected to make his final appearances in the Springbok jersey against the Lions.

The tried and tested Freddy Turner and Dai Williams were selected on the wings. Turner and Williams had already played against the tourists and both would now make their sixth international appearance. Williams had three international tries to his credit, Turner two and the threat these potent finishers posed out wide would need to be covered if the Springboks continued with the adventurous, attacking style of rugby that had brought them success the previous year, a question that would remain unanswered until the Test got under way. Would South Africa take on the Lions at their own game or revert to the tighter, forward-dominated rugby of old?

There was a new face in the centre. 'Flappie' Lochner played for Eastern Province, a team the Lions would meet later in the tour. He had also been on the 1937 tour, making his international debut in the deciding third Test when partnering the departed Louis Babrow. In place of Babrow the selectors chose twenty-one-year-old Pieter de Wet, a product of the University of Cape Town and Western Province who had played against the Lions for both the province and the combined Cape Province team. There was never any doubt that Tony Harris would be the preferred choice to partner Craven at half-back and following his two games for Transvaal in which he was a constant source of irritation to the tourists his selection was academic. An accomplished all-rounder, Harris would play Test cricket when he toured England with the 1947 Springboks and again in the following year when South Africa hosted England.

The front row was as expected. The Louw brothers would pack down alongside Jan Lotz – three players who had accumulated twenty-nine caps between them. In the modern era this sounds a small number of international appearances but when one considers that South Africa played only twenty-eight Test matches in the twenty-year period between the wars the figure is put in context.

Jan Lotz had five caps, 'Fanie' Louw nine and 'Boy' Louw fifteen, having made his debut ten years earlier against New Zealand. The front row was an area where the Springboks looked nigh on invincible and the loss of Travers would be highlighted by the trio, who both individually and collectively were a force to be reckoned with.

From Paarl in the Western Cape both Boy and Fanie Louw played for Western Province before Fanie moved to the Transvaal to work in the gold mines. He had captained Transvaal against the Lions. Boy remained in the Cape to pursue a career in banking, playing his rugby with Western Province. His knowledge of the Laws of the game was particularly comprehensive and Boy Louw would later become a first class referee. A keen student of the game, his assessment of opponents and the way in which they would approach a game was rarely proved wrong and Louw's in-depth knowledge was welcomed by the selectors, who were always prepared to listen to the senior player, one of the first to seriously investigate the game beyond his own immediate involvement. Between the brothers in the front row was Jan Lotz, without doubt the finest hooker in the land. Lotz was deemed so good that he was the only hooker taken on the 1937 tour, playing in twenty-four of the twenty-eight matches, and, since replacing Bert Kipling in the Transvaal and national sides, he had become a permanent fixture in both.

Behind this formidable trio were the Northern Transvaal quartet, Ferdie Bergh, Roger Sherriff, Ben du Toit and Louis Strachan. Sherriff and du Toit would win first caps against the Lions but they had gained experience touring with the Springboks in the previous year. Ferdie Bergh stood alone in his claim as the most travelled of the Springboks. His fourteen consecutive appearances began with South West Districts, continued following a move to Griqualand West from where he joined Transvaal before becoming attached to the newly formed Northern Transvaal. Louis Strachan was introduced to international rugby on the tour to the British Isles in 1931–32 and by 1938 had won seven caps. Finally there was William Eberhardt 'Ebbo' Bastard. An unfamiliar face but an unforgettable name. Ebbo Bastard was captain of the Natal provincial team, which the Lions would play in ten days, and was yet another who started his Test career in 1937. It was Bastard's try that clinched the all important second Test at Christchurch to level the series.

Northern Transvaal had the biggest representation with five players, Western Province and Transvaal each provided four, Eastern Province and Natal both providing one. Boy Louw was the eldest and Pieter de Wet the youngest and between them the team could boast eighty-eight caps with Boy Louw and Gerry Brand the most experienced. Solid in every department, on paper the Springboks certainly looked the finished article.

Neither did the Lions' team include any surprises. Of the players ruled out of contention through injury it is likely that Bill Clement would have been included if fit and Bunner Travers' place in the team had been assured prior to his most unfortunate head injury but these two players aside the team reflected the performances on tour to date and there was no suggestion that the Lions were significantly below strength.

Sam Walker would lead from the second row where he would continue alongside Mayne. Graves, replacing Travers at hooker, would be supported by Eddie Morgan and the uncapped Gerald Dancer. As expected Russell Taylor, Bob Alexander and Bill Howard made up the eight. Howard was another uncapped player in a pack that included four Irishmen. Vivian Jenkins was at full-back with Elvet Jones and Charles Unwin on the wings. Roy Leyland had performed well against Transvaal but the selectors continued to favour the Macrae and McKibbin centre partnership At half-back, Jeff Reynolds had come through the Transvaal game intact and though it had been far from his best performance his earlier form earned him his place alongside Jimmy Giles who must have been seriously challenged for the scrum-half berth by Tanner. The team was made up of five Englishmen, five Irishmen, four players from Wales and a solitary Scot.

Long gone are the days when spectators could simply turn up at the ground and pay at the gate, particularly for the big matches such as Tests. The last of the home countries to dispense with a pay at the gate policy was Scotland following a turnout at Murrayfield in excess of 100,000 in 1975 but in 1938 it was universally accepted that all one had to do was turn up on the day to be guaranteed entrance. Little attention was given to accurately recording the number of spectators attending matches at the time, estimates often arriving at different totals, and the fact that attendances were more often than not measured to the nearest thousand shows how unreliable they were. Press reports varied in their assessment of the crowd that filled Ellis Park on 6 August, from a lowly 26,000 to a more realistic 36,000, with one paper pushing the ante up in declaring the total at 40,000. Whatever the final figure, Johannesburg was full of supporters who had arrived by road and rail throughout the night, some from as far as Northern Rhodesia and the Western and Eastern Capes. There was not a hotel room to be had in the city. The local department of municipal transport, having anticipated the numbers, laid on fifty-five extra tram cars and twenty buses to ferry passengers from the city centre to the ground and these would be waiting to make the return journey at the final whistle.

Winter days on the Transvaal can see the thermometer reach the heights and plummet the depths with bitterly cold nights which continue into the morning, followed by a glorious few hours before the sun disappears in the late afternoon. With this in mind the first people to arrive at the ground before dawn were wrapped up in overcoats and armed with blankets, rugs and thermos flasks to keep out the cold until the gates opened at 10.00 a.m., five and a half hours before kick-off. One hour later both ends of the ground were full and all the unreserved seating areas were quickly filling until the point arrived when the officials began to realise they may have a problem. Several thousand spectators were invited to sit five or six deep in front of the terraces and the rows of bench seats that ran up both touchlines, the area surrounding the pitch fortunately wide enough to accommodate the overflow. Such desperate last-minute arrangements made it inevitable that tempers would soon become frayed and with less than an hour to go attempts were made to turn people away, the ground declared full to capacity. Even with an extra police presence and the obvious problem inside the stadium, hundreds of people forced their way through the entrances while many others climbed the perimeter fencing surrounding the ground.

While the huge crowd made its way to Ellis Park the two teams spent the morning trying to fill in the hours until kick-off. The Springboks were invited to take morning tea with Mayor Fotheringham at the Automobile Club and later held a reception at their hotel to which many ex-players were welcomed while the Lions stayed in their hotel rooms away from the excitement, leaving those players not involved in the match to welcome the never ending stream of well wishers who descended on the Carlton Hotel.

Match 15, South Africa – First Test, Saturday 6 August, Ellis Park, Johannesburg

Ellis Park was full. Every inch of space taken up by spectators straining to get a view of the playing area. If it was climbable it was climbed; if it could be sat on people sat on it regardless of the elevation or risk to life and limb; and if there was room for two people on a seat there were more likely to be three people on it – Ellis Park was full. Among the last spectators to take his seat was a dejected Bunner Travers who had spent the week in a nursing home but after promising his doctor that 'I will be good' was allowed to attend the match in the company of a nurse and with the proviso that he would return to the nursing home immediately following the final whistle. The scene was set.

A great roar greeted Sam Walker and his team as they took the field, the spectators letting out all the pent-up emotion which the last few hours had produced. When Danie Craven and the Springboks followed, the Ellis Park crowd rose as one, as much in recognition of the team's great deeds the previous year as in expectation of what was to follow. Bearing in mind that the average South African rugby supporter was only likely to see the Springboks in action once every five years, Test match rugby was a scarce commodity. This first Test against the Lions was only the seventh time South Africa had played in Johannesburg in more than forty years.

The man the Lions' management selected to officiate was A.M. Horak, who had been in control when the Lions defeated OFS. The referee tossed the coin, Sam Walker gave the wrong call and the visitors would face the sun in the first half. Macrae got proceedings under way only to see his kick go straight into touch, resulting in a Springbok scrum on halfway. There were immediate problems with the crowd spilling over onto the pitch and the police had their work cut out trying to contain the huge numbers that were now straddling the touchlines on both sides of the field. Play was held up until order was restored and a replacement ball found as the crowd had held onto the original used by Macrae. On the resumption of play it was the Lions who had the first chance to put points on the board after South Africa infringed at a scrum. Russell Taylor made no mistake with the kick to give the visitors an early 3-0 advantage. Moments later Brand had an opportunity to level the scores when the Lions forwards were penalised following a line-out infringement but from forty-five yards the full-back could only look on as his effort rebounded off an upright into the grateful arms of Bob Alexander, who cleared with a fine kick.

Both teams struggled to get into any early rhythm and it was very much a case of kick and chase in the hope that one of the full-backs would be found wanting. Neither Brand nor Jenkins failed in their defensive responsibilities, both coping well with all that was thrown at them and able to put in good relieving touch kicks of some considerable distance in the rarefied atmosphere. Up front it was the Springbok forwards who held the upper hand in the early exchanges, particularly at the line-out where their technique of catching the ball proved to be much more effective than the Lions, who favoured knocking it back to the scrum-half, a practice which often saw them in retreat as the Springbok forwards burst through on the hapless Giles. Match forecasts had suggested the

Lions' pack would cause the Springboks problems but this was not happening. It was apparent that the visitors were going to have their work cut out if the South African eight were to be contained and the Lions' backs would have to ensure that what good possession came their way did not go to waste.

When Giles was penalised for a crooked feed at a scrum thirty-five yards out, Gerry Brand had the chance to make amends for his earlier miss and this time the full-back made no mistake. From the restart Macrae kicked deep into Springbok territory and Brand was forced to minor the ball behind his goal line. Both teams had been guilty of giving away needless penalties and now it was the turn of South Africa to infringe, presenting the Lions with an immediate opportunity to regain the lead. Jenkins made no mistake from forty yards.

The Springboks began to display some of the open rugby that had served them well in New Zealand. Twice in as many minutes Vivian Jenkins had to produce try-saving tackles, first on Tony Harris, after the outside-half had linked with Craven on a blind side run from a scrum, and then when Craven again exposed the blind side to link with Dai Williams for the wing to make ground before handing on to Boy Louw, whom the full-back brought down just short of the line.

The Lions were now under intense pressure and from a scrum wide out Fred Turner threw the defence into confusion, coming in off his wing to take Harris' pass and break through before linking with Lochner who immediately cut back infield. Williams was in support and, once he had the ball under his arm, the wing executed a dazzling side step, his electric pace taking him beyond the reach of four defenders to touch down wide out. Brand goaled the difficult conversion to put the Springboks ahead for the first time. The South African forwards and backs were linking together well, supporting each other in a way not previously witnessed by their home supporters and after twenty-five minutes' play the score may have been close but the tourists were living off scraps.

Unable to get any ascendancy in the scrums, the Lions were happy to kick the ball into touch and they took every opportunity to take a line-out where the chance of securing possession was greatly improved even if the quality was often poor. The Springboks elected to do exactly the opposite, taking scrums whenever they were on offer. The Lions hung on but were playing much of the game penned back in their own half, unable to gain any territorial advantage. If they could not play the game in the Springbok half then points were going to be hard to come by so when South Africa conceded a penalty at a scrum positioned eight yards inside the Lions' half of the field Vivian Jenkins elected to go for goal. Even allowing for the altitude this was a speculative option that brought appropriate calls from the crowd but these were soon silenced when the full-back sent the ball sailing high between the posts to put the Lions ahead for the third time.

Finding themselves in front again, although very much against the run of play, the Lions forwards stepped up a gear. Walker, Mayne and Howard led spirited attacks deep into South African territory but the home defence was not found wanting, Gerry Brand proving equal to his opposite number when it came to producing try-saving tackles. Of the thirty players on show it was the two full-backs who consistently caught the eye with their competent all-round play, excellent kicking out of defence, sure tackling and prodigious goal kicking.

Jenkins in particular had cast off the demons that had prevented him producing his true form and went on to give a wonderful display in the art of full-back play that would long be remembered by those who witnessed it.

As the half-time whistle approached the Lions were hanging on to the one point lead and enjoying something of a charmed existence. This was highlighted when Dai Williams intercepted a loose pass from Macrae on halfway and broke clear to touch down under the posts, only to be recalled by the referee for a fumble which was interpreted as a knock-on much to the disgust of the celebrating crowd. But the Springboks were not to be denied, such minor indiscretions only adding to their purpose and intent. One final attack before the break saw some good interplay between the forwards. Fanie Louw hacked on a loose ball before gathering it up to cross for a try that Brand converted, giving South Africa a deserved 13-9 half-time lead.

Belying their years, the South African forwards began the second period full of adventure and several passages of play created try scoring opportunities but it was another penalty from Brand that provided the next points. On the rare occasions the Lions threatened, the full-back kept them at bay with long touch finders and a certain inevitability about the outcome began to descend on Ellis Park. Again the Springbok forwards took play into the Lions' half. Led by du Toit, the outstanding forward on the field, the move ended when Boy Louw was unceremoniously dumped by another courageous tackle from Jenkins but the thin blue line was looking ever more stretched. Danie Craven triggered a series of movements that saw play move back and forth across the field before

Tony Harris capitalised on a gap in the defence to score near the posts for Brand to add the conversion. At 21-9 there was sufficient daylight between the two sides to suggest that the game was won and, despite another excellent penalty from Jenkins, the Springboks were now enjoying superiority in all aspects of play. The only surprise was that the Lions managed to create try-scoring opportunities by running the ball at every opportunity.

A move started from in front of their posts saw Alexander, Macrae and Jones all make ground before being brought down but it was to no avail as the stronger home forwards continued to dominate a now visibly tired British eight. From a scrum on the Lions' 25 the speed with which the ball was moved through the hands to Dai Williams gave the wing the necessary room to cross in the corner for his second try and after such a masterful performance Gerry Brand was not going to miss the difficult conversion following which the referee blew for full time – the Springboks were more comfortable winners than the 26-12 final score suggests.

Post-match reaction from the two captains saw Danie Craven '…very satisfied with the performance of the Springbok side and pleased that the old team spirit of 1937 is still in existence. I hope the crowds will be satisfied now that we can play open rugby.' And Sam Walker was in no doubt which was the better side, '…it was a terrifically hard game and the Springboks played really magnificently. They told me the Springbok forwards were old and past their best but I have never seen forwards play better. I congratulate Craven and his team on playing such a splendid game. They were much too good for us.'

Philip Nel, who led the Springboks in 1937 and who many saw as particularly instrumental in the open, running game the team was now adopting, commented, '...the most pleasing thing to me was that our players were not reluctant to open up the game and played the Britons in a style which they consider their strong point. In the first half I think we were unlucky not to have led by a larger score... The kicking on both sides was remarkably good. Our passing on the whole was much cleaner among both forwards and backs. The Britons surprised me in their marked superiority in the line-outs where our taking of scrums was an admission of weakness.'

Weakness in the line-out or strength in the scrum? This is a debatable point but the statistics do confirm that the scrums were comfortably won by the Springboks who took thirty-six of the fifty contested. What the watching Bunner Travers made of this or what impact on the figures his presence would have had cannot be speculated upon but the fact that the Lions won the line-outs 22-16 could be interpreted as a weakness in the Springbok armoury. Or were they perhaps happy to let the visitors win ball which was often scrappy and then follow through and make life difficult for the half-backs?

Asked about his long penalty, Vivian Jenkins confirmed that at training sessions during the week he had been practising such long-range kicks and was regularly converting goals from fully sixty-five yards. There was no doubting the assistance he was receiving from the high altitude and when the opportunity presented itself in the Test he had no hesitation in going for goal, confident he could kick the distance, leaving him with just the direction to worry about.

British Lions – V.G.J. Jenkins, London Welsh and Wales, E.J. Unwin, Rosslyn Park and England, D.J. Macrae, St Andrew's University and Scotland, H.R. McKibbin, Queen's University, Belfast and Ireland, E.L. Jones, Llanelli, F.J. Reynolds, Army and England, J.L. Giles, Coventry and England, M.E. Morgan, Swansea and Wales, C.R.A. Graves, Wanderers and Ireland, G.T. Dancer, Bedford, S. Walker, captain, Instonians and Ireland, R.B. Mayne, Queen's University, Belfast and Ireland, R. Alexander, North of Ireland and Ireland, W.G. Howard, Old Birkonians, A.R. Taylor, Cross Keys and Wales.
Scorers – Jenkins 3P, Taylor P.
South Africa – G.H. Brand, Western Province, F.G. Turner, Transvaal, G.P. Lochner, Eastern Province, P. de Wet, Western Province, D.O. Williams, Western Province, T.A. Harris, Transvaal, D.H. Craven, captain, Northern Transvaal, S.C. Louw, Transvaal, J.W. Lotz, Transvaal, M.M. Louw, Western Province, B.A. du Toit, Northern Transvaal, W.F. Bergh, Northern Transvaal, A.R. Sherriff, Northern Transvaal, W.E. Bastard, Natal, L.C. Strachan, Northern Transvaal.
Scorers – Brand 4C, 2P, Harris T, Williams 2T, S.C. Louw T.
British Lions 12, South Africa 26 (half-time 9-13)
Referee – A.M. Horak

While Johannesburg set about enjoying one great big party the visitors were left to wonder what might have been and their chances of gaining parity or better in the remaining two Tests. The result was a huge disappointment and the manner of the defeat even more so. For the first time on tour they had failed to score a try, in contrast to the four scored by the Springboks whose twenty-six points was the most scored by South Africa at home, confirmation if any was needed that they had continued where they had left off in New Zealand. The open, entertaining rugby which the supporters had only read about was now very much established, some 30,000 plus spectators having witnessed it with their own eyes.

On the injury front Jenkins aggravated the leg muscle that had given him trouble earlier in the tour and Macrae who, alongside McKibbin, was tireless in the Lions' mid-field defensive effort, picked up a bad leg injury. There was some internal bleeding and it was expected to keep him out of action for three weeks but time would prove that, like Bill Clement, he too had played his last game.

Following the Test, it was revealed that the tour was likely to be extended. The last match was scheduled to take place at Newlands against a Combined Universities XV on 14 September, following which the party were due to leave Cape Town on 16 September aboard the *Edinburgh Castle*. This was one of the older vessels in the Union-Castle fleet and would not arrive in Southampton until 3 October, but the *Athlone Castle*, which would depart on 23 September, would complete the journey more quickly, arriving home on 7 October. If it was decided to delay their departure a week, plans were in place to move the Universities game to Saturday 17 September and play the additional fixture against a Western Province Country combination on 21 September, also at Newlands. Obviously the Lions management and players would have to be included in the discussions but it seemed likely that their stay in South Africa would be longer than expected.

CHAPTER SIX

FROM THE PARK TO THE BEACH

A bit of animal watching – To the Indian
Ocean – Ambushed – Two men on a mission
– Ebbo is foiled – Covered in blood – A buck
is shot and a Lion is grounded – A return to
Border country – A gathering of the clans
– A new captain and a record score – A
celebratory dinner.

With a week before the next match the itinerary
included a visit to the Kruger National Park.
Major Hartley and Haigh Smith decided to
remain in Johannesburg with the injured players,
who needed as much medical attention and time to
recuperate as possible, while the rest of the party set off
into the unknown. They would return to Johannesburg
on Thursday for the onward journey to Durban.

In 1898 Paul Kruger designated an area of land in
the Eastern Transvaal for the preservation of wildlife.
Aware that animal numbers were dwindling along
the well-beaten track to the coast, a result of excessive
hunting for food or simply the thrill of the kill and the
potential profiteering to be had from the trophies, the
Sabi Game Reserve was set aside by the government to
allow the animal population to recover. Unsuitable for
settlement due to the high risk of malaria, the reserve
covering 2,000 square miles was adopted by the British
following the Boer War and the first warden was
appointed with the responsibility of controlling the
wholesale poaching still prevalent.

Major James Stevenson-Hamilton, together with two rangers, took control of the reserve and over the following years its area was extended to the north, taking in the vast majority of what has since become known as the Kruger National Park, the name introduced in 1925 in recognition of Paul Kruger's insistence that efforts should be made towards ensuring the preservation of the nation's wildlife. The park first opened its gates to the public in 1928 and ten years later it welcomed 38,014 visitors – twenty-seven lions of a different sort among them.

The party left Johannesburg on Sunday, the train taking them from Pretoria due east through Middleburg, Belfast and on to Nelspruit where they disembarked and completed the final forty miles by road to the Pretorius Kop Gate at the south-west corner of the park. Bordered on the east by Portuguese East Africa (Mozambique), the Kruger Park covered the 200-mile stretch from the Limpopo River in the north to the Crocodile River in the south. Up to sixty miles wide, the park covers 8,000 square miles. Unlike much of the park, open to the public only between 16 October and 15 June, the period when the threat of malaria and rivers in full flow following the rainy season was at its lowest, Pretorius Kop remained open to visitors all year round. It was possible to travel through this corner of the park by road and track and the eighty-mile round trip was deemed safe enough not to necessitate visitors being accompanied by guides, although there were many signs advising patrons that they entered the park at their own risk.

On their excursion into the interior the party would have experienced close encounters with giraffes, zebra, lions, eland, kudu, the original springbok and in the rivers there was every chance of sighting crocodiles and hippopotami. The likelihood of seeing elephants was remote as these were mainly to be found much further to the north. Whatever sightings they may have enjoyed it is certain that the tourists would not previously have witnessed nature in such a glorious, uncommercialised environment.

Back in Johannesburg the decision to extend the tour had been confirmed and arrangements were put in place through Thomas Cook for an extended stay at the Arthur's Seat Hotel on the return to Cape Town but there was bad news on the injury front. Jenkins was likely to be out of action for two weeks and the true extent of Macrae's problem confirmed that it would be several weeks before he could expect to resume playing. Roy Leyland's injury sustained against Transvaal was showing no sign of improving and with nine matches remaining Clement, Leyland and Macrae had to be viewed as long-term casualties. It was beginning to look as if they would be spectators for the rest of the tour. The selectors now had a maximum of twenty-six players at their immediate disposal and so it would remain, a problem compounded by the fact that the three players were all three-quarters.

On a more positive note, Charles Grieve, who had not appeared since the third game, was now available for selection, which was a timely return in view of Vivian Jenkins' further problems. Gamely as George Morgan had performed in his run of four games at full-back he was not an ideal replacement for the vice-captain and although both his appearances for Scotland were at outside-half, Grieve could be expected to bring more experience to the role of last line of defence and after such a lengthy absence he was keen to experience some game time. With two centres unavailable for immediate selection, Jimmy Giles could expect to continue playing out of position, leaving George Morgan and Haydn Tanner to share the scrum-half duties.

The 500-mile journey to Durban took the party south-east to the coast, passing through Standerton, Volksrust, Ladysmith, famous as a target for the Boers during the war, and through Pietermaritzburg before heading down to the Indian Ocean and a very different South Africa from the already varied aspects of life in the Union encountered on their travels to date.

Durban was established in the 1820s largely because of its natural harbour, which provided an ideal base for trading with the native Zulus. Traders from the Cape Colony had tried to persuade the government that the location was perfect for their purposes but to no avail and in its infancy the development was privately funded. Over the following years many people arrived from Europe but it was the plantation owners from Mauritius who would have the biggest impact on the area. Sugar cane provided their livelihood but years of poor harvests at home had forced them to look overseas and the suitability of the area north of Durban, which enjoyed the ideal climate and soil for the plant, attracted them in numbers. There were also the added benefits provided by the rapidly expanding harbour, which would help the distribution of the produce.

The first problem encountered by the new arrivals was the recruitment of a suitable workforce. This was an issue that would change the demographic structure of the region for ever, most noticeably in Durban itself. The sugar barons elected to bring manual workers from the Indian subcontinent and the first boat arrived in 1860 and, despite local objections to the use of immigrant labour, many more would follow. Evidence of the number of immigrants to arrive over the following years is well documented, including in 1893 the visit of a young lawyer, in South Africa to defend a lawsuit due to be heard in the Transvaal. Bad as some of them were, the encounters the young man experienced in South Africa made a lasting impression on someone destined to become one of the leading figures of the twentieth century – Mahatma Gandhi.

In 1938 the population of Durban was approximately 270,000, made up of 70,000 natives and coloured with 100,000 Europeans and a similar number of Asians. The city had an established Indian community centred around a large mosque and markets located in busy Victoria Street. As well as being a thriving commercial port, Durban was also a popular holiday resort favoured by South Africans. Many hotels had sprung up along the promenades facing the ocean and it was here at the Empress Hotel that the Lions next unpacked their bags.

The seafront stretched from Ocean Beach in the south through Marine Parade, ending in Snell Parade to the north and one of its main features was the rickshaw – a two-wheeled open carriage in which passengers sat while being pulled along by Zulus dressed in their native costume of feathered skirts and horned headwear. The waters were a warm 60 degrees Fahrenheit even in the winter months and the Indian Ocean presented the first opportunity for the tourists to get their feet wet, while the local cuisine largely based on the curries and associated spiced dishes of India offered another new experience. Durban was certainly different but when it came to rugby the Lions would find the men from Natal to be no less compromising in their approach than any other of their fellow countrymen. This was 'Bastard' country and Ebbo was looking to inflict another defeat on the visitors.

Northern Provinces may have looked fairly innocuous on the itinerary but in reality this was a combination team that drew on players from Transvaal, Northern Transvaal, Western Transvaal, Orange Free State and Natal. Chosen by the national selectors, the team included six Springboks: Bastard and Roger Sherriff of the current team and Frank Waring, J.A. 'Tallie' Broodryk, Tiny Francis and Fred Smollan from recent years. All names with which the Lions were familiar as each player had made an individual impact against the tourists in matches earlier in the tour. Five others had also played against the Lions and the remaining four would represent Natal in four days' time. This combination posed a serious threat and coming on the back of the Test it was clear that the Lions would have to pick a strong team and include players who could have done with a longer rest.

Come match day, seven Test players were in the starting line-up and there was a welcome return for Travers, who declared himself fully recovered, but behind the scrum the backs looked vulnerable. Charles Grieve was included but lacked match practice. Ves Boyle and Bas Nicholson were yet to produce their best form although Nicholson's cause had not been helped by his selection out of position in two games. Elvet Jones continued on the wing but it was the selection of Jeff Reynolds in the centre and Harry McKibbin at outside-half that attracted most attention in the press. This was a strange reversal of roles at a time when experimentation was probably a luxury the Lions could no longer afford but if needs must it could be corrected on the field. Haydn Tanner would partner the Irishman and it remained to be seen if McKibbin could exploit the longer pass that Tanner brought to the game.

Dancer and Walker joined Travers in a strong front row. Couchman and Waters formed a new second row partnership with Taylor and Purchas on the flanks and there was a first appearance at No. 8 for Blair Mayne. Although on the face of it a pack which saw players in unfamiliar positions, most of them had proved their adaptability and could be called upon to adopt a different role if circumstances dictated. However they were used, the forwards were expected to contest the scrum and line-out but there were big question marks behind.

Union officials in Natal were bitterly disappointed when the Test matches were awarded to Johannesburg, Port Elizabeth and Cape Town and it was only fitting that the Northern Provinces should play in Durban. There was little to choose between the major provinces in terms of seniority. Northern Transvaal apart, they had all been formed during the 1880s and 1890s but with only three Test matches built into the itinerary it was unavoidable that some unions would be disappointed and in 1938 Natal was among them. The matches played at Durban and Pietermaritzburg in 1938 made more than £1,000 for the Natal Rugby Union, a great financial boost when one considers that the accounts reported a loss of £300 in the previous season. Profitable as these two fixtures were, the benefits to be had from hosting a Test match were enormous but with fewer Tests on offer than unions hoping to host them the problem would be ongoing.

Match 16, Northern Provinces, Saturday 13 August, Durban

Until the opening of King's Park in 1958, Natal's matches were historically shared between the city and the capital of the province, Pietermaritzburg seventy miles inland. For the first match in the province the Lions would play at Kingsmead, the famous old ground which now plays host to provincial and Test match cricket and it was there on 13 August that 10,000 spectators filled the seating areas and popular banks to welcome the tourists.

From the moment Tiny Walker kicked off for the Provinces the crowd were entertained to a feast of open rugby. The Lions' adventurous rugby may have won them much acclaim but it had not always won them games and the truth is that at Durban the Lions were ambushed. Ambushed by a much stronger team than they may have expected to face after a Test match and ambushed by a team which led them into a rugby extravaganza that in hindsight they should have avoided. Early pressure saw Russell Taylor convert a penalty which was followed by a piece of enterprising play by Elvet Jones, who intercepted inside his own half and set off on a direct route to the corner flag. With two defenders heading in the same direction, the wing showed a delightful side step that took him inside the covering defence, leaving him with a clear run to the posts for his ninth try in eight appearances and one which Taylor had no trouble converting.

Eight points up the tourist may have been but two things were patently clear from the first twenty minutes: the home team was obviously taking time to settle into a pattern of play and the Lions half-backs, regardless of the fact they had been on tour for two months, looked as if they had just been introduced. Tanner was finding difficulty getting the line moving as McKibbin was electing to take the ball standing still, which in turn meant the three-quarter play was fairly static, allowing the home forwards to get among the Lions' backs and stop any constructed moves developing.

Slowly the game began to swing in the Province's favour and from a line-out deep in the Lions' half Ebbo Bastard broke for the line. Faced by Grieve, he found van Rensburg on his inside to take the scoring pass for a simple try that Francis converted. The Lions were now on the back foot after what had been a promising start and it was not long before Francis opened up the blind side of a scrum to give Broodryk a clear run for the corner. At 8-8 Walker decide to swap Reynolds and McKibbin. Once they had reverted to their normal positions the tourists' back line immediately began to function, presenting the home defence with problems. Only some inspired tackling prevented Boyle from crossing in the corner. Why Reynolds and McKibbin had been selected out of position is open to conjecture, but the decision had been a costly one. When the home team were struggling in the first twenty minutes the Lions had not been able to capitalise on their overall superiority and with the scores level at half-time the signs were ominous.

A long discontinued feature of rugby union but one that was an integral part of the game in the 1930s was the controlled dribbling attacks that saw individuals or small groups of forwards advance upfield with the ball at their feet. This was a difficult ploy to stop without the defending team conceding a penalty and it was a big part of the British game where the soft, muddy grounds made the ball relatively easy to control. However, on the firm, dry surfaces in South Africa the design of the rugby ball allowed it to develop a mind of its own, forwards losing possession because of the many idiosyncrasies that an oval-shaped ball possesses. In much the same way that knowledgeable supporters in the twenty-first century will applaud a well-organised rolling maul so too would crowds in the 1930s respond to controlled footwork by the forwards. In the opening minutes of the second half it was Sam Walker who gave an exhibition of deft footwork which failed to produce a try but did bring the Kingsmead crowd to its feet. One match report described '... the performance of a master ... here in a moment the British captain showed his immense capability... it was the worst of bad luck that he should not have been able to score from so noticeable a piece of work.' It is a long-lost-skill which has no part in the modern game, but Walker's dribbling aside there was little to encourage the tourists as the Province began to exert a stranglehold on the game.

A penalty from Grobler gave the home side the lead for the first time. A cross kick from Lyster on the wing saw Sherriff gather the ball to run unopposed to the line for a try that Francis converted. Never a man to throw in the towel, Walker rallied his forwards and they responded magnificently, camping inside the home 25 for long periods only to be denied by some magnificent defence. As so often happens following such a promising passage of play it was the Northern Province backs who broke out and scored, Francis cutting through to miss out his centre and release Broodryk, the wing needing no encouragement to race away for his second try which the outside-half converted.

Reynolds made some telling breaks but there were also occasions when he showed a return to the bad habits displayed earlier in the tour when he had all too often been found guilty of losing contact with his supporting players and invariably forfeiting possession.

McKibbin came closest to adding to the Lions' score when he followed up his own kick ahead only to be beaten in the race to touch down by the covering Broodryk, and it was the pacey wing who ended the game at the other end of the field, finishing off a move started by the ever present Ebbo Bastard, who linked with Francis. The outside-half put the wing away for a well-deserved hat-trick. The conversion brought the match to an end and at 26-8 the Lions had suffered their biggest defeat of the tour, conceding five tries in the process.

British Lions – C.F. Grieve, E.L. Jones, B.E. Nicholson, F.J. Reynolds, C.V. Boyle, H.R. McKibbin, H. Tanner, S.Walker, captain, W.H. Travers, G.T. Dancer, S.R. Couchman, J.A. Waters, A.R. Taylor, R.B. Mayne, A.H.G Purchas.

Scorers – Taylor P, C, Jones T.

Northern Provinces – W. Rivers, T.J. Lyster, R.A. Wallace, F. Waring, J.A. Broodryk, M.G. Francis, J.E. Todd, T.R.H. Gafney, P. van Niekerk, P.J. van Rensburg, H. Grobler, J. Louw, W.E. Bastard, captain, A.R. Sheriff, F.C. Smollan.

Scorers – Broodryk 3T, Francis 4C, van Rensburg T, Grobler P, Sherriff T.

British Lions 8, Northern Provinces 26 (half-time 8-8)
Referee – J.W. Hudson

This defeat, coming immediately after the first Test, was a major setback. Not only had the Lions lost consecutive games for the first time but the comprehensive manner of both defeats was particularly concerning. Both the Springboks and Northern Provinces had scored twenty-six points against them which included nine tries, while the Lions only had Elvet Jones' try against the Northern Provinces and five penalty goals to show for their efforts. With seven official games remaining, including two Tests, there were several issues to be addressed and hard work to be done if the momentum was to be regained. This had to start with the first of the four matches to be played in the build-up to second Test and if the Lions were to meet the Springboks in three weeks' time with any degree of confidence, all four matches had to be won.

Before moving inland to Pietermaritzburg the Lions spent three days in Durban licking their wounds. The way individuals choose to spend their leisure time varies considerably and among the party the golfers would undoubtedly have found their way to one of the city's courses, deep-sea fishing trips were available and there were the usual cinemas and theatres but for some there was the need for another form of amusement which needed to be approached tactfully and with no little subterfuge and discretion.

As was once found at all the world's major ports, the immediate vicinity of the docks evolves naturally into a concentration of bars, bordellos, cheap hostels and chop houses and Durban was no exception to this. Anybody looking for trouble would be guaranteed to find it in dockland and it was there that two 'sailors' were reported to have been at the centre of a barroom brawl that caused untold damage and resulted in many cuts and bruises, both delivered and received. It is the nature of the beast that after long periods at sea with little source of entertainment pent-up energy is released in a matter of moments once acquaintance is renewed with terra firma. Why these particular individuals found the need to set off in search of physical confrontation remains a mystery as there had been plenty of opportunities to rumble in recent months but go in search of trouble they did and it was not hard to find.

Once the dust had settled, the two protagonists made their way back to the town and up to the beach area. Dressed in their striped T-shirts and berets they certainly looked to have come off one of the new arrivals in the docks; maybe from France, Italy or the USA. It did not really matter where the pair were from but any passing resemblance they may have had to a Welshman and an Ulsterman was pure coincidence – Bunner Travers and Blair Mayne were undoubtedly tucked up in their beds at such a late hour.

On Tuesday afternoon, after a short two-hour journey, the party checked in at the Imperial Hotel, Pietermaritzburg, a modern three-storey building on Loop Street and another facility that catered for their every need. Wednesday's game at Woodburn would see five of the victorious Northerns team included in the Natal line-up, captain Ebbo Bastard among them in what would be his third consecutive outing against the tourists, the Springbok in search of a third victory that would make a unique individual achievement were his team to succeed. Natal had yet to defeat a touring team but had held the 1924 British visitors to a 3-3 draw and local expectations were high with a general optimism that the clearly dispirited Lions were there for the taking.

These were difficult times for the Lions' selectors. Somehow they had to ensure that a winning combination was found as a third consecutive defeat was not an option they wished to contemplate. Such a result would bring the tour to a grinding halt and reduce morale to a level from which it would be difficult to recover. The selected pack had a solid look about it. A front five made up of Eddie Morgan, Bunner Travers and Charles Graves with the now established second row pairing of Sam Walker and Blair Mayne together for the sixth time. Loose forwards Russell Taylor, Ivor Williams and Jock Waters could normally be relied on to shore up the defence and harass the Natal half-backs but with Williams selected for only his fifth game and Waters his fourth these were two players desperately short of match time.

Jimmy Giles and George Cromey were paired at half-back for the first time and the selection of Harry McKibbin and Jeff Reynolds in the centre suggested that the selectors, without Macrae and Leyland at their disposal, were prepared to explore all avenues before declaring their hand in Port Elizabeth. Ves Boyle and James Unwin took their places on the wing and Charles Grieve continued at full-back in Vivian Jenkins' absence in what was only his third match.

Match 17, Natal, Wednesday 17 August, Pietermaritzburg

The Lions set about their task with a purpose and intent that had been missing in Durban. The forwards dictated all aspects of the tight play and for much of the first half the tourists were camped in Natal territory. Against the Northern Provinces it was the collective effort of the forwards that attracted most of the post-match criticism but it was clear that a repeat of that disappointing performance was not on the agenda as they continually took the game to the Natal eight and gained immediate supremacy in all phases of play. Russell Taylor opened the scoring with a penalty which was soon followed by the opening try. Jeff Reynolds broke on the outside and with only Egner to beat he committed the full-back before sending a perfectly timed pass to Unwin, who scored beneath the posts. With the easiest of conversions Taylor somehow contrived to hit an upright and the score remained at 6-0 until the interval. That the tourists had only managed six first-half points gave little indication of how dominant they had been but yet again they were let down by some poor handling.

Soon after the restart Heenan kicked a penalty for the home side which triggered their best passage of play and only some solid defending prevented further scores. Having weathered the storm, the Lions gradually worked their way back into their opponents' half and from a scrum Jimmy Giles dummied his way past two defenders to release Reynolds, who kicked on. Enger fielded the ball but found Unwin arriving at the same time and lost possession in the tackle, allowing Reynolds to hack on and touch down near the posts. For the second time Taylor had to watch in disbelief as his conversion attempt from the easiest of positions came back off the woodwork but at 9-3 the Lions were starting to see their efforts reflected on the scoreboard.

Finding themselves almost permanently camped in the Natal half of the field, the Lions forwards continued to pressurise the home pack and from a line-out on the goal line Bunner Travers secured possession to force his way over for his first try of the tour, which was greatly applauded by his teammates. With Russell Taylor's inexplicable loss of form with the boot, Harry McKibbin took over the place kicking duties but he also failed with the more difficult conversion attempt from the touchline.

The Lions should have had things sown up but missed kicks and poor finishing meant that as the game entered its final quarter there were only nine points separating the teams before a fourth try helped to calm the nerves. This followed a break by Cromey and good support work from Walker, who cleared the way for Waters to cross, but yet another missed conversion continued to give Natal a glimmer of hope. A second Heenan penalty reduced the deficit and when this was immediately followed by a try from Fairweather, who was the first to an ambitious cross kick by his captain, Heenan's successful conversion brought the score to 15-11. The closing minutes were far from comfortable for the visitors, Natal now within a converted try of stealing the game, but it was not to be and the Lions held out for the much-needed win.

Easily the better side, the Lions would have been fully aware that they had failed to secure what should have been a comfortable victory but there were some positives to build on. Grieve was outstanding at full-back and his line kicking ensured that much of the game was played in Natal territory. The forwards had produced a much better performance when it was most needed, showing a more cohesive collective effort than seen in Durban and of course, first and foremost there was the win which had been viewed as being so critical to the Lions' cause. For the moment the pressure was off.

British Lions – C.F. Grieve, E.J. Unwin, H.R. McKibbin, F.J. Reynolds, C.V. Boyle, G.E. Cromey, J.L. Giles, M.E. Morgan, W.H. Travers, C.R.A. Graves, S. Walker, captain, R.B. Mayne, A.R. Taylor, J.A. Waters, I. Williams.
Scorers – Unwin T, Reynolds T, Travers T, Waters T, Taylor P.
Natal – R.C. Egner, P.J. Lyster, R.A. Wallace, A.G. Tungay, J.F.C. Heenan, W.G.M. Seymour, J.E. Todd, T.R.H. Gafney, R.A.H. Millar, W.E. Bastard, captain, C. Williamson, P.J. van Rensburg, R.D. Wilson, A. Fairweather, C.C. Bastard.
Scorers – Heenan 2P, C, Fairweather T.
British Lions 15, Natal 11 (half-time 6-0)
Referee – P.B. Klopper

'What goes on tour stays on tour' – a saying as relevant in the 1930s as it is today. When one considers that twenty-seven of the players were single men who were expected to attend any number of official social events where they would have been introduced to a multitude of attractive females it can safely be assumed that two plus two was always going to make four. The situation could not be misread by the most naive and neither should it be. Why couldn't a group of young men thousands of miles away from home enjoy the fruits of their labours, so to speak?

Though single, Blair Mayne was not a party animal. The Irish Universities' heavyweight boxing champion made no secret of the fact that he revelled in the confrontational aspect of rugby but off the field he was a reserved individual. Despite his apparent reluctance to party, Paddy Mayne was something of a rebel, a non conformist who would often appear at functions improperly dressed. If the order of the day was number ones – i.e. formal dress – Mayne would turn up in blazer and slacks and if the Lions were attending a low key function that allowed the players to relax in their blazers and greys then Blair would appear in his tuxedo and black tie. It is not known if the striped T-shirt and beret ever saw the light of day again but it should come as no surprise to learn that Paddy Mayne gave the management some cause for concern following the victory against Natal.

The stories relating to his escapade in Pietermaritzburg vary considerably, making the actual sequence of events uncertain, but that Blair Mayne put his future tour prospects on the line is beyond doubt.

Following the official after match dinner, Blair Mayne disappeared. He was last seen going out of the hotel dressed in his formal attire and did not return until the early hours (version one); mid morning (version two); or not at all (version three). It seems certain that he did return to the hotel because he was sighted walking through the reception area with a buck draped over his shoulders, his clothes covered in the animal's blood. He headed for Sam Walker's room where he proudly put the dead animal on the bed.

Mayne had met up with some Afrikaners earlier in the tour and he was reunited with them in Pietermaritzburg. Not suitably dressed, they could not join him in the official function so Mayne took up an offer to join them on a night shoot and the dead buck was the result – the animal shot by the Lion. There is no little credence to this part of the story but where version three comes into the equation is that the player was reportedly absent when the party left Pietermaritzburg aboard the 6.34 a.m. train bound for Durban where on arrival they went directly to the docks to board the *Arundel Castle* which would take them along the coast to East London. Arriving at the quay, who should be looking down at them over the ship's rail? – the missing Ulsterman, Blair Mayne.

The mid-morning return to the hotel can be ruled out because of the early departure and the truth is probably found somewhere between the other two versions. Mayne undoubtedly went on a night shoot and proudly presented his kill to Sam Walker, whose reaction is not known. He then possibly packed his bags for Strachan's attention and rejoined the Afrikaners, who got him to Durban docks ahead of the official party. One source suggested that at some stage of the tour Mayne was severely reprimanded by Major Hartley, who threatened to send him home, but Sam Walker intervened, stressing how important the player was to the cause. If this is true, it is likely to have happened on board the *Arundel*, which would continue on to Britain after dropping off the Lions in East London, and presumably it would have been of little consequence if there was an extra passenger on board.

East London must have been a distant memory after the events of the past two months but the Lions' return now gave Border a chance to improve on their narrow 11-8 defeat in the opening game. One of the oldest provinces, Border had fourteen affiliated clubs from which the team was selected. Three of the clubs, the Queenstown-based Swifts, the Alberts from King William's Town and the East London-based Buffaloes were among the six founder clubs and together with Cambridge and Hamiltons, two clubs based in East London, provided the majority of the Border XV which for this second encounter included ten of the players who had appeared in that opening game.

The Lions' selection gave a clear indication of the trials and tribulations of the past two months. Among the backs only James Unwin had played in the tour opener, the other three-quarters on that distant day, Roy Leyland, Duncan Macrae and Bill Clement, all now resigned to the fact that their tours were over. Jeff Reynolds, Harry McKibbin and Elvet Jones replaced them alongside Unwin and once again it was Charles Grieve who was asked to continue at full-back with Cromey and Morgan selected at half-back. After all the physical pounding and exertion that their bodies had been subjected to it was surprising that seven of the forwards who featured in the opening game were included. The only change from the first match saw Dancer introduced into the front row, allowing Walker to continue with Mayne in the second row, the knock-on effect seeing Waters moved back to No. 8 in place of Duff. Travers, Graves, Taylor and Alexander made up the numbers.

Match 18, Border, Saturday 20 August, East London

A faultless performance by Charles Grieve was the highlight of another game which the Lions should have won with some ease. Grieve was credited as being the best player on the field by the local press, his outstanding defence, fine tackling and kicking out of hand denied the home team on several occasions and his favourable reviews were certainly well earned but in front of him the other backs had a mixed afternoon. The link between Morgan and Cromey was often disrupted which drew unfavourable comparisons with Giles and Reynolds but it was in the centre, where Reynolds and McKibbin were totally outplayed by their opposite numbers, that the real problems arose. They failed to put to good use the embarrassment of riches that came their way, leaving Jones and Unwin kicking their heels in frustration on the wing.

The forward effort ensured the game would not produce another unwelcome defeat, their cause considerably assisted when Border effectively lost the services of Petzer with a broken collarbone in the first five minutes. Although the player returned after having it strapped he was no longer able to fully commit himself to the forward effort, which suffered accordingly as the end of match statistics confirm. The Lions won eighteen of the twenty-seven scrums and twenty-five out of thirty-six contested line-outs, ample possession to have secured a bigger winning margin and one feels it was not only the Lions' jerseys which were blue on another sunny South African winter's day.

Playing with a strong wind behind them in the first half, the visitors missed early try-scoring opportunities. Moments into the game a touch finder by Bunny Reid at full-back was charged down and the Lions' forwards appeared to be deciding among themselves who should take the ball and score when Border captain Sibby Reid kicked it dead from under their feet. Unwin and Walker were both brought down short of the line and with the home side looking dangerous whenever they got their hands on the ball nothing could be taken for granted. There were several instances when questions were asked of Grieve's defence, the full-back never found wanting. With the strong wind behind him he regularly sent the home team back into its own half and with one 60-yard effort took play to the corner flag. The Lions forwards secured the ball from the line-out and it was fed back to the full-back who shaved the upright with a drop goal attempt.

Twenty minutes had been played before the Lions were able to capitalise on their forward supremacy. A blind-side break by Cromey from inside his own half saw him link with Jones, the wing able to make his way deep into Border territory before a well-judged tackle brought him to ground. Russell Taylor was first to the breakdown and the forward kicked on, beating two defenders to the ball for a try which McKibbin converted. Immediately from the restart the home team responded with a forward rush that saw the ball dribbled over the goal line but when a try looked inevitable, in a repeat of events at the other end of the field earlier in the half, Taylor appeared from nowhere to fly kick the ball over the dead ball line and the situation was saved. Border continued a period of pressure but a poor pass from Evans went to ground in midfield and Bob Alexander hacked on, took advantage of a favourable bounce and touched down beneath the posts for a try which McKibbin had no difficulty converting.

They may not have troubled the scoreboard but Border were playing much better than their nil return suggested. Only solid defence by Grieve had kept them out and the end to end rugby saw the crowd in good vocal spirit. The forward effort from the tourists was outstanding and the loose forwards in particular were looking much sharper than in recent matches. They were first to capitalise on any loose ball, the trio regularly taking the ball forward at their feet to cause the home defence a multitude of problems. One such rush took play to the goal line allowing Morgan to collect and break around the blind side to score out wide. McKibbin was unable to add the points and half-time arrived with the tourists holding a comfortable 13-0 lead.

With the wind now at their backs but playing into a low sun, the Border half-backs put some searching kicks into the Lions' territory only for Grieve to return them, very often with interest. The general flow of play suggested that there was little to choose between the teams, the Lions perhaps getting the rub of the green when a score depended on a favourable bounce, something which the gods and Charles Grieve managed to deny Border. That said there was nothing fortunate about the Lions' fourth try. From a move started in their own half McKibbin and Taylor stormed up the touchline with some clever inter-passing between themselves that left a trail of would be tacklers in their wake. This led to no little confusion inside the Border 25 and when McKibbin was brought to a halt by the determined Bunny Reid the Lions' forwards were in support to hack on to the goal line. Beef Dancer scored one of those classic prop forward tries, scooping up the ball just short of the try line for an effort which in time would probably become a twenty or thirty-yard run-in with a few side steps and dummies thrown in for good measure. The missed conversion left the score at 16-0 but the home side continued to threaten and were finally rewarded for the part they had played in the game when the outstanding Hardwich on the right wing was put over in the corner following a good passage of play involving both forwards and backs.

Correspondents who had followed the tour from the start later claimed this second meeting with Border as the outstanding provincial game and in response to the Border try the Lions certainly produced some spectacular play. The forwards were all involved in one sweeping attack that saw the ball passed between them as they covered much of the field only for Sam Walker to knock-on with the line at his mercy. A further score was inevitable and it came from the backs. Cromey received quick ball from a scrum and made a telling outside break before linking with Reynolds who had space in which to free McKibbin on the outside and the centre timed his pass to Unwin perfectly to give the wing a clear run to the corner for a fifth try which Taylor failed to convert. If the centres had combined as efficiently with the men outside them earlier in the match the scoreboard would have rattled along.

To their great credit Border refused to accept that they were a beaten team, playing as if they were within a score of victory. They continued to threaten and some attractive interplay between the three-quarters ended with Moore committing Grieve to the tackle before giving a well judged pass to Wegener who had a clear run to the line. The wing scored beneath the posts making life easy for Evans and the outside-half obliged by adding the extra points. More was to come and when the Lions were penalised ten yards inside their half it was Kopke who stepped up to take advantage of the following wind and drill the ball between the uprights.

There was sufficient time remaining for each team to mount one final attack but both were brought to a halt by determined defence and at the final whistle the Lions had deservedly won a thrilling contest 19-11. Deservedly because they had outscored Border by five tries to two but this failed to paper over the cracks of what was yet another far from convincing performance by the backs. With two games remaining before the second Test, full-back apart, every position behind the scrum was up for grabs and nobody was more aware of this than the players themselves.

British Lions – C.F. Grieve, E.L. Jones, F.J. Reynolds, H.R. McKibbin, E.J. Unwin, G.E. Cromey, G. J. Morgan, G.T. Dancer, W.H. Travers, C.R. Graves, S. Walker, captain, R.B. Mayne, A.R. Taylor, J.A. Waters, R. Alexander.
Scorers – McKibbin 2C, Unwin T, Morgan T, Dancer T, Taylor T, Alexander T.
Border – B.C. Reid, N. Hardwick, S. Reid, captain, M. Moore, B.H. Wegener, R.J. Evans, R. Gordon, C. Wilhelm, H. Maarsdorp, O. Kopke, H.J. Petzer, J. Maartens, F. Woodford, R. Lancaster, J. Lewis.
Scorers – Hardwick T, Wegener T, Kopke P, Evans C.
British Lions 19, Border 11 (half-time 13-0)
Referee – R.S. Wakefield

North of East London, the Transkei is an area of land covering 16,000 square miles stretching from the Natal border in the north to the Kei river in the south, a distance of some 270 miles varying between forty and eighty miles inland from the Indian Ocean. Broadly speaking it was divided into three principal regions: the Transkei proper in the south stretching between the Kei and Bashe Rivers; Tembuland, the central district, continuing north to the Mtata River; and Pondoland, ending at the Natal border.

The migration of thousands from the north saw the Zulu settle in Natal and what in time became the Xhosa move further down the coast to the area that is now the Transkei. The Tembu and the Pondo gave their names to the two northern regions but, with a migration of a different sort moving up from the south, conflict was inevitable and in 1879 what became known as the Frontier Wars led to the annexation of the area to the Cape Province. A certain amount of autonomy was granted to the tribal leaders and the region would in due course become the tribe's first independent homeland. In 1938 there were more than one million natives living in the area compared to little more than 17,000 Europeans, who were primarily involved in farming and trading but working within strict limitations.

It was north into this unique territory that a convoy of cars set off on the Monday following the Border game, their destination Idutywa, a small town eighty miles from East London and some fifty miles into the Transkei. Guests of the Border Union, the tourists enjoyed lunch at the Idutywa Hotel before continuing north in the afternoon to the village of Chief Poni and his Abakaweta tribesmen. Here they were entertained to what was described as the '...biggest Abakaweta dance in living memory.' Inside a huge human circle made up of more than 2,000 natives and 500 Europeans the dancers moved to the sound of '...thudding feet, rhythmically beaten ox hides (stretched over dried thorn bushes), the chanting of women's voices and the weird high sound of whistles.' Dressed in traditional palm leaf skirts and masks, their bodies covered in clay, the best dancer from each community had his body daubed with large blue spots patterned with red ochre. Tassels, spoons and dead birds dangled from their waists and encouraged by their leaders and elders they put on a memorable performance. They were joined in the circle by Xhosa and Ndlambe women who wove intricate patterns among them but the highlight was thought by many to be the involvement of Major Hartley and Sam Walker, who delighted their hosts by offering their own interpretation of the ceremonial dancing.

Sam Walker presented a prize of ten shillings to each of the three dancers deemed to be the best by their peers. The celebration had been organised by the mayor of Idutywa, Mr F. Richardson, together with some local businessmen, among them Colin Geach, who presented Sam Walker with a century-old dagger that was found on a battlefield and had remained in the Geach family for generations. The weapon had a thick ivory handle inlaid with patterns and designs and was kept in a sheaf made from hide. A wonderful memento of a very special day. Following the departure of the guests, the natives ate the two oxen and three sheep that had been provided by the organisers and enjoyed the fifteen, fifty-gallon barrels of beer they had been allowed to brew especially for the occasion – 6,000 pints of ale and not a Lion in sight!

While there was still a lot of rugby to be played, when the Lions left East London railway station headed for Burgersdorp, 240 miles inland, they must have started to think that they were on their way home. Following Burgersdorp and the game against the North Eastern Districts they would drop down to Port Elizabeth on what would be their last railway journey and following the second Test sail along the coast to Cape Town where three games would be played before they departed for Southampton and onwards to their final destinations. It may well have seemed like the start of the homeward journey but a glance at the itinerary would have confirmed that it was another six weeks before their great adventure would come to an end.

The North Eastern Districts was a perfect example of the problems that faced the towns and smaller centres distanced from the main cities and focal points of rugby throughout South Africa. In an area that stretched 200 miles from east to west and 100 miles in a north–south direction the clubs from which the selectors would pick a team to play the Lions were long distances apart. As a consequence games were very infrequent affairs, rarely more than one a month played, with only the three clubs based in Burgersdorp meeting on a home and away basis during the season. The network of railways and roads was totally inadequate and away matches could involve two or three days' travelling. Consequently the team selected to represent the region was not expected to threaten the tourists. That said, a look through the record books would show that in 1910 the North Eastern Districts earned a creditable 8-8 draw with Tom Smyth's British team, which included twelve of the players who had been present in the team narrowly defeated (14-10) by the Springboks in Johannesburg four days earlier. And in 1924 the tourists had won 20-12, a close enough encounter to confirm that there was no such thing as an easy match in South Africa.

Well, perhaps there was. Unable to emulate the heroic deeds of their predecessors the home side were comprehensively beaten by the Lions 42-3, the visitors running in eight tries for their highest score in the Union. With Walker taking a well-earned rest and Jenkins still unavailable it was Irish scrum-half George Morgan who captained the side, which also included Grieve in his fourth consecutive game at full-back. Nicholson and Boyle were chosen on the wing with Giles and Reynolds, an international half-back partnership now paired in the centre, allowing Cromey and Morgan to continue at half-back. The Lions' problems in midfield were highlighted by the fact that in this, the nineteenth game, the Giles–Reynolds pairing was the tenth selected. Injuries had without doubt played their part but to have to call on ten different centre partnerships – there would be another before the tour ended – goes some way in explaining why the backs had struggled to hit form as the tour unfolded. A problem exacerbated by the nine different half-back partnerships that had also been introduced.

All departments up front had shown greater stability and any enforced changes were comfortably accommodated, mainly as a result of the regular inclusion of Walker, Travers, Taylor and Mayne. With Walker rested, only Travers of the quartet was selected to play at Burgersdorp with Eddie Morgan and Jock Waters alongside him, Couchman and Purchas in the second row, Williams and Duff on the flanks with Howard as eighth man.

Match 19, North Eastern Districts, Wednesday 24 August, Burgersdorp

The smallest crowd of the tour it may have been but the 2,500 spectators were treated to an exhibition of open rugby from the visitors which comfortably surpassed the performances of all the previous touring teams to visit the region. The 1933 Australians had scored seven tries in winning 31-11 and the 1928 All Blacks ran in five in their 27-0 victory but the eight tries and forty-two points scored by the 1938 Lions improved on both these performances. There is no better confidence booster than to see tries being scored with some regularity and after the five in East London this was a performance both reassuring and timely and one from which the Lions could take great heart.

The opening exchanges gave no indication of what was to come, the much lighter home pack causing all manner of problems for the visitors, who did not look at all comfortable, but it was short-lived and once the Lions' forwards began to assert themselves the outcome was never in doubt. The first points came in unexpected fashion, Bill Howard converting a drop goal from a mark and it was the same player who claimed a try after a blind-side break by Morgan saw the scrum-half make inroads into home territory before handing on to Boyle, who found Duff supporting on the inside with Howard on hand to take the scoring pass. Further tries by Reynolds and George Morgan and a conversion by Giles opened up a 14-0 lead but the Lions were unable to add to the try total in what remained of the first half, only a penalty by Giles and a Reynolds drop goal adding to the score, which stood at 21-0 at half-time.

The Districts centre pairing of Baker and Morrison had struggled to contain their opposite numbers and for the second half Pretorius moved up from full-back, Morrison replacing him, and Bekker was taken out of the set piece exchanges to help shore up the fragile defence but it was to no avail. Boyle and Cromey scored in quick succession, both tries converted by Grieve, before Baker finished off a good handling move by the home side, the centre on hand to take van Straten's scoring pass and cross in the corner after initiating the move with a break from inside his own 25. The Lions response was immediate. Puchas readily accepted a scoring pass for his first try of the tour, quickly followed by Reynolds and Boyle, who both claimed their second tries of the afternoon. When the final whistle arrived the 42-3 victory was twenty points better than any other gained on South African soil and the 39-point margin, the most comprehensive.

British Lions – C.F. Grieve, C.V. Boyle, F.J. Reynolds, J.L. Giles, B.E. Nicholson, G.E. Cromey, G.J. Morgan, captain, M.E. Morgan, W.H. Travers, J.A. Waters, S.R. Couchman, A.H.G. Purchas, P.L. Duff, W.G. Howard, I. Williams.
Scorers – Grieve 2C, Giles P,C, Reynolds 2T, DG, Boyle 2T, Cromey T, G. Morgan T, Purchas T, Howard T, C, DP.
North Eastern Districts – D. Pretorius, G. van Straaten, W. Baker, D. Morrison, J. van Straaten, T. Farr, G. Pelser, C.J. Lennard, J. Shorten, J. Hutton, V. Cronje, C. van Straaten, V. Campbell, G. Bekker, M. van Straaten. Scorer – Baker T.
British Lions 42, North Eastern Districts 3 (half-time 21-0)
Referee – P.J.J. van der Walt

The following morning there was an early start for what was to be the last leg of the exhausting odyssey by train that had taken the party the length and breadth of the land. A 270-mile trip took them across country through Stormberg to Rosmead before making the connection that would continue south to Port Elizabeth. Including this final journey, more than 7,500 miles had been travelled by train, which had taken more than 350 hours to complete. Apart from the train journeys in Rhodesia the Lions had been guests of the South African Railways and on this final leg their hosts laid on a celebration dinner.

Fresh pineapple was followed by consommé royal and fried kingklip before the main course of lamb cutlets with asparagus in butter and a selection of vegetables. Desserts and cheeses brought the dinner to an end and having enjoyed the appropriate wines with each of the courses and the customary port and brandy the Lions settled down to their final night listening to the wheels rattling over the rails before they drifted off to sleep. When the train pulled in at Port Elizabeth station at 7.30 a.m. on Friday 26 August what at many times must have seemed a never-ending ritual was over.

For their stay in the city the party took up residence at the Elizabeth Hotel in Humewood, a southern suburb located two miles from the centre, the hotel fronting the Indian Ocean and its extensive beaches – a perfect location in which to spend the next nine days.

CHAPTER SEVEN

THE TEMPERATURE RISES

A Springbok speaks out – A close encounter
– Injuries force the Springboks' selectors to
make changes – The Lions ring the changes
– The sun rises – The temperature rises –
The tempo of the Test rises – The Lions
struggle and the series is lost – A meeting
on board ship and some unexpected help.

The train journeys behind them, the Lions could
now look forward to an extended stay in Port
Elizabeth. The matches against Eastern Province
and the Springboks would both take place at the
famous old Crusaders ground in St George's Park. It
was at this ground on 30 July 1891 that South Africa
first competed on the international stage, losing 4-0
to W.E. Maclagan's British tourists. On 3 September
1938 South Africa would play her forty-ninth Test
having won twenty-nine of the previous forty-eight,
with five of the matches drawn. When one considers
that the first six Tests all ended in defeat the results
since had been very much in the Springboks' favour.
The landmark fiftieth Test would be played in Cape
Town but in the first Test at Ellis Park another notable
milestone had been reached when Fanie Louw scored
his country's one hundredth try in a Test match.

Published every Friday, The *Outspan* was South
Africa's most widely read magazine. The *Outspan*
appealed to male and female readers alike and the
edition that hit the shelves the day the tourists arrived

in Port Elizabeth contained an article by Philip Nel in which he discussed the state of the game in South Africa, his thoughts on the Lions and much else besides. Under the banner heading 'We Should Never Hesitate to Play the Open Game', the former Springbok captain expounded the theory that rugby was a handling game, not one controlled by kicking, and that with ball in hand the options available to attacking teams were obviously greater than when the ball was in the air or at the feet of the forwards.

'I have always been an admirer of open rugby and have privately been a little hurt when I have been in a winning Springbok side and found that we have had to win the game by keeping the ball tight and kicking. Rugby is a game of passing and running with the ball and this is the style of rugby I have always liked and I am glad to say we were able to win our matches in New Zealand with open play which not only pleased the crowds but gave ourselves a lot of pleasure. I am happy to think that our play did a bit of good for the game. All the members of the 1937 side which toured New Zealand were convinced that we wanted less kicking in South African rugby and as I have always had the welfare of the game close to my heart I was anxious to see open methods adopted against the British team... the fact that we were able to play them at their own game and beat them is evidence that our team in New Zealand did not make mental resolutions in vain and will stick to open play which, I think, will have a healthy influence on the game in the Union for many years to come.'

Nel's observations on the British team were in the main addressed to the forwards. He was of the opinion that '...their forwards were very good at times but I thought they played spasmodically. Two or three of them were often breaking away dangerously with the ball but the other forwards were not up with them and did not make any attempt to get up... I have always liked to remember that a pack consists of eight men and only when all eight men realise that they are part of a whole is that pack as effective as it might be.'

The comments were largely based on what the ex-captain had witnessed in the first Test and as such cannot be taken as a reflection of the tour as a whole. There were some reporters who had attended most of the matches played and who may have disagreed with Nel but the Test match had seen the Lions comprehensively beaten and if things were to improve in the remaining two Tests then without doubt the forwards would have to improve on their performance in Johannesburg. Overall the control in the scrums and line-outs was acceptable but Nel was undoubtedly right in his comments regarding the lack of a collective effort in the loose where individuals and small groups of forwards frequently found themselves in isolation at critical moments, the supporting forwards generally some distance off the play. It was this breakdown in continuity that would have to be addressed if the Springbok pack were to be outplayed. The Lions had to support the man in possession and get players in the right position for the full eighty minutes.

Eastern Province were not considered one of the stronger regional teams as their representation in recent Springbok selections confirmed. Only four players had caught the selectors' eye in the post-war period: wing Jack Slater in the 1920s; current Springboks Danie Craven and Fred Turner, who were now playing for Northern Transvaal and Transvaal respectively; and centre Flappie Lochner, like Slater a product of the Albany club in Grahamstown.

The Lions had achieved their objective by winning the three matches played following the defeat in Durban and it was essential that there was not a loss of form in this final outing before the second Test. As in the selection for the second encounter with Transvaal the selectors again opted for what looked to be the likely Test team. There was a welcome return for Jenkins but Grieve had already done enough in recent matches to suggest that he might yet be the better option at full-back. Unwin and Nicholson were on the wings with McKibbin and Giles filling the problem positions at centre. Tanner and Reynolds were reunited at half-back for the first time since playing against the OFS at Kroonstad. The forwards had that familiar feel about them with the Walker, Travers, Taylor and Mayne quartet joined by Morgan, the consistently improving Dancer, Bob Alexander and 'Plum' Duff.

Match 20, Eastern Province, Saturday 27 August, Port Elizabeth

It was both the lowest scoring match of the tour and the closest, with one point separating the sides at the final whistle, all of which ensured that the 10,000-strong crowd were mightily entertained for the full eighty minutes. Each team scored one try but there could so easily have been many more, only desperate defence or a lapse of concentration denying attacks at both ends of the field. For the visitors the contest provided a hard, physical forward battle which the home side narrowly won in the tight but for once the Lions proved to be much more accomplished in the loose.

The game was little more than ten minutes old when Vivian Jenkins suffered another leg injury and although he remained on the field it effectively brought his tour to an end. This necessitated Russell Taylor being taken from the pack and used as an extra back, which partly accounts for the success Gerber, the Eastern Province hooker, had in his duel with Travers, who lost six of the first seven scrums.

On the positive side there was a welcome return to form for Jeff Reynolds, at last resembling something like the player seen in the early part of the tour. He thrilled the crowd with his electrifying breaks through the middle and it was unfortunate that on at least two occasions what should have been straightforward try-scoring passes went to ground. There was no doubt the outside-half benefited from the extra time and space Haydn Tanner's longer pass provided and he exploited it to the full. Harry McKibbin and Jimmy Giles in the centre cancelled out the threat posed by Lochner and Meyer, who were unable to make any impression against the Lions' organised defence, while out wide Jimmy Unwin and Bas Nicholson made the most of their limited opportunities.

From the start things looked ominous for the Lions with Eastern Province taking the early initiative and the first four scrums. The visitors were kept on the back foot until a rare attack took play to the home 25 where the Province forwards infringed, giving Jenkins an opportunity to open the scoring with a penalty kick fifteen yards in from touch. His effort was both short and wide, missing so badly that Nicholson was able to gather the ball and it was only desperate defending by full-back Smith that prevented the wing crossing for a try.

The pressure continued and from the ensuing scrum Reynolds looked to have worked his way clear to the line, only for Smith to repeat his heroics of moments earlier with another fine try-saving tackle. Gerber won another scrum which allowed the ball to be cleared upfield, allowing the home side the chance to regroup only for a forward to drift offside, giving Jenkins a second kick at goal, this from the half-way line. Having returned to sea level there was no rarefied atmosphere to help the goal kickers and Jenkins' effort, though straight and true, fell short of the target and into the arms of Smith who set off on a counter-attack that brought the crowd to its feet. The Lions hung on desperately, some fine defensive tackling the only thing preventing Eastern Province registering the game's opening score. The home side continued to threaten and an enterprising phase of play saw loose forward Marais put clear to touch down under the posts only for the referee to call him back for a forward pass.

This was a time for cool heads. Slow the game down, let the forwards win possession allowing one of the backs time and space to put in a relieving touch kick. The forwards did their bit, winning the ball for Tanner who passed back to Reynolds and there the simplest of strategies ended. Was it ever any different? Jeff Reynolds elected to run the ball out of the 25 leaving five or six would-be tacklers in his wake and made his way forty yards upfield before an opponent collared him. The Lions' centres were up in support and Reynolds was able to offload to Nicholson, who linked with McKibbin only for the Irishman to be brought down inches short of the line by another fine tackle from Smith. More points went begging when

Taylor missed a penalty but the Lions kept Province in their own half and when the outstanding Flappie Lochner made his only error of the afternoon in failing to collect a loose ball at the second attempt Jeff Unwin was on hand to gather and score an opportunist try wide out that went unconverted.

The remainder of the first half continued in the same breathless fashion with perhaps the best chance of a try falling to Bob Alexander, who failed to hold on to the ball after '...Reynolds on one occasion cut through the opposition like a streak on one of the greatest swerve runs ever seen at the Crusader Ground and it looked all over a score because he had Unwin on one side of him and Alexander in support on the other. He gave the ball to Alexander instead of the safe handling Unwin and Britain's chance of another try – this time almost under the posts – went a begging.' So the local paper reported and the half ended with the Lions holding onto a rather fragile looking three-point advantage.

Vivian Jenkins did not take his place at the start of the second half but an injury to Taylor prompted his return. Taylor insisted on continuing but it was obvious that neither player was able to contribute much to the team effort. There were clear chances at both ends of the field but players were denied by grand defensive tackles, handling errors or the bounce of the ball but it all added up to an entertainment which kept the spectators on the edge of their seats. The second score came midway through the half, the home forwards adjudged offside inside their 25. Taylor made no mistake with the kick and the home side now had to score twice to salvage anything from the game.

Their moment came following a line-out on halfway.

Flappie Lochner made an incisive break, cutting between the flat-footed Giles and McKibbin to get within ten yards of the line before offloading to Marais who in turn found prop forward Venter in support to take the try-scoring pass and scramble over at the corner. George Smith made the difficult conversion and with five minutes remaining and the score standing at 6-5 to the visitors there was all to play for. After such a hard-fought battle the Lions were in no mood to let the game slip from their grasp in the dying moments and they proceeded to set up camp inside the Province half of the field. Unwin had a chance to make the game safe but was cut down a yard short before Smith's clearance kick finally brought proceedings to an end. The Lions had secured the narrowest of victories but the intensity and closeness of the match had kept the crowd enthralled until the final whistle and the tough examination of the Lions' resilience under pressure and their ability to grind out a close-fought victory could only stand them in good stead in seven days' time.

The critics were quick to point out that there remained a tendency among the tourists to throw the ball about when in dangerous positions on the field and there was still an obvious problem in finishing. Poorly directed passes were far too numerous and the use of the lobbed pass all too often led to interceptions, giving the opposition the opportunity to turn defence into attack. Reynolds was declared the best back on the field despite being singled out as the biggest culprit when it came to risk-taking. Mayne was the best forward and Tanner also came in for some praise, his passing in particular earning him the plaudits and a probable Test place alongside Reynolds. For Vivian

Jenkins the match marked the end of a disappointing tour. The full-back had arrived in South Africa with a glowing reputation and those who saw him play appreciated his great talent but the sequence of injuries restricted his involvement to eleven appearances. The Lions' management were fortunate that in Charles Grieve they had a capable alternative and it would be for the Scot to play the remaining four matches at full-back.

British Lions – V.G.J. Jenkins, E.J. Unwin, H.R. McKibbin, J.L. Giles, B.E. Nicholson, F.J. Reynolds, H. Tanner, M.E. Morgan, W.H. Travers, G.T. Dancer, S. Walker, captain, R.B. Mayne, A.R. Taylor, P.L. Duff, R. Alexander.
Scorers – Unwin T, Taylor P.
Eastern Province – G.A.C Smith, J. Louw, A. Meyer, G.P. Lochner, G. Webster, T. Reed, N.D. Parent, G. Venter, F. Gerber, T. Phelan, M.C. Marais, L. Froneman, captain, G. du Plessis, J.Phelan, G. Pringle.
Scorers – Venter T, Smith C.
British Lions 6, Eastern Province 5 (half-time 3-0)
Referee – D.P. Thomas

Wherever international rugby is played, the week leading up to the game is one of great expectancy, discussion and debate. Who should play? Are there any fitness concerns? What will the weather be like? The week leading up to the second Test of the 1938 series was no exception with both camps having injury concerns. Following the first Test, the South African team would certainly have been selected en bloc but for injury; however, the Lions had not only to work around the various absentees but come up with a new combination that would have to improve on the performance at

Johannesburg if the rubber was to be decided in the third Test in Cape Town. And the weather would have no small part to play in proceedings come Saturday, the temperatures unusually high for the time of year.

At a civic reception held early in the week Major Hartley spoke of the benefits gained from such an extensive tour, the development of good relations between the host country and its guests. An editorial in the local press expanded on this theme and argued that if it had not been for the early visits by teams from the British Isles the current state of the game in South Africa would not be at the level it was; '... we can never forget that we owe our prowess to the earlier teams of British players who came to this country and taught us the game by the most excellent method of administering a series of generous drubbings.' Hartley's comments extended beyond the field of play which was expanded on in the paper's editorial; '...but skill apart, there is something for which we are infinitely more grateful to our visitors and their forerunners. It is the fine spirit of sportsmanship with which they have invested the game and which, through their example, the players of South Africa have been imbued. We look forward to the Test match in the spirit of sportsmen who are conscious that it is not the winning of the game that counts.'

Fine words, but words which in the climate of Test match rugby in the twenty-first century seem particularly naive at a time when any national coach will categorically state that the winning is all that matters.

What has changed? The truthful answer to that question is that nothing has changed. When South Africa first visited the British Isles in 1906 the first 'Springboks', as captain Paul Roos christened them, arrived following three consecutive tours to South Africa by British teams which had gradually seen their initial dominance disappear until it was the South Africans who were the stronger. Playing on distant shores for the first time the Springboks lost two matches and drew one but while there was no doubting their gentlemanly conduct both on and off the field, the post-tour analysis highlighted the poor weather conditions in Glasgow where Scotland had won 6-0 and in the last match of the tour at Cardiff where the home team had controlled the muddy field to gain an emphatic 17-0 victory. These were not comments made by poor losers, these were comments made on behalf of a team which had played to win and been denied that opportunity due to conditions for which they were ill prepared. Losing in Glasgow and Cardiff had obviously hurt the players, dented their national pride and on their return to South Africa Roos was the first to admit that there were lessons to be learnt from the tour – and learn them they did.

South African rugby went from strength to strength and six years later the second Springboks lost three matches but won the five Tests played. The culmination of a comprehensive development into one of the game's superpowers was seen in 1937 in New Zealand where it can confidently be argued that, while not detracting from a gentlemanly and sportsmanlike approach to the game, all that mattered was the winning and in 1938 one gets the feeling that the same measurement would be used to gauge how good the Springboks were.

By Wednesday it was clear that the South African selectors were not going to be able to field the team that had won the first Test. Ebbo Bastard was the first casualty, John Apsey his likely replacement. Apsey had been outstanding in two appearances against the Lions in the early part of the tour when he was prominent in helping Western Province Town and Country and Western Province down the Lions' colours. He was no stranger to international rugby, having been capped twice against Australia in 1933 and although he had not featured since, Apsey would not be found wanting. Thursday brought further bad news when Gerry Brand pulled up in training and was immediately declared unavailable but his misfortune presented an opportunity for another Newlands' favourite to make his first Test appearance.

Johnny Bester had toured Australia and New Zealand in 1937 but his thirteen appearances had all been in provincial games where his time was divided between the centre and the wing. He scored eleven tries on tour and like Apsey had appeared in the two earlier games together with a third appearance when he led the Cape Provinces at Kimberley.

His two tries for Western Province early in the second half at Newlands had helped turn the game in the home team's favour and the Lions were well aware of the pace Bester brought to the game and that he would have to be closely marked. His inclusion on the wing meant that Freddy Turner would replace the injured Brand at full-back and return to St George's Park where he had once worn the colours of Crusaders and Eastern Province before moving to the Transvaal. These two changes aside it was 'same again' for the Springboks with Danie Craven, another ex-Eastern Province star who had migrated north, continuing as captain.

How Major Hartley and his fellow selectors must have envied the relative ease with which the Springbok team was chosen. In many ways the selection of the Lions team was also a fairly straightforward exercise but for all the wrong reasons, with the number of injured players dictating that in certain positions there were not any real options available. Charles Grieve had hit a rich vein of form which made his selection at full-back automatic following Jenkins' continuing misfortune and the forwards had performed well as a unit against Eastern Transvaal, which encouraged the committee to continue with the same eight, but the remaining positions among the backs were a selector's nightmare.

All five of the half-backs were available. With the diminutive George Cromey still considered an obvious target for the marauding Springbok forwards, Jeff Reynolds looked certain to play at outside-half but who should partner him? His international partner Giles had enjoyed a good tour, proving equally adept in the centre, where he had featured in five games together with one start at outside-half. Similarly, George Morgan had been played out of position at full-back in four games but his inclusion at scrum-half would be a gamble, particularly as he was yet to be partnered with Reynolds. All of which left Haydn Tanner, whose nine appearances had all been at scrum-half, three of them with Reynolds outside him, and it would not have gone unnoticed that the Lions had won the three matches when the pair were in tandem. There was no doubt that the English fly-half benefited from Tanner's longer pass and it was probably this that swung the selectors in his favour but the biggest selection headache remained with the three-quarters where the problems that had first reared their head in the early days of the tour showed no sign of going away.

The party included four wings and four centres

of whom much had been expected but finding the best combination from the three Englishmen, two Welshmen, two Irishmen and Scot had proved nigh on impossible largely as a result of the injuries picked up by the various players. The late arrival of Nicholson was an added factor but those early injuries to McKibbin and Clement in particular had hampered the selectors and now, with Macrae and Leyland also ruled out of the rest of the tour, the problems were compounded. Unwin and McKibbin both played in the first Test and regardless of the injury problems these two players would have probably been first choice. Neither had underperformed on tour and the selectors went with them again, leaving the search for a centre and wing before the team was finalised.

Of all the three-quarters it was perhaps Ireland's Vesey Boyle who had yet to reproduce his true form on tour. A seasoned international with eight caps to his name, Boyle had featured in eight matches and been on the losing side only once and he was given his chance ahead of Elvet Jones. In the centre it was a straightforward choice between Basil Nicholson and Jimmy Giles, the vote going to the orthodox centre despite McKibbin and Giles linking well together against Eastern Transvaal, particularly in defence. The team was made up of five Irishmen, four players from England, four Welshmen and two Scots. The selectors had taken one or two gambles in their selection behind the scrum but overall the team looked good on paper – but how would it perform on the field?

As match day approached Port Elizabeth braced itself for an influx of rugby supporters. Weather predictions earlier in the week had suggested the possibility of rain and with figures taken over the previous sixty years confirming that September was the wettest month in the province the Lions began to look forward to conditions with which they were more familiar and that could perhaps give them an unexpected advantage. But the rain did not arrive. In its place was a heatwave, one of such intensity that it broke all records, making the first weekend of September 1938 in Port Elizabeth the hottest to date.

The tourists had arrived in South Africa at the start of winter. Their three-month journey had seen them take in all the major regions and cities and nowhere had the weather been less inviting than an average British summer. The cooler nights were the only reminder that these were the darker, colder months but the days remained warm throughout with temperatures averaging 65–70 degrees for most of the daylight hours, and rainfall had been at a minimum. The conditions had proved ideal for rugby and the quality of most of the games bore witness to the good playing surfaces enjoyed, even if some were hard with little grass cover. In September Port Elizabeth would expect to see average daytime temperatures of 60 degrees, perfect for rugby, but add another 40 degrees and you have a problem.

The heatwave that arrived in Port Elizabeth on match day was unexplained. A fluke. One of those meteorological conundrums which defy all that has gone before. Temperatures of 95 degrees and upwards in the shade were reported and everybody was looking for somewhere to hide. St George's Park offered little shelter for those spectators not seated in the grandstand and the open seating areas exposed the early arrivals to the intense heat for several hours before the 3.30 kick-off. For the Lions this was to be an unwelcome new experience, one which undoubtedly had an effect on performance but, as was the case at Johannesburg, the Springboks would again prove too strong in all departments.

Match 21, South Africa – Second Test, Saturday 3 September, Crusaders Ground, Port Elizabeth

More than 20,000 supporters made their way into the Crusaders Ground, a marked increase on the 6,000 present at that first Test back in 1891. In anticipation of a record attendance, officials went to great lengths to ensure those attending knew where they could enter the ground and plans of the area were placed in the local press to help avoid any uncertainty. Schoolchildren and students would be refused entry if they were not accompanied by an adult or part of an organised group and following the game they were to remain in their seats until the rest of the ground had been vacated. Press photographs of the game show hundreds of uniformed schoolchildren sitting in ringside seats situated in front of the main seating areas and particularly close to the action.

Pre-match preliminaries saw the teams introduced to Vice Admiral D'Oyly Lyon, an ex- England international full-back and captain who was Commander in Chief of the Africa Station based at Simonstown in the Western Cape. Looking at the teams as they waited to be presented it was obvious to those who had been in Johannesburg for the first Test that the British forwards had beefed up in the last four weeks, which was perfectly understandable following the endless round of hospitality to which they had been subjected. The additional weight may even help them in the forward exchanges but it would also be a telling factor in the scorching heat that was beating down on the ground.

The pace of the game from the kick-off belied the temperature and it appeared as if both teams were looking to make early headway in the almost certain knowledge that as the game unfolded so would the physical effort become harder to maintain in such uncompromising conditions. Travers' return to the team had a noticeable impact and the hooker took three scrums in succession before Lotz took his first strike, only for the shove from the Lions eight to put Craven under pressure. The scrum-half sent a poor pass out to Harris which bounced before reaching the outside-half who was immediately enveloped by a sea of blue jerseys.

That the Springbok half-backs took time to settle was a direct result of how well the Lions' forwards had set about their task and early indications suggested that the tourists were a much improved team as the large part of the opening quarter was spent inside Springbok territory. In such conditions it was important that the Lions capitalised on their early advantage but unfortunately their efforts in the first twenty minutes were not reflected on the scoreboard, staunch midfield defence denying them any try-scoring opportunities. Blair Mayne, Russell Taylor and Bunner Travers were all prominent in the early exchanges but as the game began to unfold so did the intense heat begin to take its toll on the tourists. All the Lions had to show for their early supremacy was a solitary penalty in front of the posts, which Taylor missed badly from thirty yards, and with that went what proved to be the Lions' only chance of taking the lead.

With several players on both sides struggling, the game was failing to live up to expectations and in danger of becoming something of an anti-climax after events at Ellis Park. Springbok wing Dai Williams finally broke the monotony when he latched on to a pass from Lochner to take play deep into the Lions' half but when the move broke down Reynolds was quick to counter-attack, making the most of a long pass from Tanner to cut through the middle of the field. Reynolds passed to McKibbin who made further inroads into South African territory but when Nicholson received the ball de Wet arrived with it, the Springbok's tackle bringing the promising attack to an end. Two penalties in succession forced the visitors back, Harris finding touch on the halfway line before taking play deep into Lions territory with the second, and slowly but surely with the tourists on the back foot the Springbok forwards began to assert their authority.

Ferdie Bergh led the first of a series of forward raids on the Lions line and it was only sound tackling by Grieve that kept the Springboks out. Flappie Lochner and Piet de Wet combined well to create some space in the middle of the field but again it was Grieve who produced a brilliant tackle on de Wet when a try looked certain. From a lethargic opening quarter the game was suddenly transformed into the spectacle the press had predicted but it was very much one-way traffic as the Springboks' new found confidence saw them raise their game to a level that the tourists were unable to match. A score seemed inevitable before a penalty gave the Lions the chance to relieve the pressure.

From a scrum on halfway Lochner and Williams combined well to take play back into the visitors' 25 where the supporting Boy Louw and Louis Strachan handled brilliantly to create two more try-scoring opportunities for the three-quarters but once again the Lions' defence held firm. Attacking opportunities were scarce and when Boyle did break away and make some headway up the touchline it was only to see a clever reverse pass inside to Nicholson go to ground. The forwards also had their moments. Travers, Mayne, Dancer and Alexander were at the front of a foot rush that took play deep into Springbok territory but Bester bravely gathered the ball from under their feet and put in a good relieving touch kick from a difficult position. Heroics aside it was only a matter of time before South Africa broke the deadlock. Tony Harris paved the way for the opening score, manufacturing a break from deep inside his own half before linking with the forwards, who took play on into the Lions' 25 where Ferdie Bergh committed Grieve to the tackle before passing to Ben du Toit who ran over unopposed at the posts to give Turner the simplest of conversions for a 5-0 lead.

Jeff Reynolds had been singled out as the Lions' most dangerous back but the Springboks had done their homework. His breaks were countered by the loose forwards who allowed him some room on the inside then immediately closed the gap before bringing him to ground. Immediately after South Africa had taken the lead, Reynolds set off on one of his forays back inside only to find his way blocked by the trio of loose forwards. There was a clash of heads and when play moved on two players were left on the ground in need of attention. Reynolds and John Apsey were led from the field for repairs, blood flowing freely from their wounds. Basil Nicholson took over at outside-half and Russell Taylor was withdrawn from the pack to play on the wing.

Apsey reappeared just before half-time with his

head heavily bandaged. This gave the home side a numerical advantage in the forwards as South Africa set about securing a second score that would more accurately reflect their undoubted supremacy. From a scrum Danie Craven set off on a probing run with both Harris and Louw in support. An interchange of passes ended with the forward brought to ground but the Springboks were first to the breakdown and Craven again fed Harris who passed to Lochner, the centre able to carve his way through the disorganised defence to score under the posts. With half-time approaching the Lions had a final chance to open their account but a penalty attempt by Alexander fell well short and the whistle went to signal the interval and the Springboks, at 10-0, were firmly in control.

Reynolds returned for the start of the second half, heavily bandaged and wearing a scrum cap for added protection but no sooner had play restarted than Nicholson was led from the field in some discomfort and was only able to do duty as an extra wing when he returned which saw Alexander taken out of the pack. The Springboks, sensing that victory was theirs for the taking, began to spread the ball wide at every opportunity. From a scrum inside the Lions' 25 Craven elected to use the blind side and managed to put Bester into space, the wing needing no second bidding to streak over in the corner for a try which Turner failed to convert.

Up against a team physically drained by the heat, the back three of Turner, Williams and Bester were looking particularly dangerous as the gaps began to appear in the Lions' defence. Such pressure is almost guaranteed to lead to infringements by the defending side and the next Springbok points came from the boot of Turner, who converted two penalties to increase the lead to 19-0 and put the game out of reach. But it was the visitors who had the last word. Tony Harris dropped a pass from Craven and Jeff Reynolds was able to hack on and collect before linking with Laurie Duff, who carried two despairing tacklers over the line with him for a well-deserved try which Grieve failed to improve. At the final whistle the Springboks were able to celebrate not only another Test victory but also a series victory – no matter what happened in Cape Town they had won two of the three-match rubber.

The Lions were left to lick their wounds and wonder what might have been. That the forwards, despite being reduced in number for most of the second half, contested the scrums with more success than had been achieved at Ellis Park was a clear indication of the improvement that had been made in that area. The final figures showed a 28-19 count in the Springboks' favour compared to the 36-14 in the first Test but the line-out statistics told a different story. Where the Lions had held the upper hand in the first Test the figures now read 21-18 in South Africa's favour.

The Springbok forwards had won the scrum and line-out contest and the same was seen in the loose, where the Lions were desperately exposed by the oppressive conditions. Throughout the team, few of the Lions could claim to have got the better of their opposite number but Charles Grieve received particularly good reviews for his inspired performance in the face of the Springboks' many attacks, one correspondent moved to write that the Scot had '... bordered on the heroic'. Travers' presence had made a noticeable impact on the forward effort and although the players had given their all in the extremely difficult conditions it was hard to see how they could produce an upset in Cape Town.

British Lions – C.F. Grieve, Oxford University and Scotland, C.V. Boyle, Dublin University and Ireland, B.E. Nicholson, Harlequins and England, H.R. McKibbin, Queen's University Belfast and Ireland, E.J. Unwin, Rosslyn Park and England, F.J. Reynolds, Army and England, H. Tanner, Swansea and Wales, M.E. Morgan, Swansea and Wales, W.H. Travers, Newport and Wales, G.T. Dancer, Bedford, S. Walker, Instonians and Ireland, captain, R.B. Mayne, Queen's University Belfast and Ireland, A.R. Taylor, Cross Keys and Wales, P.L. Duff, Glasgow Academicals and Scotland, R. Alexander, North of Ireland and Ireland.
Scorer – Duff T.
South Africa – F.G Turner, Transvaal, J.L.A. Bester, Western Transvaal, G.P. Lochner, Eastern Province, P. de Wet, Western Province, D.O. Williams, Western Province, T.A. Harris, Transvaal, D.H. Craven, Northern Transvaal, captain, S.C. Louw, Transvaal, J.W. Lotz, Transvaal, M.M. Louw, Western Province, B.A. du Toit, Northern Transvaal, W.F. Bergh, Northern Transvaal, A.R. Sherriff, Northern Transvaal, J.T. Apsey, Western Province, L.C. Strachan, Northern Transvaal.
Scorers – du Toit T, Lochner T, Bester T, Turner 2P, 2C.
British Lions 3, South Africa 19 (half-time 0-10)
Referee – J.J. Strasheim

Another night, another post-match function, this time at the invitation of Eastern Province and held at the Elizabeth Hotel. A large turnout for the event saw many late arrivals unable to gain admittance to the crowded function room where couples danced the night away to the music of Gaby's Orchestra. Guests of honour included the Lord Mayor, Vice Admiral D'Oyly Lyon, officers of H.M.S. *Amphibion*, recently arrived in Port Elizabeth, the Springbok selectors and their wives together with the usual representation of local dignitaries. Noticeable by their absence, however, were most of the British and South African players who were exhausted after playing eighty minutes in extreme heat and had taken to their beds.

Sunday morning saw a hive of activity at No. 2 Quay at Port Elizabeth docks as the *Windsor Castle* prepared to take on passengers and luggage for the noon departure to Cape Town. One of the older ships in the fleet, the *Windsor Castle* had been given a recent refit to bring her into line with the new demands of the mail service. Among her passengers on the twenty-four-hour journey were the tourists and their Springbok counterparts who would travel together before going their separate ways on arrival in Cape Town to prepare for the third Test. For the Lions this would take them back to the Arthur's Seat Hotel while the South Africans would head to a hotel located outside the city. The Springboks preferred a city centre base and the change of hotel would be the cause of a heated dispute between the players and the South African Rugby Union that at one point looked in danger of forcing the cancellation of the final Test.

The short journey would also raise an issue which would be well documented in the press and in time become part of the folklore of Springbok and Lions rugby – the meeting between Sam Walker and Springbok selector A.F. Markotter during which Markotter wrote on a scrap of paper what he felt should be the Lions' Test team. Rumour has it that Markotter's suggestions were followed to the letter and helped to produce not only what was regarded as the greatest Test match to have taken place in the Union to date but also the biggest upset.

CHAPTER EIGHT

THE LIONS ROAR

All change – The greatest Test – The
Greatest Springboks are beaten – The pride
of the Lions – No change – Young men on a
mission – A smoker to remember – A match
too far – The last blue Lions.

I t was three months earlier that the *Stirling Castle* had
weighed anchor outside Cape Town. The night time
arrival denied the tourists a daylight approach to the
Mother City and the spectacular views of its famous
mountain but not this time. On the morning of
Monday 5 September the *Windsor Castle* made her way
into Table Bay and the slow approach to the quay in
Victoria Basin where her passengers would disembark.

Seven miles out the vessel passed Robben Island,
which since 1936 had been used by the military with
access forbidden to the general public. The island had
a varied history. As far back as 1652 it had been the
location for the country's first sheep farm and more
recently the site of a leper colony until this particular
facility was relocated to Pretoria in 1930. In-between
times Robben Island had been used as a depository for
all manner of miscreants and criminals who were sent
there to await their eventual demise with no hope of
ever returning to the mainland.

In 1819 Chief Makana of the Xhosa tribe was
incarcerated there after leading 10,000 warriors on
a thwarted attack on Grahamstown in the Eastern
Province during the Frontier Wars. Beaten back by a

much smaller number and having sustained serious losses, Makana eventually surrendered and was taken to the island prison. Some years later he perished in a desperate attempt to make for shore on a stolen whaling vessel but many other political prisoners would end their days on the island as guests of the government. In 1938 the most famous of them all was a twenty-year-old man from the Thembu tribe. As the Lions made their way around the country, Nelson Mandela was to be found studying law at Healdtown, a Wesleyan College in Fort Beaufort, 170 miles to the south of Umtata in the Transkei. Twenty-five years later Mandela would begin his term of imprisonment on Robben Island, one which extended to more than twenty-six years before his release in 1990.

On disembarking from the *Windsor Castle*, the Lions and Springboks went their separate ways. The Lions to the familiar surroundings of Sea Point with its beaches and Mediterranean resort atmosphere, the Springboks to an unfamiliar out of town establishment with which the players were clearly not happy. Danie Craven put the players' concerns to the Union but they fell on deaf ears and it was only when it was suggested that the team may not play come Saturday that the issue was addressed. The Union, forced to review the situation, finally acceded to the players' requests and the team was relocated to their preferred accommodation, the Metropole Hotel on Long Street in the heart of the city.

Although this was the tourists' fourth time in Cape Town, the first three visits had been of such short duration there had been little time to experience the delights that South Africa's second largest city had to offer. Now with the best part of three weeks at their disposal the players had a lot of free time to fill and there was certainly no danger of boredom setting in, Cape Town having much to offer.

With a municipal population of 350,000, Cape Town was spread over seventy-five square miles and dominated by Table Mountain, a 3,500-foot-high plateau with a two-mile horizontal front from which it gets its name. In 1929 a remarkable feat of engineering was finally completed with the opening of a cable car station from which passengers could be carried to the summit along a single 4,000-foot span. Only from the top of the mountain can Cape Town's unique location be fully appreciated: the meeting of the two oceans; the coastal suburbs which run south to Cape Point; the dock development and its approach at the foot of the city and Robben Island in the distance. To the north lay the residential suburbs, Newlands among them, where the remaining three games would all be played.

With no midweek match to worry about, the focus could be firmly placed on the final Test and only following this would attention be given to the Combined Universities and Western Province Combined Country matches which would bring the curtain down on the tour. Early in the week there were suggestions that the Springbok team would include changes. Ebbo Bastard was fit for selection and there were doubts about the fitness of Flappie Lochner. If Bastard returned it would undoubtedly be at the expense of local favourite Apsey and the absence of Lochner would probably see Freddy Turner moved into the centre to make way for the inclusion of George Smith, the Eastern Province full-back who had so impressed against the tourists. Local favourite Gerry Brand had not recovered from the leg injury that had kept him out of the Port Elizabeth Test and the Western Province captain was to be denied a final appearance in front of his home supporters.

The selection of the Lions team would again present the all too familiar problems. The series lost, it was time for a radical rethink but with eight players ruled out for the remaining matches the selectors had a squad of twenty-one fit men from which to choose. Joining long-term casualties Bill Clement, Roy Leyland and Duncan Macrae were Vivian Jenkins, Jeff Reynolds, Haydn Tanner, Eddie Morgan and Russell Taylor, all destined to watch the final games from the sidelines. The decision to include fifteen backs in the twenty-nine-man party was proving to be a prudent one. In these final weeks nine backs were still available for selection with twelve forwards vying for the eight places up front but overall the resources available to the selectors were stretched to the extreme and inevitably there would be some new faces lining up against the Springboks. Only Harry McKibbin in the backs together with Sam Walker, Bunner Travers and Blair Mayne among the forwards could confidently expect to be included. Eleven places were up for grabs and when the team was announced to the press there were plenty of surprises but the question everyone wanted answered was who had chosen it?

The conversation between Sam Walker and Springbok selector A.F. Markotter now began to have some significance. The team Markotter had written on a piece of paper proved to be identical to the one which Major Hartley announced to the press. Even allowing for the small number of players certain to be included there were still plenty of surprises. The first noticeable difference between the team selected for the final Test and those which had contested the earlier matches was its composition. Whereas previously England and Wales had accounted for the majority of the players this was no longer so, with the combined representation of those two countries now reduced to four. All eight Irishmen were included together with the three Scots available for selection. Only Giles at centre and the uncapped prop Gerald Dancer would represent England while for Wales, Travers together with Elvet Jones, another player yet to be capped by his country, would be the standard bearers.

The inclusion of the three Scots was no less than the Triple Crown winners deserved although only Duff had been part of that campaign. Charles Grieves' recent performances suggested that he may even have ousted a fully fit Jenkins from the full-back berth and the experience of the underplayed Jock Waters was preferred when it came to choosing the No. 8. The inclusion of all eight Irish players in the party was remarkable as each had played some part in the Championship which had seen Ireland lose all three games, two by large margins, conceding thirteen tries in the process. That the Irishmen were all still standing and available for selection was in itself an achievement of some note but that a country with such a dismal recent record was supplying eight British Lions Test players confounded most critics.

In marked contrast to the conditions in Port Elizabeth, Saturday brought cold and windy weather with the distinct possibility of rain come the 4.00 p.m. kick-off. Defying the conditions, queues began forming at 5.00 a.m. when two lads from Rondebosch Boys' High School were the first to show, arriving at the schoolboy gates ahead of the two Jan van Riebeeck pupils who had claimed pole position for the Lions' two previous visits to the ground. The general queuing began an hour later and from 9.00 a.m. onwards the numbers increased significantly until the gates were finally opened at 11.30. Hopes of another record crowd were dashed by the prospect of bad weather, the fact that the series had already been decided, the absence of Gerry Brand and that the Lions appeared to be fielding what many saw as a scratch team with little prospect of producing an upset. The final estimate suggested that some 18,000 spectators watched the game, considerably fewer than had attended the Western Province Town and Country and Western Province games, but those who made the effort were rewarded with a dry afternoon and eighty minutes' rugby to savour.

Match 22, South Africa – Third Test, Saturday 10 September, Newlands, Cape Town

The three flags on the newly renovated pavilion representing Western Province, the Springboks and the Lions, a blue flag with a gold lion at its centre, indicated that there was a strong wind blowing downfield and having won the toss and on the advice of the groundsman, who suggested the wind would drop come the second half, Craven elected to play with it, allowing Harry McKibbin to start the game for the Lions.

The first five minutes saw the visitors camped in South African territory. Travers won four consecutive scrums and alongside Walker was prominent in a foot rush that came to a halt a few yards from the Springbok line. Some clever back play saw Giles make a telling break and give a try-scoring pass to Elvet Jones but the wing dropped the ball with the line at his mercy. Moments later a similar opportunity presented itself when Cromey broke between Harris and Turner, linked with Giles who gave another perfect pass to Jones, who this time made no mistake to open the scoring with a try in the corner which Bob Alexander failed to convert.

The Lions' tails were up with the forwards looking the more aggressive and dominant. The Springbok eight who had enjoyed a comfortable superiority in the previous encounters looked strangely subdued and it was very much against the run of play when South Africa took the lead. Johnny Bester and Jan Lotz led a foot rush deep into the visitors' half but again it was Charles Grieve who showed tremendous courage by falling on the ball and holding firm until his forwards arrived to lend support.

The situation was cleared but from a line-out Freddy Turner ghosted past his opposite number and broke clear in the middle of the field. He moved out towards the touchline and gave a reverse pass to Dai Williams whose break infield caught the Lions' defence wrong-footed. The wing made strides into the 25 before kicking the ball across field where any number of Springboks were lining up to continue the move and it fell to Turner to collect the bouncing ball and cross unopposed under the posts for a try which he converted himself to give the Springboks a 5-3 lead.

With the strong wind influencing play, the game settled in the Lions' half and the Springbok backs began to look more threatening every time they received the ball. Fred Turner again found space in midfield, belying those who doubted his ability as a centre and it was from his break that the next serious attack came. Clear of the Lions' midfield defence, Turner found Bester running at pace alongside him. The wing gratefully collected Turner's well-timed pass and immediately moved the ball on to Dai Williams who was in full flight and looking unstoppable. Only a despairing tackle by Boyle that caught Williams' heel prevented what had looked a certain try.

The Springboks were now playing more like a side that was two up in a three-match rubber. One particular passage of play saw virtually the whole team handle the ball before Craven narrowly missed with a drop goal attempt. The Lions were subjected to a prolonged period of pressure and another Springbok score seemed inevitable but unfortunately when it came it was not as a result of a piece of attacking flair but a casual lapse of concentration. From what looked to be a safe situation in the middle of the field Sam Walker flung out a long pass to Elvet Jones, only to see Bester race in to intercept with a clear run to the line for the simplest of tries which Turner once again converted.

During the tour the gay abandon with which the Lions had thrown the ball about the field had been both praised and condemned in equal measure. The more conservative observers felt that this was one area of play which should be confined to their opponents' half, particularly in the tighter games. Such comments had fallen on deaf ears, the tourists preferring to stick to their belief that first and foremost they were in South Africa to entertain and nothing was going to detract from this priority. They may have been trailing 10-3 but this was certainly not the time for any soul searching or reappraisal of their game plan. Quite simply, the show had to go on.

217

The game may have been moving away from them but by keeping faith with their enterprising brand of rugby the Lions continued to threaten and were unlucky not to get the scoreboard ticking over in their favour. Forwards and backs combined forces to take play deep into the Springboks' half but when Duff collected what appeared a try-scoring pass from Morgan the celebrations were cut short by the referee who had adjudged that the ball had gone forward earlier in the move. The bad luck continued when Walker and Boyle led a foot rush deep into Springbok territory but, having collected a favourable bounce, the wing lost possession in the act of grounding the ball. Neither was it just try-scoring opportunities which went begging. In between these two efforts firstly Alexander and then McKibbin missed relatively easy penalty kicks, the absence of a front line goal kicker yet again impacting heavily on the tourists' effort. What stood at 10-3 to the Springboks could so easily have read 14-10 or more in the Lions' favour and with the half-time whistle approaching, after a suspect start the visitors appeared to have gained the upper hand in all facets of play. Only the scoreboard disputed the fact but unfortunately it was showing the only statistic that mattered.

In the final moments of the half Tony Harris punted the ball deep into the Lions' 25 and from the resultant line-out Ferdie Bergh broke through before finding Lotz on his outside for the hooker to cross unopposed in the corner. It was a cruel blow and, while Turner failed with his conversion attempt, the score at 13-3 to the Springboks was not a true reflection of the way the game had unfolded in the first forty minutes.

Ifs and buts aside, the Lions looked to be in serious trouble but they had the consolation of knowing that, contrary to earlier predictions and much to Danie Craven's concern, the wind had shown no sign of abating and they would have the advantage of it in the second period.

The half-time interval saw Sam Walker gather his troops around him in the centre of the field and address them in what one touchline correspondent observed was '...language that must have been plain...' In the stands the non-playing members of the party had a look of resignation about them, apparently already accepting the inevitability of a third successive Test defeat. Meanwhile, the Springboks ate their oranges and watched a low-flying plane circle the ground, perhaps reassured in the knowledge that never before had a Springbok team surrendered a ten point half-time lead. But they, like the crowds in the stands and the open areas, were totally oblivious to what the next half would produce.

Late in the first half, Danie Craven had readjusted the three-quarter line. Freddy Turner was dropped to full-back, Johnny Bester moved into the centre and George Smith took his place on the wing. When play resumed South Africa continued with this formation and it was Bester who was the first to make any headway after fielding a loose kick from Mayne, who had marked the ball immediately following the restart. Bester made progress up the touchline before punting the ball into the Lions' 25 for Grieve to gather and aided by the strong wind relieve the situation with a fine touch kick. Boyle worked himself into space from the line-out only for his pass infield to McKibbin go to ground. Smith left the field for some attention to a hand injury but his absence failed to stop the Springboks playing some adventurous rugby with Craven putting Williams clear. The wing's cross kick was competently gathered by Grieve, who once again put in a long wind-assisted kick that took play back into Springbok territory.

While Grieve's defensive qualities continued to earn the plaudits from the appreciative crowd, George Morgan and George Cromey were equally instrumental in keeping the Springboks pinned back in their half for long periods. The experienced Irish half-backs brought all their nous and expertise to the table and the way in which the pair controlled play in the second half was reminiscent of a windswept Lansdowne Road in February. This was the fifth game in which the Irishmen had appeared together and as the previous four had all been won it raises the question as to why they had not been more involved. Morgan had been called up as an emergency full-back, which restricted the opportunities the pair may have had, but their time finally came at a windy Newlands. Morgan cajoled and encouraged his forwards while taking full advantage of the elements to launch a variety of kicks which kept the Springboks on the back foot and when he elected to release the ball to Cromey the outside-half adopted similar tactics. By tightening play in this manner the Lions gradually began to assert their authority on the game, one which not many minutes earlier had appeared a lost cause.

There was a scare when Dai Williams gathered a long pass from du Toit and used his great pace to outflank the stretched defence to cross in the corner only to be recalled for an earlier infringement before the Lions finally got the break they so desperately needed. George Smith managed to gather a loose ball but was pressurised into making a hasty touch finder which relieved the situation but took play only a matter of yards from the try line. Sensing their moment had arrived, the Lions forwards gathered for the line-out. Jock Waters leapt high to collect the ball, which he passed to Sam Walker for the captain to muscle his way through the Springbok forwards before passing to Beef Dancer for the prop to cross unopposed for a try which Harry McKibbin converted from wide out.

Suddenly the tempo of the game was increased with both sides aware there was all to play for. Tony Harris was the first to threaten when after spending the afternoon moving the ball on to his centres he caught the Lions' defence unawares by electing to make an inside break which took him clear with only Grieve to beat and with Craven at his elbow. As the outside-half closed on the full-back he seemed to hesitate and rather than release the ball to his captain charged on, only to be unceremoniously dumped on the ground by the Scot.

The Lions were subjected to an extended period of pressure and did well to hold out as the Springboks desperately tried to reclaim their grip on the game. A break by Craven from the base of the scrum saw him return the ball to his forwards. Ben du Toit, Ferdie Bergh, Roger Sherriff, Jan Lotz and Boy Louw each displayed some deft handling skills before involving the backs, who moved the ball wide to Bester only to see the wing hang on too long and be tackled in possession. Buoyed by their superb defensive efforts, the Lions' forwards made ground upfield and with Cromey using the wind to good effect soon found themselves back in the Springbok 25. A wayward hand in a scrum presented McKibbin with the chance to close the gap to two points. From a difficult angle he struck the ball beautifully and the Lions had scored eight unanswered points in a ten-minute period and any thoughts of a whitewash were now firmly put on hold.

Craven refused to change tactics when it was clear that the Springboks needed a period of consolidation. Rather than allow the forwards to retain possession and slow down the game, he continually gave the backs their head and there were some exciting moves that involved clever passing between forwards and backs but the Lions defence was never found wanting. There followed an intense passage of play which H. du P. Steytler, who had followed the tour throughout described. '...They went at one another hammer and tongs, running, tackling, pushing, struggling, until one marvelled at their fitness and the amount of punishment the human body can stand. The British backs who had started rather shakily, settled down to some real three-quarter play and for a time Britain had the better of the Springboks in all departments of the game...'

That the Lions were able take advantage of this important period of play proved to be critical to the final outcome. Such was their determination to succeed in this final clash it was nothing less than they deserved when they reclaimed the lead midway through the half. Both sets of forwards were involved in a period of mauling in the middle of the field when the ball was suddenly brought away by Eddie Morgan, who fed George Cromey. The smallest man on the field, the one who it was felt may have suffered if exposed to the South African forwards earlier in the tour, somehow escaped the clutches of several Springbok forwards to find himself in acres of space with only George Smith to beat. Unlike his counterpart minutes earlier, Cromey did commit the full-back and released the ball to the supporting Bob Alexander, who made the line with three tacklers desperately trying to bring him to ground. McKibbin failed with the conversion but at 14-13 the Lions were ahead for the first time since Jones' try early in the first half.

The Springboks now knew that they were in a game and one that was not going the way most had predicted. The Lions were playing arguably their best rugby of the tour and it was going to take a huge effort from the home side if they were to gain the expected whitewash. Dai Williams had been a constant problem throughout the series and midway through the second half he made several probing runs but was well marshalled by Boyle, who forced him into touch. The Springboks were making a concerted effort to regain the lead and appeared to have done so following a move that saw Williams come off his wing to link with Piet de Wet, who crossed following a break in midfield, but the centre was penalised, adjudged to have made a double movement in his bid for the line, Grieve's tackle bringing him down short of his objective. The pressure continued and when Giles was penalised for hanging on to the ball in front of the posts Turner's kick was a formality and the lead had changed hands again, the Springboks now enjoying a two-point advantage.

Time was running out but from somewhere deep down the Lions' forwards found the stamina to mount a sustained attack on the Springbok line. They threw themselves at their opponents but the defence held firm and when Lotz won a scrum it was Harris who received the ball from Craven with plenty of room to kick for touch and take play away from the danger area. He mistimed his clearance and it fell into the welcoming arms of Grieve some forty yards out. The full-back had time to steady himself, look up at the posts and take aim with a drop goal that sailed high above the crossbar to restore the Lions' lead. A slender one but with little more than five minutes remaining on the clock an important one.

The 18,000 spectators knew they were witnessing one of the great Test matches and when the tourists again took play deep into Springbok territory the most partisan among them must have sensed that the men in blue were not going to be denied. Another line-out deep into Springbok territory saw the Lions' forwards confirm their supremacy as Jock Waters and Blair Mayne, now playing like men inspired, set off in search of the score that would decide the game. They took the ball on, sweeping despairing tacklers aside and it was Laurie Duff who was on hand to take the scoring pass from Mayne and force his way over with the Springbok defence in total disarray. McKibbin's failure to convert gave the home side a glimmer of hope that they could perhaps salvage a draw but the Lions were in no mood to let their wonderful effort go unrewarded and in the game's dying moments proved equal to everything the Springboks threw at them. Dai Williams had one final chance for glory when he dived over in the corner but again the referee blew up for a forward pass earlier in the move. The scrum was set in the middle of the field. Travers hooked, Morgan found Cromey, the outside-half found touch and referee Nick Pretorius blew his whistle for full time.

The spectators poured onto the field and it was

fitting tribute to Sam Walker's magnificent leadership throughout the tour that he should be carried shoulder high from the field. The other British players were lost among the crowd, who were all looking to congratulate them on their great victory, and it took a while before they could retire to the safety of the dressing room. The series had been lost the week before and there could be no denying that over the three games South Africa had proved the better team but the circumstances which had seen an unlikely selection take the field at Newlands left everyone asking the same question. What would have happened if the Lions had found this winning combination earlier in the tour?

British Lions – C.F. Grieve, Oxford University and Scotland, C.V. Boyle, Dublin University and Ireland, J.L. Giles, Coventry and England, H.R. McKibbin, Queen's University Belfast and Ireland, E.L. Jones, Llanelli, G.E. Cromey, Queen's University Belfast and Ireland, G.J. Morgan, Clontarf and Ireland, C.R.A. Graves, Wanderers and Ireland, W.H. Travers, Newport and Wales, G.T. Dancer, Bedford, S.Walker, Instonians and Ireland, captain, R.B. Mayne, Queen's University Belfast and Ireland, R. Alexander, North of Ireland and Ireland, J.A. Waters, Selkirk and Scotland, P.L. Duff, Glasgow Academicals and Scotland.
Scorers – Grieve DG, Jones T, McKibbin P. C, Dancer T, Duff T, Alexander T.
South Africa – G.A.C. Smith, Eastern Province, J.L.A. Bester, Western Province, F.G. Turner, Transvaal, P. de Wet, Western Transvaal, D.O. Williams, Western Province, T.A. Harris, Transvaal, D.H. Craven, Northern Transvaal, captain, S.C. Louw, Transvaal, J.W. Lotz, Transvaal, M.M. Louw, Western Province, B.A. du Toit,

Northern Transvaal, W.F. Bergh, Northern Transvaal,
A.R. Sherriff, Northern Transvaal, W.E. Bastard, Natal,
L.C. Strachan, Northern Transvaal.
Scorers – Turner T. P. 2C, Lotz T, Bester T.
British Lions 21, South Africa 16 (half-time 3-13)
Referee – N.F. Pretorius

Reviewing the game for the *Cape Argus*, H.B Keartland
enthused over not just the victory but the manner
in which it had been gained. The Lions' forwards,
although marginally beaten in both scrum and line-
out, had proved the more effective in the loose where
the game was perceived to be won and lost. Walker led
by example with Travers, Mayne and Alexander always
prominent, the quartet ably abetted by Dancer, Graves,
Duff and Waters, who in his first Test had a particularly
fine game. George Cromey's performance at outside-
half was rated the best by any player in that position
throughout the series and at full-back Charles Grieve
was again picked as the best player on the field.

That the Lions had outscored the Springboks by four
tries to three was a remarkable turnaround following
the first two Tests, which had produced a cumulative
try count of 7-1 in South Africa's favour. The half-time
13-3 deficit meant that the Lions had scored eighteen
second-half points, a record against the Springboks
which would not be equalled until the second Test in
1974 and then beaten in the third Test of that series
when the Lions improved a 7-3 half-time score into a
26-9 victory.

South Africa's fiftieth Test match had produced
eighty minutes of wonderful rugby and was one
against which all others would be compared for many
years to come. Unfortunately it had not ended with

the expected victory that would have unequivocally confirmed the country's status as the number one rugby nation in the world and there would have to be some rebuilding before the All Blacks arrived in 1940. Some of the great forwards who had served South Africa so well would be retired, there would be the need to find a new captain and the selectors would have to decide who of the leading candidates would replace Gerry Brand at full-back. These were all questions that could be put on hold and subsequent events elsewhere would decree that for the Springboks who had played against the Lions there would be no more Test rugby, but for the moment the players could take comfort from the fact that over an eighteen-month period they had taken the Springboks to the pinnacle of the world game by playing a style which had not only won them Test matches but many admirers along the way.

Danie Craven took his leave of South African rugby in a beaten team but there were no excuses. '...I heartily congratulate Sam Walker and his men on their splendid victory. The Springboks have no complaints to make for they were beaten by a better team. I wonder why the British side did not start earlier to play the type of rugby they showed us today. Perhaps it was just as well for us that they didn't do so. People have said they always want to see clean, open rugby – well, they have got their wish throughout this tour but more particularly today...'

The proud Lions captain commented '...I am overjoyed our lads were able to pull it off and that we were able to win a game which I think delighted the crowd and which I have already been told will be remembered as one of the most exciting international games that have been played in this country. It was just the hard sort of game that we like to play in Britain and we enjoyed every moment of it. Speaking for all my boys I can say that we are very proud of being able to beat South Africa on this very historic ground which I understand is the home of South African rugby. I hope the Springboks enjoyed the game as much as we did ... but the biggest thrill of my career was when the final whistle went and Ben du Toit and Louis Strachan and others hoisted me on their shoulders and chaired me off. That is real sportsmanship...'

The after-match function was a low-key affair in comparison to some that had gone before. Held at the famous Del Monico restaurant, the Western Province Rugby Union hosted a dinner at which 150 guests saluted the Lions and their wonderful achievement in downing the Springbok colours. Mr J.D. de Villiers, senior vice president of the union, applauded the tourists and the manner in which they played the game. That they had been hugely popular visitors was beyond question and he concluded by commenting, 'We are proud to know that the founders of the game in South Africa can, after all these years, be the best winners and losers we have met.'

Brought to his feet by loud calls of 'We want Sam', the popular captain made the appropriate comments on behalf of the team, thanking their hosts for the hospitality shown towards them, but before he sat down he took the opportunity of '... publicly acknowledging the unswerving and ever ready support given to me as captain by my teammates and to thank them for a loyalty that has been remarkable...' There was never any doubting that it had been a happy tour and the captain's role in maintaining a standard both on and off the field can never be understated. That Sam Walker had succeeded in bringing together a party of players drawn from four countries and helped produce a side capable of beating one of the best teams the game had seen was a true testament to the genial Ulsterman's character.

More than twenty years later Sam Walker wrote about what it meant to captain the British Lions. He placed great emphasis on team spirit and how he felt it had been his responsibility as captain to nurture this essential ingredient. He placed great value on the time spent aboard the *Stirling Castle* and emphasised that the greatest responsibility he held was to ensure that all players were given sufficient match time to keep them involved. He was also aware of the dangers of allowing cliques to form and went to great lengths to avoid such potentially disruptive factions materialising. But through all the highs and lows, good times and bad, it was the final Test in Cape Town which stood above all else.

'The second half of the match is one that will never be forgotten by anyone who was privileged either to play in it or witness it, for the British Lions played like men inspired... To this day my most treasured rugby possessions are a blue No. 14 jersey and a tattered pair of shorts, both unwashed and still retaining traces of mud from a famous ground to associate as it were, a truly Homeric struggle between two great rugby teams... That epic game made all my efforts well worth while but the things that matter most to any successful touring captain are not the great moments on the field of play but the friendship and mutual respect of the members of the team.'

The additional fixture with a Combined Country XV had long since been confirmed, which meant that the Combined Universities game was now scheduled for the following Saturday, giving the party time to prepare for the journey home and the prospect of a return to normality; life as a rugby tourist in a foreign land was anything but representative of a normal lifestyle. But for the late change to the schedule the Lions would have left Cape Town on Friday 16 September aboard the *Edinburgh Castle* in the company of Danie Craven and his wife, who were on their way to Europe where Craven would continue his studies.

Realistically, Craven was aware that his international rugby career had ended at Newlands but his biggest disappointment was not the defeat or the fact that his distinguished career had come to an end, rather that Gerry Brand was unable to take his place in the team for a final swansong in front of his home crowd. If Brand had played Craven was insistent that he would have handed the captaincy to one of South Africa's finest, a gesture which sums up the magnanimous nature of a man for whom the game of rugby was bigger than any of its component parts, as his later involvement administering it at the highest level would confirm.

Craven was now twenty-seven. His international career had started on the 1930–31 visit to the British Isles. He played rugby in Australia and New Zealand and captained the Springboks in a Test series in South Africa, thereby completing what in the 1930s was a near perfect playing record: a grand slam in Britain followed by a home series win against Australia and the golden period of 1937–38. This enabled Craven to go on record as saying, 'I leave the stage with no regrets.'

With time to reflect on the Test defeat Craven was

of the opinion that the Springboks were a little over confident at Newlands. '... I believe Sam Walker told his men before they went onto the field that they had to win the match or the tour would be regarded a failure and he asked them to play as they had never played before, even if they had to leave Newlands in an ambulance. That was the right spirit and he was supported loyally. We, on the other hand, simply could not envisage defeat. We had beaten them so comfortably in the first two Tests that it did not seem possible for them to give us anything but a good, hard game. I confess quite frankly that some of our fellows went onto the field with the idea of running up a record score...

'I feel that having won the first two Tests so decisively we should not have lost this match, but we did and it was a good lesson. Some of the fellows wanted me to close the game down but I did not feel justified in doing this. Open rugby is South Africa's traditional game and I think we have shown the South African public we can play it well and effectively... I went into Springbok rugby when the game was dull and stodgy and I leave it with a feeling that the methods of 1931–32 will not return. With the example of the 1937 and 1938 Springboks to inspire them I feel sure that future generations of South African rugby players will always try to keep alive the true spirit of the game.

'I am glad to have been associated with the game in this revival of open play and I am glad too, to have been associated with such a fine lot of sportsmen as the British team. On behalf of the Springboks I can say that we all enjoyed playing against them immensely. It has been a fine experience and we shall all be sorry when they leave.'

Danie Craven was destined to be one of rugby

union's great administrators and his massive contribution in that field often consigns his playing career to something of an afterthought, which should not be the case. Even before those days of attrition and political strife in the boardroom, here was a man who people recognised as a major figure in the game, none more so than the British players who had met him on and off the field. In the hours leading up to the *Edinburgh Castle*'s departure, several of the tourists spent time on board with Craven, Sam Walker and Bunner Travers among them. A fitting gesture to a man who knew his international days were over, unlike most of his teammates who were now looking forward to the visit of the 1940 New Zealand All Blacks. That tour would not take place and it would be eleven years before South Africa would play international rugby again.

After the excitement of the final Test there was every indication that the interest in the remaining matches would be high. Certainly the Universities game would benefit from being played on a Saturday. The third Test was the twenty-second match of the tour but as yet no two games had seen the Lions field the same team. The twenty-two games had seen twenty-two different combinations take to the field but that was about to change. Following their performance in the third Test, Major Hartley called it same again when he announced the team to face the Combined Universities.

Drawn from the University of Cape Town and Stellenbosch University, the combined team was expected to mount a serious challenge to the Lions, even if it was the successful Test team that would face them. The inter-varsity match played at Newlands earlier in the season had attracted a crowd in excess of 25,000 and the students had produced one of the finest varsity contests in living memory, Stellenbosch claiming a 14-8 victory over their greatest rivals. Now these two grand academic institutions would join forces in an effort to succeed where their predecessors had failed. The 1910 and 1924 British teams both defeated the students, as did the 1928 All Blacks, but in 1933 the Australians were held to a 3-3 draw and it was felt that despite what had happened seven days earlier the Lions could be beaten. The students were full of optimism and captain Koos Smit was quoted as saying, '... if we cannot get the ball in the tight or line-outs we'll go and pinch it from their backs.' Simple as that.

The two universities both boasted impressive honours boards. Among those who had played for Stellenbosch RFC before the formation of a university team were Japie Krige, Paul Roos and Bob Loubser and Danie Craven had completed his doctorate there in 1935. The Osler brothers, Bennie and Stan, were among the notables at the University of Cape Town and more recent alumni included Morris Zimerman and Louis Babrow. The current team would include Springbok Piet de Wet in the centre and the outstanding North 'Porky' Wells at hooker. Wells had been a Springbok trialist in 1937 but the decision to take only one specialist hooker to New Zealand denied him and his playing career was unfortunately overshadowed by Jan Lotz.

Match 23, Western Province Universities, Saturday 17 September, Cape Town

As at Port Elizabeth two weeks earlier, the temperature was well into the nineties and the estimated crowd of 15,000 sat in shirt sleeves, many of them in improvised sun hats crafted from the match day programme. There had been suggestions that de Wet might not be able to take his place but much to the delight of his home crowd, after a run-out before kick-off, he was declared fit by Oobus Markotter who had selected and organised the combined team. Among the many great traditions preserved by the universities was one which respected that when they combined forces the players would wear the colours of the team not represented by the captain. Koos Smit was studying at Stellenbosch, therefore when the team appeared at Newlands it was in the zebra white and dark blue striped jerseys of the University of Cape Town.

With the enthusiasm one expects from varsity teams the students set about the task of competing with their more 'senior' opponents with relish. From de Wet's kick-off the Lions moved the ball only for Harry McKibbin to knock on in midfield and from the ensuing scrum the visitors were penalised but from forty yards full-back Wahl failed with the attempt at goal. McKibbin fielded the kick but rather uncharacteristically knocked on again and the Lions were forced to defend a 5-yard scrum, Travers heeling to give his scrum-half the chance to clear the ball. The first opportunity of points for the tourists came from a penalty on halfway but Bob Alexander was short with his effort and it was McKibbin who finally opened the scoring with a penalty kick from wide out after Nel had fallen offside.

With no regard for the oppressive heat, the Varsities ran the ball at every opportunity and when the Lions tried to respond with their own particular brand of running rugby the students showed great courage and commitment in defence. The intensity of the play ensured there were plenty of opportunities for referee Tunbridge to blow up and following missed kicks at goal at both ends of the field it was Wahl who succeeded with a penalty from just inside the Lions' half, his drop kick sailing high between the posts to level the scores at 3-3. These early exchanges suggested there was little to choose between the teams, which were both getting their share of possession and enjoying equal territorial advantage, and throughout the first quarter it was the two defences who were asked the most questions.

They may have been the same fifteen players who had beaten the Springboks, but the Lions were given little opportunity to display their craft as the students met them head-on in all areas of play. Such was their enthusiasm for the task, errors were unavoidable and from a scrum inside the home 25, the visitors were awarded a penalty which gave McKibbin the chance to put the Lions in front on the stroke of half-time. His well-struck kick took the score to 6-3 but any thoughts that they were in for an easy afternoon's work had long since disappeared and when the whistle went the Lions had much to contemplate as they sucked on their oranges.

Sam Walker must have chosen his words well because from the restart the Lions' forwards took play to the goal line but wave after wave of determined attacks were repelled, even the strength of Blair Mayne not enough to enable him to force his way over. Scrum-half Ehlers somehow managed to get under Mayne as he dived to score, then added insult to injury by picking him up and unceremoniously throwing him into touch, much to the chagrin of the Ulsterman. A misjudged touch kick by Ehlers failed to find its target and was fielded by Grieve, who attempted a long-range drop goal which was wide of the mark, but the receiving player fumbled in the in-goal area and the resultant 5-yard scrum saw the Lions' forwards successfully drive and wheel, which gave Sam Walker the chance to pick up the ball and fling himself over the line for a try which McKibbin converted.

For the first time in the match the students began to look vulnerable in defence and it was a basic error which led to the next Lions score. Loose forward Oberholster picked up the ball at the base of a scrum and opted to pass it to Gonin but his effort gave the outside-half little chance as it went well above and behind him. It was the sort of opportunity a player with such speed off the mark as Jimmy Giles relished and the scrum-half-cum-centre made no mistake in gathering the loose ball to run directly at the full-back, knowing that McKibbin was in support. He committed Wahl to the tackle before releasing a perfectly timed pass to his centre partner, who scored under the posts and made no mistake with the easiest of conversions.

Throughout the game the Lions had struggled in the scrums. Their line-out work had been excellent, denying the opposition much ball from this area of play, but if the Varsity team was going to make any impact on the game they needed to get more possession and it was now that Smit made the decision to opt for scrums at every opportunity. A decision that in the space of twenty minutes turned the game on its head. Slowly but surely the younger forwards began to assert their authority. Whether the arduous tour was finally taking its toll, particularly after the effort needed to beat the Springbok pack, or whether the heat was affecting the Lions more than the local team is irrelevant. For the final quarter of the game the students were very much in control and the crowd began to sense that despite trailing 16-3, they were not beaten yet.

Wahl converted a penalty from wide out to reduce the lead to ten points and after some frantic defence had stopped Travers and then Walker a matter of inches from the line the students once more worked their way into the visitors' half. Little George Cromey was caught by Tromp Nel and the big flanker robbed him of possession and hacked on into the 25. Laurie Duff fell on the ball but van Niekerk somehow managed to get a boot to it and kicked it nearer the try line with Grieve and de Wet giving chase. It was the centre who benefited from the bounce to collect and score under the posts and with Wahl making no mistake with the conversion Newlands erupted. The lead was now reduced to five points – a converted try would level the scores.

After twenty-two games in which the Lions had never attempted to play negative rugby there was no possibility of them trying to defend a lead in the twenty-third. Play moved back into home territory but no matter what the tourists came up with the students were prepared and after soaking up five minutes of constant pressure eventually made their way back upfield. Sensing their opponents might be tiring, the students kept the ball alive and moved it at pace across the width of the field and then back, a sweeping attack which ended with right wing Miller eventually running out of space. With few options available to him Miller put in an innocuous grubber kick, the type that Charles Grieve had been coping admirably with match after match, but not this time. The full-back missed the ball and Miller was past him in a flash to continue hacking it towards the line, only to collide with the covering McKibbin, both players going to ground and the ball left bouncing freely in the in-goal area. First up was loose forward Wilson who touched down a few yards in from the corner flag, leaving a difficult conversion to tie the scores. In a matter of moments Newlands went from a deafening roar to a deafening silence as Wahr placed the ball and stepped back to appraise what he had to do. There was never any doubting the ball's destiny as it sailed high and true between the uprights and with five minutes remaining, sensationally, the scores were level.

The Lions were playing for their pride, the students for the long overdue scalp of a major touring team and it was pride that proved the stronger incentive as the clock ticked down. Vesey Boyle was tackled into touch at the corner flag as he dived for what would surely be the winning score. The tackler, the tackled player, the corner flag and the ball all ended up in the front row of the touchline seats with touch judge Haigh Smith reluctantly indicating to the referee that it was touch in-goal.

From the restart, Bunner Travers made one final, desperate charge for the line, the ball gripped firmly under his arm. He could not complete his mission but handed on to Bob Alexander, who looked certain to score in the corner only for the diminutive Miller to bring him to ground with a fine tackle. But the Lions were not to be denied. Following a line-out play once again entered the 25 and of all the noise that was now reverberating around the ground it was the shrill blast of the referee's whistle that indicated there had been an infringement and that a penalty was about to be awarded. But to which team?

The referee pointed in the Lions' favour and the crowd remained silenced for what was clearly going to be the last kick of the game and it was Harry McKibbin who was stepping up to take it. Not the best struck penalty – to many it looked as if it was heading left of the posts – but the ball corrected itself and the Lions had won a desperate victory with that final kick. The Combined Universities had given their all in what was another of the great games of the tour but it ended in disappointment, a feeling with which the tourists could empathise having lost to Western Province Town and Country at the same ground in identical circumstances.

British Lions – C.F. Grieve, E.L. Jones, H.R. McKibbin, J.L. Giles, G.V. Boyle, G.E. Cromey, G.J. Morgan, G.T. Dancer, W.H. Travers, C.R.A. Graves, S.Walker, captain, R.B. Mayne, P.L. Duff, J.A. Waters, R. Alexander.
Scorers – McKibbin T, 3P, 2C, Walker T.
Western Province Universities – F. Wahl, H. de Vos, P. de Wet, H. Brunow, D. Miller, A. Gonin, J. Ehlers, G. Osler, N. Wells, J. Oberholster, J.N. van Niekerk, J.N. Smit, captain, J. Koch, T. Nel, H.R.H. Wilson.
Scorers – Wahl 2P, 2C, de Wet T, Wilson T.
British Lions 19, Western Province Universities 16 (half-time 6-3)
Referee – P.D. Tunbridge

Officially the great adventure was over. There was one remaining game to be played before the party sailed for home but it would not be included in the final analysis and would only be referred to in the record books as an unofficial match. All the statistics pertaining to the tour would exclude the outcome of the game against the Western Province Combined Country XV, which meant that the 1938 British Isles team had won seventeen of their twenty-three games but the fact that they had failed to win the all-important Test series would always weigh against how successful the team was. They had played entertaining, open rugby at every opportunity, which the accumulation of seventy-nine tries lays testament to, an average of 3.4 per match which was better than any previous touring side had achieved in South Africa since the introduction of modern scoring values. The 407 points scored was also a record for any touring side in South Africa.

Elvet Jones was top try scorer with ten, followed by Unwin, nine, and all bar three of the party crossed the line at least once. Those who failed to score a try were the two full-backs, Vivian Jenkins and Charles Grieve, and surprisingly Blair Mayne who, despite making nineteen appearances, was the only member of the party not to register any points at all. Equally surprising was the elevation of Russell Taylor to top points scorer. The fifty-three points he accumulated in sixteen appearances topped Jenkins' fifty which had come from five fewer matches, but that eight players were called upon to take over the goal kicking duties at some stage of the tour confirms this was a department in which there was a disappointing weakness. Fewer than fifty per cent of the tries were converted and the total of twenty-four successful penalties, barely one per game, suggests that this was a feature of the Lions' game that does not bear close inspection, although to suggest that any of the defeats could have been avoided if the place kicking had been more reliable would be unrealistic.

As the tour entered its final week so began the traditional round of goodbyes. Mac Strachan did his job well as baggage master. The total 3,300 lbs free allowance was not expected to be exceeded as that had not happened on any previous tours but in 1938 from as early as the journey from Johannesburg to Durban there had been excess baggage charges incurred. It meant Strachan's task grew harder over the final seven weeks. For his labours he received the same stipend as the players, one guinea per week, plus all board and meals.

Only Vivian Jenkins had lost a suitcase, at Pietermaritzburg, but local Cape Town merchants J.W. Jagger and Co. did surprisingly good business during the final week with Ivor Williams, George Morgan, Unwin and Duff all needing new trunks while Russell Taylor's needed running repairs. In addition to his defined responsibilities, Mac Strachan became more of a general factotum to the players with his local knowledge and experience often being called upon. It was fitting then that the tourists recognised the part he had played in their great journey by holding a 'smoker' at the hotel in his honour. A 'smoker' can loosely be described as a social gathering of men at which pipes, cigars and cigarettes could be enjoyed without apologies having to be made to ladies or non-approving, non participants. In other words a thing of the past, but as the Lions included many pipe smokers among their number the opportunity to enjoy the occasional pow wow was never passed up.

As the evening unfolded, the players took turns at entertaining the gathering, a favourite song being the usual choice and when it was the turn of Bob Graves to take the spotlight he delighted his team mates with a rendering of 'Paddy McGinty's Goat' to which he had added an extra verse:

At Newlands the rugby team, all from the British Isles

Fought against the Springboks their faces wreathed in smiles.
The Springboks relied upon a strong and heavy pack
And bet their bottom dollars they would shove Great Britain back.
They were surprised when they found the thing went wrong
And, instead of pushing they were pushed by men more strong.
This fact they didn't know about, I'll bet you a five pound note,
The ninth man in the British pack was Paddy McGinty's goat!

A grand night helped to cement friendships that would last a lifetime, Sam Walker acknowledging in his presentation speech to John Strachan that '...we wouldn't have been able to tour if it hadn't been for Mac.'

The last few days had given the Lions the opportunity to completely unwind and there is no doubting the fact that come Wednesday they were probably not mentally prepared for a final eighty minutes of rugby. Drawn from the Western Province clubs outside the Cape Town catchment area, the Combined Country side included one player, outside-half D. van der Vyver, who had played against the tourists in their first defeat. For those Lions selected to play it was a final chance to pull on the famous jersey – time would show that it was the last game in which the blue jersey would be worn by a British touring team – and it is certain that those not involved would have been bitterly disappointed. Included among the forwards were Couchman, Williams,

Howard and Purchas, none of whom had played in the last four games, and they joined Walker, Travers, Mayne and Waters in a solid-looking pack. Cromey and Morgan continued at half-back, Grieve at full-back, Jones and Unwin were on the wing with Nicholson alongside McKibbin in the centre, the Irishman making his thirteenth start in the last fifteen matches.

Unofficial Match, Western Province Country, Wednesday 21 September, Cape Town

It was a game too far. There was a disappointing turnout estimated at 5,000 and the match was saved from being consigned to those instantly forgotten encounters by some enterprising play from the tourists in the closing minutes, but overall it was a dull affair. That notwithstanding it was a tremendous victory for the home team, whose backs quite simply made better use of the limited possession they received than their counterparts did with the embarrassment of riches made available to them. The Lions forwards dominated the game, winning twenty-two of the thirty-five scrums and twenty of the twenty-four line-outs, but for the first time in a provincial game the tourists failed to score a try.

The first half produced some of the most negative rugby of the tour with both sides seemingly content to wait for the opposition to make mistakes, and neither did referee Mr G. Brink help matters with his whistle far too regularly bringing play to a stop, often to the astonishment of both teams. The interval approached with the score at 3-3, each side having converted a penalty, but there had been more opportunities for the combined side to trouble the scoreboard and but for a succession of missed kicks the home team would have held a comfortable half-time lead.

Undeterred, the combined side continued to hammer away at the Lions' line, and from a ruck van der Vyver attempted what should have been a relatively simple drop at goal only to see his effort bounce nearer the corner flag than the goalposts. What was fast becoming a comedy of errors was stabilised when Goosen on the left wing followed up a speculative kick ahead, gathered the ball after a favourable bounce and crossed unchallenged in the corner for a try that went unconverted. Combined Country now led 6-3, a big lead in the light of the inept play which the first forty minutes had produced.

Things were slow to improve once the second half got under way. A penalty award took the Country XV to 9-3 but there was a noticeable absence of expansive rugby and a try from an organised attacking move never looked likely. The second try of the afternoon came after the diminutive Cromey was caught in possession, lost the ball to van Blomenstein, who hacked on and beat Grieve in the race for the touchdown. At 12-3 the Lions had no option other than to throw caution to the wind, move the ball about in a last-ditch attempt to retrieve the situation. The crowd thrilled to their enterprising rugby and other than not actually scoring a try many of the moves were as good as had been seen on tour, but all they could manage was a drop goal by Elvet Jones who had spent the whole tour telling those prepared to listen that he would get one. Jones had his moment of glory and the score now stood at 12-7 but unofficial match or otherwise, those were the last points scored by the 1938 British Isles rugby team in South Africa.

A final try and the chance of a conversion to tie the game was denied them by some staunch defence and some of the party may have been forgiven if they did not wonder why they were not somewhere off the west coast of Africa, five days into their journey home.

British Lions – C.F. Grieve, E.L. Jones, H.R. McKibbin, B.E. Nicholson, E.J. Unwin, G.E. Cromey, G.J Morgan, S. Walker, captain, W.H. Travers, J.A. Waters, R.B. Mayne, S.R. Couchman, A.H.G. Purchas, W.G. Howard, I. Williams.
Scorers – McKibbin P, Jones DG.
Western Province Country – D. Steyl, C.B Louw, S. Hofmeyer, A. van Blommestein, P. Goosen, D. van der Vyver, captain, D. Slabbert, G. Kellerman, A. Botha, P. van Blommestein, H. Retief, B. Claasens, D. de Koch, A. van der Merve, M. Loubscher.
Scorers – A. van Blommestein T, P, Louw P, Goosen T.
British Lions 7, Western Province Country 12 (half-time 3-6)
Referee – G. Brink

It was over. Three months had passed since Sam Walker led his men out at East London for the opening match against Border. Much had happened in that three-month period but most importantly the relationship between the rugby-playing fraternities in the British Isles and South Africa had been strengthened. It would be seventeen years before the Lions and Springboks would once again contest a Test series and when the day arrived there would be one significant difference from the class of '38 – the Lions would wear the now famous red jersey. The days of the 'Blue Lions' were over.

AFTERWORD

When the *Athlone Castle* entered Southampton docks in the first week of October it signalled the end of the great adventure. The departure aboard the *Stirling Castle* on 21 May must have seemed a lifetime ago to the management and players as they made their way down the gangway to terra firma – British terra firma. Matches had been won, matches had been lost. And there were the unforgettable experiences enjoyed away from the field of play – the Victoria Falls and Kruger National Park prominent among them. But above all else there were the many friendships that had been forged, friendships which would last a lifetime.

The 1938–39 season was already well under way and the players could look forward to returning to their clubs, taking up the cudgels of domestic rugby and on occasion squaring up to men with whom they had recently stood side by side against the best that South African rugby had to offer. For some, such encounters would have to be put on hold until the International Championship started in the new year but even then there would be those whom the various selection panels would not call upon.

On 21 January 1939, England defeated Wales 3-0 at Twickenham in the opening match of the Championship. Included in the Welsh team were Vivian Jenkins, Haydn Tanner, Eddie Morgan, Bunner Travers and Russell Taylor but not one of England's representatives in South Africa was selected. In fact, none of the nine English Lions would play for their country again and Stanley Couchman, Gerald Dancer, Bill Howard and A.H.G. Purchas remained uncapped. Neither would

Wales' Ivor Williams play for his country. Of the six uncapped players who toured South Africa only Elvet Jones gained international honours when he was selected against Scotland later in the Championship.

Six of the eight Irish Lions appeared in the Championship. George Morgan was reinstated as captain and together with Bob Alexander, George Cromey, Blair Mayne and Harry McKibbin took part in all three matches with Vesey Boyle selected for the final game of the campaign against Wales. But for Sam Walker and Charles Graves, their international rugby-playing days had ended at Newlands. In Scotland, Duncan Macrae played throughout the Championship and there was one further cap for Laurie Duff but neither Charles Grieve nor Jock Waters were called upon again. For those Lions who had missed out on international honours in 1939 there was usually next year to look forward to but not this time. It would be eight years before the next Championship took place and when that happened the international arena would welcome a host of new faces looking to make their mark.

The outbreak of war on 3 September 1939 saw the players who had represented Britain on the rugby field twelve months earlier now take up arms to represent their country in a much more hostile arena. On the resumption of international fixtures in 1947 the playing personnel of the home unions would be very different and in the 1947 Championship, England, Ireland, Scotland and Wales would between them introduce seventy-six new caps. Haydn Tanner was the baby of the 1938 Lions and on the resumption of international rugby it was Tanner who the Welsh selectors invited to lead Wales' first post-war team. He remained in charge for three seasons, helping to bring together the new generation of young Welsh stars who would go on to great deeds in the 1950s but they weren't all young men. In 1949 the thirty-five-year-old Bunner Travers was recalled to the team ten years after winning his last cap and went on to play in all four Championship matches.

The first official international match following the Second World War was played at Eden Park, Auckland on 14 September 1946 and saw New Zealand defeat Australia 31-8. The wait for the resumption of international fixtures in the northern hemisphere was a little longer, the 1947 Championship starting in Paris on New Year's Day. After an enforced sixteen-year absence France celebrated a return to the tournament with an 8-3 victory over Scotland. England and Wales resumed international rugby when they met in Cardiff on 18 January and Ireland returned to the fray against the French in Dublin a week later. For South Africa the wait to resume international fixtures would extend until 16 July 1949 when the Springboks defeated the All Blacks 15-11 in Cape Town. This was the first Test of a four-match series which South Africa went on to win 4-0, thereby emphatically reaffirming their pre-war position as unofficial world champions. This was confirmed during the 1951–52 season when the Springboks defeated the four home countries and France on a fourth visit to Europe and in 1953 Australia lost a Test series in South Africa 3-1. But what of the British Lions?

The first post-war tour was to New Zealand and Australia in 1950 and only confirmed what had been seen between the wars – that the combined strength of the four home countries was not equal to the task of overcoming one of the juggernauts of the game in their

own back yard. Neither were there the ready made excuses regarding the availability of leading players etc.
– on paper this was a great Lions team but following a
spirited draw in the first Test they went on to lose the
series 3-0 and also experienced defeat against three of
the provincial teams. Remember, twelve months earlier the All Blacks had been comprehensively beaten by
the Springboks.

In 1955 the British Lions returned to South Africa.
Much had changed. These Lions were the first to fly
to their long-haul destination and used the domestic
airline network to move about the country, avoiding the
long train journeys experienced by their predecessors
in 1938. For the first time journalists from the British
national press accompanied the tour, including Vivian
Jenkins of *The Sunday Times* who had been a Lion
in 1938. The Test series would be decided over four
matches and gone were the blue jerseys, replaced in
1950 by the now familiar red. With white shorts and
blue stockings with green tops the playing strip was at
last representative of the four home countries.

The 1955 Lions fared better than their predecessors,
drawing the series 2-2 and losing only three of the
provincial matches. Like the 1938 tourists they were
applauded for the style of rugby played – fast, open,
attacking rugby that would not only entertain but was
also capable of gaining the desired results in the Test
matches. The drawn series in 1955 remained the best
post-war performance by a Lions team until the early
1970s when both New Zealand and South Africa had to
concede second best but since the heady days of John
Dawes and his 1971 Lions, followed by Willie John
McBride's unbeaten squad of 1974, only the 1989 and
1997 Lions in Australia and South Africa respectively

have won a Test series. The record books confirm that of the sixteen post-war British Lions tours to date the all-important Test series has been lost 11 times. The statistics make no allowance for the hard luck stories attached to each tour, and there have been many of those, but overall the Lions have had a tough time in the southern hemisphere.

All of which gives no small cause for concern when reappraising the 2005 tour to New Zealand. This included the largest contingency of players who were accompanied by the biggest backroom staff in Lions history and the squad was supposedly the best prepared with nothing having been left to chance. And what did this army of players and coaches together with the spin doctor, the kicking guru, the medicine men, the chef, the lawyer and Uncle Tom Cobley and all achieve in New Zealand? Nothing!

So what does this say about the 1938 Lions? Where do they stand in the history of what has become the British and Irish Lions? Why do Sam Walker and his men warrant attention on the printed page? What makes them so special?

Such questions could be answered by stating the obvious. That if the 2005 Lions deserved the media hype that preceded their tour, the press reporting and television coverage of every minute of every match and the post mortems that followed the debacle, then at the very least the 1938 tour to South Africa is deserving of at least one document which records its achievements. But the real reasons why Sam Walker and his men should not be forgotten go much deeper than that. Theirs is not a tour that should be remembered solely by the results of twenty-four games of rugby, results which in fact suggest that the 1938 Lions were not a great success. Rather, it should be viewed as representative of a period in the game's history that was brought to a premature end by events way beyond its control. The Second World War determined that the 1938 British Isles tour to South Africa would bring to a close the second of four distinct periods in the development of the Lions. The inter-war period was preceded by the formative years of touring that came to an end with the outbreak of the First World War and it was followed by the post-war period that saw rugby football begin to emerge as a global sport. This inevitably led to the professional era and the many changes that accompanied such a momentous development in the game of rugby union, but it would be remiss to forget that which went before and the inter-war years remain as important in the game's global development as any other period in its history.

The period 1918–1939 is particularly memorable because it heralded the start of the New Zealand/South African rivalry on the rugby field. That it took some years before the Springboks could lay claim to being the best team in the world shows how little there was to choose between the two countries but when a 'champion' was declared the intensity of the rivalry only increased. That it took one of South Africa's greatest teams, maybe one of rugby's greatest teams, to finally break the deadlock has long since been a matter of record but what has not been so readily accepted is the fact that a combination of twenty-nine English, Irish, Scots and Welshmen were the first to challenge the Springboks' rugby supremacy – and how spirited a contest they fought.

Far from being the best-prepared team to leave these shores, they showed a character of spirit and adventure which made them many friends off the field while on it they never knew when they were beaten and got their just rewards at Newlands in the final Test. The succession of injuries was unprecedented and the tedium of the long journeys by rail must have tested the strongest fibres but through it all emerged twenty-nine men of fine character and mettle – theirs is a contribution to the game of rugby union football in Britain and Ireland that should never be forgotten.

APPENDIX 1
PLAYER PROFILES

BRITISH LIONS

Players may have represented more than one club during their career but are identified as a member of the club to which they were attached at the time of the tour. Similarly, the positions listed are those in which the players were selected in South Africa. The number of appearances and points scored on tour are included. The annotation + indicates the player appeared/scored in the unofficial match against Western Province Country.

HARTLEY, MAJOR BERNARD CHARLES CB OBE
b 16 March 1879, d 24 April 1960
Cambridge University, Blackheath, England
Manager

Jock Hartley was a much respected figure within the game when he was appointed manager of the 1938 British Isles team. As a player, Hartley won his Blue in 1900 before representing England against Scotland in 1901 and 1902. He was club captain at Blackheath. Hartley also won an athletics Blue at Cambridge and was a competent oarsman and golfer but it was as a leading rugby administrator that perhaps he is best remembered. He represented Cambridge University on the RFU and later the Army. He was an England selector and following the Second World War became a senior vice-president of the RFU before becoming its thirty-ninth president in 1947.

Jock Hartley proved to be immensely popular with the players and he was never less than accommodating when it came to the many demands placed on the Lions by their hosts. An excellent after dinner speaker, he entertained gatherings at many functions across the country and left South Africa with many fond memories of a true English gentleman. Jock Hartley was a stockbroker.

HAIGH SMITH, HAMILTON AUGUSTUS
b 21 October 1884, d 28 October 1955
Blackheath
Assistant manager

Like Jock Hartley, Jack Haigh Smith was also a much respected administrator. He had served on the RFU committee but it was as a member of the Barbarians that he was best known. In 1925 Haigh Smith was elected as Honorary Secretary of the famous club, remaining in office for thirty years before he was chosen to succeed Emile de Lissa as president in 1955. Sadly, Haigh Smith died shortly after his new appointment was announced.

Jack Haigh Smith was a front row forward. He played for Blackheath and Hampshire and became secretary of the county in 1925, serving until the outbreak of war in 1939. Together with Hartley he formed a hugely successful management team and the involvement of both in the running of the tour, team selection and the many problems that arise when extensively travelling a foreign country with twenty-nine energetic young men in tow ensured the operation ran smoothly.

WALKER, SAMUEL
b 21 April 1912, d 27 January 1972
Instonians, Ireland
Prop, lock
15 caps
Lions – 19 + 1 appearances, 3 Tests, 12 points
Sam Walker's leadership credentials were never in doubt despite his having captained Ireland only once, against Wales at Swansea a week before the Lions squad was announced. Ireland lost the match but seven of the team were selected to tour and Walker was appointed captain. It proved to be an inspired choice, the personable Ulsterman proving a great success both on and off the field and he very quickly brought players from four countries together as one.

Walker's fifteen appearances for Ireland began against England in 1934 but after two defeats he was replaced in the front row. An inspired performance for Ulster against the All Blacks a year later earned him a recall against the same opponents and he went on to feature in thirteen consecutive matches culminating in the game at Swansea which proved to be his last in an Irish jersey.

Sam Walker was a bank employee and following the war and his retirement from the game he became a well-respected radio commentator for the BBC before his premature death in 1972.

ALEXANDER, ROBERT
b 24 September 1910, d 19 July 1943
North of Ireland, Ireland
Wing forward
11 caps
Lions – 14 appearances, 3 Tests, 18 points
Bob Alexander adapted well to the hard playing surfaces experienced in South Africa and was the leading try scorer among the forwards, indeed only Jones and Unwin on the wing scored more. A police officer with the Royal Ulster Constabulary on the outbreak of war, Alexander enlisted with the Royal Inniskillen Fusiliers attaining the rank of captain. He was killed in action in Sicily.

BOYLE, CHARLES VESEY DFC
b 2 July 1915, d 3 March 2007
Dublin University, Ireland
Wing
9 caps
Lions – 12 appearances, 2 Tests, 18 points
Vesey Boyle won his first cap against New Zealand in 1935. Eight more followed in the next three seasons, during which he moved from the right wing over to the left. He was accommodated in both positions in South Africa and scored six tries in his twelve appearances. Boyle was awarded the Distinguished Flying Cross in the Second World War and on his return to civilian life became a barrister and high court judge, serving in the colonial division before retiring to live in Devon.

CLEMENT, WILLIAM HARRIES OBE, MC, TD
b 9 April 1915, d 10 February 2007
Llanelli, Wales
Wing
6 caps
Lions – 6 appearances, 12 points
Bill Clement's tour ended when he was injured in the first encounter with Transvaal, by which time he had featured in six matches and scored four tries, making him a likely Test player but it was not to be. Clement first played for Wales in 1937 and won six consecutive caps before the outbreak of the Second World War. Serving with the Welsh Regiment he attained the rank of Major and was awarded the Military Cross in 1944. After his retirement Bill Clem-

ent continued his involvement in the game as an administrator and in 1956 he became secretary of the Welsh Rugby Union, remaining in office until the centenary season of 1980–81. In the 1981 New Year's Honours List he was awarded the OBE for services to rugby. Bill Clement worked in local government.

COUCHMAN, STANLEY RANDALL
b 1913, d November 1992
Old Cranleighans
Lock
Uncapped
Lions – 10 + 1 appearances, 6 points
Stanley Couchman was an England trialist and reserve but he remained uncapped by his country. A stalwart of the Surrey side, he played his club rugby with Old Cranleighans alongside Jeff Reynolds, another Lion in 1938. Following his retirement from the game, Couchman served as an administrator for the county and on the RFU committee. His contribution to English rugby may not have been rewarded on the field of play but in 1978 Stanley Couchman was elected as the seventy-first president of the RFU.

CROMEY, GEORGE ERNEST
b 8 May 1913, d 2007
Queen's University Belfast, Ireland
Outside-half
9 caps
Lions – 10 + 1 appearances, 1 Test, 6 points
George Cromey was ordained as a Methodist minister the day before the Lions departed from Southampton. He won his first cap against England in 1937 and partnered George Morgan in nine consecutive matches. Lacking in stature he may have been, but Cromey featured in six official matches alongside his Irish half-back partner, all of which were won by the Lions including the third Test.

DANCER, GERALD THOMAS
b 15 January 1911, d
Bedford
Prop
Uncapped
Lions – 15 appearances, 3 Tests, 6 points

Beef Dancer was drafted into the squad following the withdrawal of Eddie Watkins, a Welsh international who had been capped at second row and No. 8. Dancer was comfortable at lock but was selected as a prop in each of his fifteen tour appearances. He played in the three Tests but his performances in South Africa counted for nothing with the England selectors and despite playing in several England trials Dancer was one of five 1938 Lions not capped by his country.

DUFF, PETER LAURENCE
b 12 November 1912, d
Glasgow Academicals, Scotland
Lock, wing forward, No. 8
6 caps
Lions – 14 appearances, 2 Tests, 12 points
Laurie Duff won his six Scotland caps as a No. 8. In South Africa his versatility saw him included in the second row and on the flank. In the third Test he played at wing forward alongside fellow Scot Jock Waters, the player he had replaced at No. 8 in the Triple Crown winning Scottish team of 1938. Duff scored tries in both his Test appearances against the Springboks, crossing for the final score in the third Test which secured the historic victory. Laurie Duff was a farmer.

GILES, JAMES LEONARD
b 5 January 1912, d 28 March 1967
Coventry, England
Scrum-half, outside-half, centre
6 caps
Lions – 15 appearances, 2 Tests, 20 points
Of all the Lions backs Jimmy Giles was perhaps the most blessed. At no time during the tour was he absent from the team for more than one match. Be it in his usual position of scrum-half or in the less familiar roles of outside-half and centre Giles proved equal to the task. Late in the tour he formed a formidable centre partnership with Harry McKibbin, the pair playing together in three of the last four official matches that saw Eastern Province, South Africa and Western Province Universities all defeated.

Giles won his first cap in 1935 but for the following three seasons opportunities were limited, England captain Bernard Gadney the preferred choice. In 1939, Giles led Warwickshire to the County Championship.

257

GRAVES, CHARLES ROBERT ARTHUR
b 23 May 1909, d 14 October 1990
Wanderers, Ireland
Prop, hooker, wing forward
15 caps
Lions – 13 appearances, 2 Tests, 3 points
Bob Graves was a versatile forward equally at home in the front row
or at wing forward. He was introduced to the Ireland team in 1934,
playing three matches at wing forward, but the next two seasons
saw him win seven caps at hooker. In 1937 he made two appearances at prop before winning three more caps from the hooking
berth in 1938. The Lions selectors made full use of his all-round
ability and he played in each position on tour. His knowledge of
several aspects of forward play were put to good use when he
was made an Ireland selector in 1949, serving until 1952 and again
between 1959 and 1961. Bob Graves was employed in banking.

GRIEVE, CHARLES FREDERICK
b 1 October 1913, d
The Army, Scotland
Full-back
2 caps
Lions – 8 + 1 appearances, 2 Tests, 8 points
Not among the original selection, Charles Grieve was called into
the squad when Scotland full-back George Roberts was forced to
withdraw. Grieve had won two caps as an outside-half in 1935 and
1936, but he excelled at full-back in South Africa and by the end
of the tour he was being hailed as one of the Lions' outstanding
backs. Injured in the third match, Grieve was sidelined until the
Northern Provinces fixture two months later, following which he
featured in eight of the last nine matches, including the unofficial
game against Western Province Country. He scored a 40-yard drop
goal in the third Test which put the Lions ahead late in the game.
Charles Grieve was an Army officer.

HOWARD, WILLIAM G
b 13 July 1909, d
Old Birkonians
No. 8
Uncapped
Lions – 9 + 1 appearances, 1 Test, 8 points

Player Profiles

Bill Howard took his place in the squad following the withdrawal of Dudley Kemp. He was the only forward regularly playing at No. 8 for his club and this was reflected when he appeared in five consecutive matches early in the tour. Injury then played a part in restricting his appearances but, after featuring in the first match in Rhodesia, Howard played a prominent part in the victory over Transvaal and earned his place in the first Test. Bill Howard is one of four English forwards on the tour who never played for his country.

JENKINS, VIVIAN GORDON JAMES
b 2 November 1911, d 5 January 2004
London Welsh, Wales
Full-back
14 caps
Lions – 11 appearances, 1 Test, 50 points
Vivian Jenkins won rugby and cricket Blues during his time at Oxford University and in addition to his first class rugby career played county cricket for Glamorgan. He won his first cap against England in 1933, and against Ireland the following year was the first Welsh full-back to score an international try. Appointed vice-captain of the Lions, Jenkins led the team in three matches but was rarely seen at his best in South Africa, a direct result of the string of injuries that plagued his tour.

A teacher in 1938, Jenkins later became a member of the press, writing for *The Sunday Times*, and he was that newspaper's representative on the Lions tours to Australia and New Zealand in 1950 and South Africa in 1955. His books *Lions Down Under* and *Lions Rampant* provide comprehensive insights into the two tours. Jenkins was a regular contributor to *Rugby World* magazine and Editor of the *Rothmans Rugby Yearbook*.

JONES, ELVET LEWIS MBE
b 16 April 1912, d 5 October 1989
Llanelli, Wales
Wing
1 cap
Lions – 11 + 1 appearances, 2 Tests, 30 + 4 points
Elvet Jones was not among those players originally selected to tour South Africa but following the withdrawal of F.J.V. Ford he was drafted into the squad. Yet to be capped by his country, Jones played in two Tests and was the Lions' top try scorer with ten. He

won his only Welsh cap against Scotland in 1939. Following the Second World War, Jones continued his association with Llanelli RFC in an administrative capacity and later became chairman and president of the famous club.

LEYLAND, ROY OBE
b 6 March 1912, d 4 January 1984
The Army, England
Centre
3 caps
Lions – 5 appearances, 6 points
No player appeared in fewer matches on tour than the unfortunate Roy Leyland. After playing in four of the first six matches, injury ruled him out of contention until the second match with Transvaal when he picked up another injury that brought his tour to an end. That he had not been on a losing side in his five matches would have been no consolation.

A schoolteacher by profession, Leyland joined the Army Educational Corps. He served with various regiments during the war, following which he served in Malaya and Iraq. He ended his military career as an instructor at Sandhurst and was awarded the OBE in 1957. Roy Leyland was also the Army's representative on the RFU.

MACRAE, DUNCAN JAMES MC
b 4 November 1914, d
St. Andrew's University, Scotland
Centre
9 caps
Lions – 11 appearances, 1 Test, 18 points
Duncan Macrae was introduced into the Scotland team in 1937 and alongside Wilson Shaw and Charles Dick completed a midfield trio that initiated the attractive, attacking rugby that took Scotland to the Triple Crown in 1938. That Shaw and Dick were unable to tour was unfortunate but much was expected of Macrae and in his eleven matches he showed his midfield craft, scoring six tries before injury in the first Test brought his campaign to a premature end. Duncan Macrae served in the medical corps during the Second World War and was awarded the Military Cross.

MAYNE, ROBERT BLAIR DSO
b 11 January 1915, d 15 December 1955
Queen's University Belfast, Ireland
Lock, No. 8
6 caps
Lions – 19 + 1 appearances, 3 Tests, 0 points

Blair 'Paddy' Mayne won the first of his six caps against Wales in 1937 and had three to his name when he was selected to tour with the Lions. Remaining injury free, his place in the team was never in doubt and he played in twenty matches, including all three Tests. Perhaps the only surprising statistic is that Mayne was the only Lion not to score any points. He played throughout the 1939 Championship but it was on a much bigger stage that Blair Mayne would gain the greatest recognition. During the Second World War he was awarded four DSOs, the Croix de Guerre and the Légion dé honneur, making him the most decorated British soldier. But for all his heroics Mayne was very much a nonconformist who preferred to do things his own way. He was under close arrest for hitting his commanding officer when invited to join a new squadron and he is recognised as one of the founder members of the SAS.

Following the war Mayne took up a post with the Law Society. He was killed when the car he was driving collided with a parked vehicle in his home town of Newtownards in the early hours of 15 December 1955.

MCKIBBIN, HENRY ROGER
b 13 July 1915, d 3 September 2001
Queen's University Belfast
Centre, outside-half
4 caps
Lions – 15 + 1 appearances, 3 Tests, 29 + 3 points

Harry McKibbin won his first cap against Wales in 1938 under new captain Sam Walker and a week later was selected for the British Lions tour. He proved to be essential to the Lions' cause after numerous injuries ruled several three-quarters out of contention for large parts of the tour. McKibbin suffered concussion playing against Western Province which prevented him appearing in the next four matches but he only missed two of the remaining fifteen following his return to action. Harry McKibbin became a Belfast solicitor and revisited South Africa in 1962 as assistant manager of that Lions tour. A long-time committee member, he was elected president of the

IRFU in the centenary season of 1974–75. In 1975 Harry McKibbin was made CBE in recognition of his services to rugby.

MORGAN, GEORGE JOSEPH
b 24 March 1912, d 16 April 1979
Clontarf, Ireland
Scrum-half, full-back
19 caps
Lions – 10 + 1 appearances, 1 Test, 12 points
George Morgan won the first of nineteen consecutive caps against England in 1934. Three years later he took over the captaincy from Jack Siggins and led Ireland in five matches before Sam Walker was given his chance, Morgan reclaiming the mantle in 1939. His experience leading Ireland made him the ideal candidate to captain the Lions in the absence of Walker and Jenkins and he led the team to victory against North East Districts. He had the dubious distinction of being asked to play out of position at full-back in four consecutive matches. George Morgan was a bank employee.

MORGAN, MORGAN EDWARD
b 18 December 1913, d 16 April 1978
Swansea, Wales
Prop forward
4 caps
Lions – 14 appearances, 2 Tests, 3 points
Not surprisingly this serving police officer from the Swansea Valley was known as Eddie Morgan. He made his international debut in the 1938 Championship, playing in all three matches, and won a further cap on his return from South Africa. Morgan was one of the unsung heroes of the Lions pack and but for an injury picked up in the second Test he may well have played at Newlands.

NICHOLSON, BASIL ELLARD
b 1 January 1913, d
Harlequins, England
Outside-half, centre, wing
2 caps
Lions – 9 + 1 appearances, 1 Test, 6 points
Basil Nicholson joined the party late. He had to remain in England to sit his final engineering examinations and joined the tour in time to take his place in the eighth match against Orange Free State

Country at Kroonstad. With an ever increasing injury list, Nicholson was used in three positions behind the scrum and perhaps the best of this exciting prospect was not seen in South Africa.

On the outbreak of war Nicholson was commissioned to the Royal Engineers involved in the construction of ports and installations. He became Lieutenant Colonel and Group Commander of the regiment and was actively involved in the planning of the Normandy landings.

PURCHAS, A.H.G.
Coventry
Lock, wing forward, No. 8
Uncapped
Lions – 7 + 1 appearances, 3 points
Selected in place of Scottish prop forward Bill Inglis, Purchas proved to be a versatile forward, playing in both the second and back rows but never at prop. At the time of his selection Purchas was playing for Coventry which was widely regarded as one of the best clubs in the country. Another of the uncapped English forwards who toured South Africa.

REYNOLDS, FRANK JEFFREY
b 2 January 1916, d 1 August 1996
Old Cranleighans, the Army, England
Outside-half, centre
3 caps
Lions – 14 appearances, 2 Tests, 19 points
Jeff Reynolds experienced several injuries on tour but this did not prevent him playing fourteen matches, including the first and second Tests, and it was only after the defeat in Port Elizabeth that his tour came to an end. On the top of his game there was no more exciting player in the Lions team and his adventurous approach delighted the home supporters but on occasion led to problems his fellow players had to address.

After attending Sandhurst, Reynolds served with the Duke of Wellington's Regiment in World War Two and after resigning in 1947 took a course in hotel management which led him back to South Africa where he married a girl he met on the 1938 tour.

TANNER, HAYDN
b 9 January 1917

Swansea, Wales
Scrum-half
25 caps
Lions – 10 appearances, 1 Test, 3 points
Still only eighteen, Haydn Tanner won his first cap on the occasion of Wales' defeat of New Zealand in December 1935. Three months earlier he had been a member of the Swansea team that also triumphed against the All Blacks. He won thirteen consecutive caps before the Second World War and became Wales' first post-war captain, leading the team twelve times. The only match he missed between winning his first cap in 1935 and his last in 1949 was against Australia when he was forced to withdraw from the side through injury. The 'baby' of the 1938 team, Tanner impressed onlookers with his quick, long service from set pieces and was unfortunate not to have played more matches on tour. A schoolmaster, Tanner later became employed in the chemical industry and at the time of writing he is believed to be the only surviving member of the 1938 Lions.

TAYLOR, ALBERT RUSSELL
b 2 December 1914, d 9 October 1965
Cross Keys, Wales
Wing forward
3 caps
Lions – 16 appearances, 2 Tests, 53 points
Russell Taylor is the only representative of Cross Keys to tour with the British Lions. His three Welsh caps were won over three season and the try he scored against Ireland in 1938 certainly didn't suggest that Taylor would be the Lions' top points scorer in South Africa. But his 53 points elevated him to that position ahead of the unfortunate Vivian Jenkins. His prowess with the boot should not have come as a surprise, Taylor having been a competent outside-half earlier in his playing career. Russell Taylor was a member of the local constabulary.

TRAVERS, WILLIAM
b 2 December 1913, d 4 June 1999
Newport, Wales
Hooker
12 caps
Lions – 19 + 1 appearances, 2 Tests, 3 points

Player Profiles

The son of Welsh hooker George Travers, Bunner Travers made his Welsh debut against Scotland in 1937. He quickly became established in the team, winning eight consecutive caps before the outbreak of war. In 1949 he earned a surprise recall and is one of only four players who represented Wales before and after the war. Travers gave up his job as a coal trimmer to tour with the Lions. Named 'The Prince of Hookers' by the South African press he appeared in twenty matches, more than any other player, and only injury prevented him playing in the three Tests. Later in life Bunner Travers became a well-known licensee in his home town of Newport.

UNWIN, ERNEST JAMES
b 18 September 1912, d
Rosslyn Park, Army, England
Wing
4 caps
Lions – 14 + 1 appearances, 2 Tests, 31 points
James Unwin was no stranger to the demands of touring, having been a member of the British team that visited Argentina in 1936, on which he was joined by Vesey Boyle and Jock Waters. One of the few three-quarters to avoid serious injury in South Africa, Unwin scored the opening try of the tour against Border and his total of nine tries was second only to Elvet Jones. Unwin won his first cap against Scotland in 1937, the first player from Rosslyn Park to be capped by England. In beating the Scots England won the Triple Crown, Unwin scoring a try on his debut.

An army officer, Unwin served with the Middlesex regiment in the Second World War and later joined the family business of seed and corn merchants.

WATERS, JOHN ALEXANDER
b 11 November 1908, d 29 September 1990
Selkirk, Scotland
Prop, lock, No. 8
16 caps
Lions – 8 + 1 appearances, 1 Test, 9 points
At twenty-nine, Jock Waters was the elder statesman of the Lions party. He won his first cap as a prop forward in 1934 and played throughout the Championship in an unchanged pack that helped Scotland to a Triple Crown. The following season he was moved to No. 8, arguably his best position, and he won seven more caps be-

fore being restored to the front row to accommodate Laurie Duff. Another six caps followed at both prop and No. 8 but Waters was deemed surplus to requirements in 1938.

Injured in the opening match of the tour, Waters did not play again until the party arrived in Rhodesia, from when he featured in eight of the last twelve matches, including the unofficial fixture at the end of the tour. Jock Waters was a master butcher.

WILLIAMS, IVOR
Cardiff
Wing forward, No. 8
Uncapped
Lions – 6 + 1 appearances, 3 points
Ivor Williams' appearances were few in number largely as a result of his fall in the dark at the Cango Caves. Later in the tour he showed his worth in the victories against Northern Transvaal and Natal but could not force his way into the Test team. Neither did his talents go unnoticed in Wales but despite being selected as a Welsh reserve Ivor Williams remained uncapped.

SOUTH AFRICAN TEST PLAYERS

CRAVEN, DANIEL HARTMAN
b 11 October 1910, d 4 January 1993
Western Province, Eastern Province, Northern Transvaal.
Scrum-half, outside-half, centre, fullback, No. 8.
16 Caps
The multi-talented Danie Craven was first capped on the 1931–32 Springbok tour of the British Isles. He captained South Africa in the first Test against New Zealand in 1937 and throughout the series against the Lions a year later. Great player most definitely, but it was in his role as one of the game's leading administrators that Craven is best remembered. He was assistant manager of the fourth Springboks tour of Britain and France in 1951–52 and manager of the party that toured Australia and New Zealand in 1956, the year in which he was elected president of the South African Rugby Board. With the formation of the South African Rugby Football Union in 1992 Craven became joint president.

APSEY, JOHN TRAVERS
b 16 April 1911, d 12 November 1987

Western Province
No. 8 and wing forward
3 caps
After playing for the Junior Springboks against Argentina in 1932, John Apsey made his international debut against Australia a year later. He was selected for the fourth and fifth Tests but had to wait five years and one day before winning his third and final cap. This was in the second Test against Sam Walker's Lions, Apsey being called into the side in place of the injured Ebbo Bastard.

BASTARD, WILLIAM EBERHARDT
b 10 December 1912, d 14 February 1949
Natal
Wing forward
6 caps
Ebbo Bastard toured with the 1937 Springboks, scoring a try on his debut in the first Test against Australia. He played in all three Tests in New Zealand and scored the try that secured victory in the second Test. Bastard continued in the team a year later but injury kept him out of the second Test when he was replaced by Apsey. Bastard captained Natal in 1935 and 1936 and continued in the role in 1938 and 1939. Only his involvement with the touring Springboks in 1937 stopped him having a run of five consecutive seasons. He returned to lead the province in 1947.

BERGH, WILLEM FERDINAND
b 2 November 1906, d 28 May 1973
South Western Districts, Griqualand West, Transvaal, Northern Transvaal
Lock and No. 8
17 caps
From winning his first cap against Wales in 1931, Ferdie Bergh played in seventeen consecutive Tests before the outbreak of the Second World War. He scored seven tries in his international career, four of which were against Australia, including a brace in the first Test in 1933. This was a South African record which Bergh held until 1965 when it was broken by John Gainsford, a centre playing in his twenty-ninth Test. Ferdie Bergh was manager of the fifth Springboks tour of Britain and France in 1960–61.

BESTER, JOHANNES LODEWYK AUGUSTINUS
b 25 December 1917, d 14 May 1977
Western Province
Wing
2 caps
Johnny Bester won his two caps against the Lions and scored tries
in both matches. A tourist in 1937, he failed to make the Test team
but scored eight tries in twelve games and added a further three in
the unofficial match against South Australia.

BRAND, GERHARD HAMILTON
b 8 October 1906, d 4 February 1996
Western Province
Full-back and wing
16 caps
Of all the Springboks who played against the 1938 Lions Gerry
Brand's international career was the longest. Although first capped
as a wing against New Zealand in 1928, Brand is best remembered as one of his country's finest full-backs. He toured Britain
in 1931–32 and Australia and New Zealand in 1937 and scored a
total of 293 points in 46 matches, including 55 points in sixteen
Test appearances. Of all the points scored, perhaps the drop goal
against England at Twickenham stands out. In the final minutes
Brand fielded the ball wide out on the halfway line and launched a
drop kick that sailed between the posts, the ball estimated to have
travelled more than eighty yards from Brand's boot to where it
landed. Injury prevented him playing in the second and third Tests
in 1938 and it seems certain that if he had been available for selection, Craven would have invited the Newlands favourite to lead the
Springboks in Cape Town.

DE WET, PIETER
b 12 March 1917, d 18 October 1968
Western Province
Centre
3 caps
With the departure of Western Province centre Louis Babrow, who
had left for Britain after the 1937 tour to continue his medical studies, the selectors had to look no further than the young pretender
who had stepped into his shoes. Piet de Wet had performed well
for Western Province and Cape Province against the Lions early in

the tour and the selectors showed faith in the young University of Cape Town student by including him in the first Test. He played throughout the series and made his sixth appearance against the tourists when he was included in the Western Province Universities team the week after the final Test.

DU TOIT, BAREND ABRAHAM
b 10 November 1912, d 25 January 1989
Transvaal, Northern Transvaal
Wing forward
3 caps
A tourist in 1937, Ben du Toit's appearances were limited by injury and he featured in only seven of the official tour matches. He won his first cap in the first Test against the Lions at the expense of Mauritz van den Berg and retained his place throughout the series, scoring a try in the second Test at Port Elizabeth.

HARRIS, TERENCE ANTHONY
b 27 August 1916, d 7 March 1993
Transvaal
Outside-half
5 caps
Tony Harris was an international rugby player and Test cricketer. Capped in the second and third Tests against New Zealand in 1937, he appeared throughout the 1938 series, partnering Craven in all five matches. Following the Second World War and ten years after he had won his first rugby cap, Harris toured England with the South African cricket team in 1947 and it was on this tour that he became a dual international. He retained his place in the South African team and also played Test cricket when England toured in 1948.

LOCHNER, GEORGE PHILLIPUS
b 11 January 1914, d 30 January 1996
Eastern Province
Centre
3 caps
Another of the 1937 tourists, Flappie Lochner won his first cap in the crucial third Test in Auckland. He played against the Lions in the first and second Tests but injury kept him out of the third. In 1971 Lochner was appointed manager of the Springboks touring party that visited Australia and won all thirteen matches.

LOTZ, JAN WILLEM
b 26 August 1910, d 13 August 1986
Transvaal
Hooker
8 caps
From the time he was selected to tour Australia and New Zealand in 1937 to the third Test in 1938, Jan Lotz appeared in the Springbok jersey more times than any other player. On tour he featured in twenty-three of the twenty-six official matches including the five Tests and he played in the three Tests in 1938. When occasions dictate that an all-time great Springbok fifteen be selected, Jan Lotz is among the first names on the sheet, his place as South Africa's greatest hooker never questioned. Lotz was a national selector in the '50s and '60s.

LOUW, MATTHYS MICHAEL
b 21 February 1906, d 3 May 1988
Western Province
Prop, lock, wing forward, No. 8
18 caps
'Boy' Louw was the elder statesman among those Springboks who played Test rugby in 1938. He won his first cap on the flank and represented his country at Test level in three other positions and when Jan Lotz was rested it was Boy Louw who replaced him at hooker. By 1938 each of the forward positions had become specialist vocations so to play Test rugby in four of them and represent the Springboks in a fifth suggests Boy Louw was a particularly talented player. In winning his eighteenth cap in the third Test against the Lions Louw became his country's most capped player. On his retirement from the game Boy Louw became a first class referee. He was selected assistant manager for the 1960–61 Springbok tour of Britain and France and asked to repeat the task for the short tour of Ireland and Scotland in 1965.

LOUW, STEPHANUS CORNELIUS
b 16 September 1909, d 13 July 1940
Western Province, Transvaal
Prop, wing forward
12 caps

Fanie Louw played alongside brother 'Boy' in ten of his twelve international appearances. A tourist in 1931–32 and 1937, Fanie Louw played a total of thirty matches for the Springboks. He scored eight tries, two in Test matches, including South Africa's one hundredth Test try which he collected against the Lions in the first Test at Johannesburg. On 13 July 1940, Fanie Louw led Transvaal to victory against Western Province. Shortly after the match he collapsed and died of heart failure.

SHERRIFF, ALFRED ROGER
b 17 March 1913, d 4 December 1951
Transvaal, Northern Transvaal
Lock
3 caps
A tourist in 1937, Roger Sherriff played in only three of the official matches and the unofficial game against South Australia. All his appearances were in Australia, injury ruling him out following the 60-0 victory against Toowoomba. It is unlikely that Sherriff would have played Test rugby on tour but with Philip Nel's retirement the opportunity was presented a year later and he was ever present in the Springbok pack during the three-match series with the Lions.

SMITH, GEORGE ALFRED CARY
b 31 August 1916, d 23 March 1978
Eastern Province
Full-back
1 cap
George Smith won his only cap in the third Test against the 1938 Lions. He was the third Springbok full-back to face the tourists following Gerry Brand and Fred Turner, who moved into the centre to replace the injured Flappie Lochner. The Eastern Province full-back was selected following an outstanding season with his province and but for the outbreak of war it is likely that he would have continued in the position following Brand's retirement.

STRACHAN, LUKAS CORNELIUS
b 12 September 1907, d 4 March 1985
Transvaal, Northern Transvaal
Wing forward and No. 8
10 caps
Louis Strachan won his first cap against England on the 1931–32

tour of the British Isles and kept his place in the team that played Scotland. Then it was a five-year wait before he was selected to tour in 1937, playing in all five Tests. Strachan was outstanding in the second Test against the All Blacks when the Springbok pack was effectively reduced to six men, the injured Ebbo Bastard and Boy Louw little more than passengers for much of the match. Strachan was one of the players drafted into the newly formed Northern Transvaal and together with Danie Craven, Ferdie Bergh, Roger Sherriff and Ben du Toit featured in the three Tests against the Lions – the first group of players to represent the now famous province on the international stage.

TURNER, FREDERICK GEORGE
b 18 March 1914, d 12 September 2003
Eastern Province, Transvaal
Wing, centre, full-back
11 caps
Freddy Turner was first capped against Australia in 1933 when he was selected on the wing, from which position he won seven of his caps. Against the Lions, he confirmed his versatility when selected as a wing in the first Test, full-back in the second and in the centre for the third. His 20 points in the series was the most scored by any player from either side. Freddy Turner scored 131 points in a Springbok jersey, of which 29 were in Test matches, and he was South Africa's record points scorer until both figures were bettered in the 1950s.

WILLIAMS, DAVID OWEN
b 16 June 1913, d 24 December 1975
Western Province
Wing
8 caps
Dai Williams played a total of eighteen matches for South Africa in which he crossed for seventeen tries. He was introduced to the Springboks when called up as a replacement on the 1931–32 tour of the British Isles but his appearances were limited and the eighteen-year-old wing played in only three matches. Six years later he won his first cap against Australia and went on to play in eight consecutive Test matches, including the three Test against the Lions, scoring a brace of tries in the encounter at Johannesburg.

APPENDIX 2
MATCH RESULTS

Sat 11 June	BORDER 1 – East London	w	11-8
Wed 15 June	GRIQUALAND WEST – Kimberley	w	22-9
Sat 18 June	W.P. TOWN AND COUNTRY – Cape Town	l	8-11
Wed 22 June	S.W. DISTRICTS – Oudtshoorn	w	19-10
Sat 25 June	WESTERN PROVINCE – Cape Town	l	11-21
Wed 29 June	WESTERN TRANSVAAL – Potchefstroom	w	26 -9
Sat 2 July	ORANGE F.S. – Bloemfontein	w	21-6
Wed 6 July	ORANGE F.S. COUNTRY – Kroonstad	w	18-3
Sat 9 July	TRANSVAAL 1 – Johannesburg	l	9-16
Wed 13 July	NORTHERN TRANSVAAL – Pretoria	w	20-12
Sat 16 July	CAPE PROVINCE – Kimberley	w	10-3
Wed 20 July	RHODESIA 1 – Salisbury	w	25-11
Sat 23 July	RHODESIA 2 – Bulawayo	w	45-11
Sat 30 July	TRANSVAAL 2 – Johannesburg	w	17-9
Sat 6 Aug	SOUTH AFRICA 1 – Johannesburg	l	12-26
Sat 13 Aug	NORTHERN PROVINCES – Durban	l	8-26
Wed 17 Aug	NATAL – Pietermaritzburg	w	15-11
Sat 20 Aug	BORDER 2 – East London	w	19-11
Wed 24 Aug	NORTH EAST DISTRICTS – Burgersdorp	w	42-3
Sat 27 Aug	EASTERN PROVINCE – Port Elizabeth	w	6-5
Sat 3 Sept	SOUTH AFRICA 2 – Port Elizabeth	l	3-19
Sat 10 Sept	SOUTH AFRICA 3 – Cape Town	w	21-16
Sat 17 Sept	W.P. UNIVERSITIES – Cape Town	w	19-16

Unofficial Match

Wed 21 Sept	W.P. COUNTRY – Cape Town	l	7-12

BIBLIOGRAPHY

Bannister, Anthony and Gordon, Rene; *The National Parks of South Africa*; New Holland 1992

Brett, R.LW.; *Makers of South Africa*; Thomas Nelson and Sons Ltd 1944

Bulpin, T.V.; *To the Shores of Natal*; Howard B. Timmins 1953

Bulpin, T.V.; *Discovering Southern Africa*; DSA Productions 2001

Chester, Rod; McMillan, Neville; Palenski, Ron; *Men In Black*; Hodder Moa Beckett 2000

Chester, R.H. & McMillan, N.A.C; *The Visitors*; Moa Publications 1990

Clayton, Keith & Greyvenstein, Chris; *The Craven Tapes*; Human & Rousseau 1995

Clayton, Keith editor; *Doc Craven's Tribute – The Legends of Springbok Rugby 1889–1989*; KC Publications 1989

Difford, Ivor; *History of South African Rugby Football*; The Specialty Press of S.A. Ltd 1933

Gibbs, Henry; *Twilight in South Africa*; Jarrolds Publishers (London) Ltd 1951

Godwin, Terry; *The International Rugby Championship 1883–1983*; Collins Willow 1984

Godwin, Terry; *The Complete Who's Who of International Rugby*; Blandford Press 1987

Greyvenstein, Chris; *Springbok Saga*; Don Nelson 1977

Griffiths, John; *British Lions*; Crowood Press 1990

Herbert, Alfred; *The Natal Rugby Story*; Shuter & Shooter 1980

Jenkins, John M; Pierce, Duncan; Auty, Timothy; *Who's Who of Welsh International Rugby Players*; Bridge Books 1991

Maule, Raymond; *The Complete Who's Who of England Rugby Union Internationals*; Breedon Books 1992

Middleton, John N; *Railways of Southern Africa*; Beyer-Garratt Publications 2002

Millin, Sarah, Gertrude; *Rhodes*; Central News Agency Ltd, South Africa 1933

Morton, H.V.; *In Search of South Africa*; Methuen & Co. Ltd 1948

Newall, Peter; *Union-Castle Line – A Fleet History*; Carmania Press 1999

Newman, Kenneth; *Birds of Southern Africa*; Struik 2002

Bibliography

Parker, A.C.; *The Springboks 1891–1970*; Cassell & Co. 1970

Reyburn, Wallace; *The Lions*; Stanley Paul 1967

Sacks, John E.; *South Africa's Greatest Springboks*; Sporting Publications 1938

Shnaps, Teddy; *A Statistical History of Springbok Rugby*; SARB Don Nelson 1989

Smuts, J.C.; *Jan Christian Smuts*; Cassell & Co. Ltd 1952

Thomas, Clem; *The History of the British Lions*; Mainstream Publishing 1996

Titley, U.A. & McWhirter, Ross; *Centenary History of the Rugby Football Union*; RFU 1970

Townsend Collins, W.J.; *Rugby Recollections*; R.H. Johns 1948

Van Esbeck, Edmund; *Irish Rugby 1874–1999*; Gill & Macmillan 1999

Walsh, Frank; *A History of South Africa*; Harper Collins 1998

Wells, A.W.; *South Africa – A Planned Tour*; J.M. Dent & Sons Ltd 1939

Winch, Jonty; *Rhodesia Rugby*; The Zimbabwe Rhodesia Rugby Union 1980

YEARBOOKS – VARIOUS EDITIONS

The Rugby Football Annual
Playfair Rugby Football Annual
Rothmans Rugby Yearbook
South African Rugby Annual
The South and East African Yearbook and Guide

NEWSPAPERS AND PERIODCALS

The Cape Times
The Times
The Western Mail
National Geographic
Outspan

Index

Natal v. 168
Nel, Philip 12, 80, 139, 152, 188, 189, 234, 237, 239, 271
Newlands 55, 56, 58, 66, 68, 69, 154, 198, 212, 215, 220, 225, 230–232, 234, 237, 238, 241, 247, 252, 262, 268
Nicholson, Basil 18, 25, 32, 74, 80, 86–89, 94, 98, 100–102, 105, 106, 118, 120, 122, 123, 130, 160, 165, 183, 185, 190, 191, 192, 195, 200, 204, 205, 206, 208, 243, 245, 262, 263
North East Districts v 183
Northern Provinces v 162
Northern Transvaal v. 105

Orange Free State v 83
Orange Free State Country v 87

Pienaar, A.J. 29, 30
Potgieter, Hennie 75, 82, 122, 123
Purchas, A.H.G. 18, 64, 65, 66, 67, 76, 79, 87, 89, 110, 113, 118, 120, 161, 165, 183, 185, 242, 245, 246, 263

Reid, Bernard 38, 39, 42, 113, 175, 177, 179
Reynolds, Jeff 18, 31, 37, 38, 39, 42, 54, 56, 57, 64, 69, 71, 73–79, 83, 84, 86, 87, 94, 97, 100, 101, 108, 114, 118, 123, 130, 134, 136, 143, 153, 160, 163, 165, 168, 169, 171, 174, 175, 178, 179, 183–185, 190–195, 199, 204–208, 213, 256, 263
RFU 15, 16, 28, 126, 253, 254, 256, 260, 275

Rhodesia v 118, 122
Roberts, George 19, 67, 258
Roos, Paul 30, 196, 197, 233

Shaw, Wilson 17, 20, 63, 260
Sherriff, Roger 93, 104, 142, 153, 160, 164, 208, 221, 226, 271, 272
Smollan, Fred 94, 100, 102, 131, 135, 136, 160, 165
Smyth, Tom 40, 63, 93, 182
South Africa v 146, 202, 215
South West Districts v 64
Stirling Castle 25, 26, 27, 28, 29, 34, 35, 43, 62, 210, 229, 246
Strachan, Louis 12, 35, 43, 44, 52, 93, 104, 106, 108, 142, 153, 173, 204, 208, 226, 228, 240, 241, 242, 271, 272

Tanner, Hadyn 1, 20, 64–67, 76, 77, 79, 83, 84, 86–89, 105, 106–109, 112–114, 122, 123, 144, 158, 161, 163, 165, 190–192, 194, 195, 199, 204, 208, 213, 246, 247, 264
Taylor, Russell 20, 37, 42, 43, 54, 58, 65, 67, 76, 77, 79, 83–86, 95, 97, 100–102, 105, 106, 108, 110, 112, 113, 122, 123, 130, 133, 136, 143, 147, 153, 161, 162, 165, 168, 169–171, 174, 176–179, 183, 190, 191, 193, 195, 203, 205, 208, 213, 240, 241, 246, 264
Transvaal v. 96, 131
Travers, Bill 1, 3, 20, 37, 42, 51, 54, 56, 58, 64, 68, 70, 72, 73, 75, 76, 79, 83, 86–89, 94, 95, 98, 101, 102, 105, 107, 108, 110, 111, 113, 114, 118, 121,